Annie Besant An Autobiography

Annie Besant

TUTIS Digital Publishing Pvt Ltd

ISBN 978-81-8456-280-4

Annie Besant An Autobiography

This impression 2007

Published by

TUTIS Digital Publishing Pvt Ltd.

26 Ramasamy Street

T. Nagar, Chennai 600 017

CONTENTS

Preface

It is a difficult thing to tell the story of a life, and yet more difficult when that life is one's own. At the best, the telling has a savour of vanity, and the only excuse for the proceeding is that the life, being an average one, reflects many others, and in troublous times like ours may give the experience of many rather than of one. And so the autobiographer does his work because he thinks that, at the cost of some unpleasantness to himself, he may throw light on some of the typical problems that are vexing the souls of his contemporaries, and perchance may stretch out a helping hand to some brother who is struggling in the darkness, and so bring him cheer when despair has him in its grip. Since all of us, men and women of this restless and eager generation—surrounded by forces we dimly see but cannot as yet understand, discontented with old ideas and half afraid of new, greedy for the material results of the knowledge brought us by Science but looking askance at her agnosticism as regards the soul, fearful of superstition but still more fearful of atheism, turning from the husks of outgrown creeds but filled with desperate hunger for spiritual ideals—since all of us have the same anxieties, the same griefs, the same yearning hopes, the same passionate desire for knowledge, it may well be that the story of one may help all, and that the tale of one should that went out alone into the darkness and on the other side found light, that struggled through the Storm and on the other side found Peace, may bring some ray of light and of peace into the darkness and the storm of other lives.

ANNIE BESANT.

THE THEOSOPHICAL SOCIETY,

17 & 19, AVENUE ROAD, REGENT'S PARK, LONDON.

August, 1893.

Illustrations

CHAPTER I

"Out of the Everywhere Into the Here"

On October 1, 1847, I am credibly informed, my baby eyes opened to the light(?) of a London afternoon at 5.39.

A friendly astrologer has drawn for me the following chart, showing the position of the planets at this, to me fateful, moment; but I know nothing of astrology, so feel no wiser as I gaze upon my horoscope.

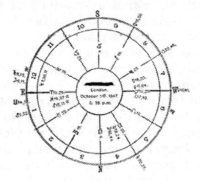

Horoscope of Annie Besant

Keeping in view the way in which sun, moon, and planets influence the physical condition of the earth, there is nothing incongruous with the orderly course of nature in the view that they also influence the physical bodies of men, these being part of the physical earth, and largely moulded by its conditions. Any one who knows the characteristics ascribed to those who are born under the several signs of the Zodiac, may very easily pick out the different types among his own acquaintances, and he may then get them to go to some astrologer and find out under what signs they were severally born. He will very quickly discover that two men of completely opposed types are not born under the same sign, and the invariability of the concurrence will convince him that law, and not chance, is at work. We are born into earthly life under certain conditions, just as we were physically affected by them pre-natally, and these will have their bearing on our subsequent physical evolution. At the most, astrology, as it is now practised, can only calculate the interaction between these physical conditions at any given moment, and the conditions brought to them by a given person whose general constitution and natal condition are known. It cannot say what the person will do, nor what will happen to him, but only what will be the physical district, so to speak, in which he will find himself, and the impulses that will play upon him from external nature and from his own body. Even on those matters modern astrology is not quite reliable—judging from the many blunders made—or else its professors are very badly instructed; but that there is a real science of astrology I have no doubt, and there are some men who are past masters in it.

It has always been somewhat of a grievance to me that I was born in London, "within the sound of Bow Bells," when three-quarters of my blood and all my heart are Irish. My dear mother was of purest Irish descent, and my father was Irish on his mother's side, though belonging to the Devonshire Woods on his father's. The Woods were yeomen of the sturdy English type, farming their own land in honest, independent fashion. Of late years they seem to have developed more in the direction of brains, from the time, in fact, that Matthew Wood became Mayor of London town, fought Queen Caroline's battles against her most religious and gracious royal husband, aided the Duke of Kent with no niggard hand, and received a baronetcy for his services from the Duke of Kent's royal daughter. Since then they have given England a Lord Chancellor in the person of the gentle-hearted and pure-living Lord Hatherley, while others have distinguished themselves in various ways in the service of their country. But I feel playfully inclined to grudge the English blood they put into my father's veins, with his Irish mother, his Galway birth, and his Trinity College, Dublin, education. For the Irish tongue is musical in my ear, and the Irish nature dear to my heart. Only in Ireland is it that if you stop to ask a worn-out ragged woman the way to some old monument, she will say: "Sure, then, my darlin', it's just up the hill and round the corner, and then any one will tell you the way. And it's there you'll see the place where the blessed Saint Patrick set his foot, and his blessing be on yer." Old women as poor as she in other nations would never be as bright and as friendly and as garrulous. And where, out of Ireland, will you see a whole town crowd into a station to say good-bye to half a dozen emigrants, till the platform is a heaving mass of men and women, struggling, climbing over each other for a last kiss, crying, keening, laughing, all in a breath, till all the air is throbbing and there's a lump in your throat and tears in your eyes as the train steams out? Where, out of Ireland, will you be bumping along the streets on an outside car, beside a taciturn Jarvey, who, on suddenly discovering that you are shadowed by "Castle" spies, becomes loquaciously friendly, and points out everything that he thinks will interest you? Blessings on the quick tongues and warm hearts, on the people so easy to lead, so hard to drive. And blessings on the ancient land once inhabited by mighty men of wisdom, that in later times became the Island of Saints, and shall once again be the Island of Sages, when the Wheel turns round.

My maternal grandfather was a typical Irishman, much admired by me and somewhat feared also, in the childish days. He belonged to a decayed Irish family, the Maurices, and in a gay youth, with a beautiful wife as light-hearted as himself, he had merrily run through what remained to him in the way of fortune. In his old age, with abundant snow-white hair, he still showed the hot Irish blood on the lightest provocation, stormily angry for a moment and easily appeased. My mother was the second daughter in a large family, in a family that grew more numerous as pounds grew fewer, and she was adopted by a maiden aunt, a quaint memory of whom came through my mother's childhood into mine, and had its moulding effect on both our characters. This maiden aunt was, as are most Irish folk of decayed families, very proud of her family tree with its roots in the inevitable "kings." Her particular kings were the "seven kings of France"—the "Milesian kings"—and the tree grew up a parchment, in all its impressive majesty, over the mantelpiece of their descendant's modest drawing-room. This heraldic monster was regarded with deep respect by child Emily, a respect in no wise deserved, I venture to suppose, by the disreputable royalties of whom she was a fortunately distant twig. Chased out of France, doubtless for cause shown, they had come over the sea to Ireland, and there continued their reckless plundering lives. But so strangely turns the wheel of time that these ill-doing and barbarous scamps became a kind of moral thermometer in the home of the gentle Irish lady in the early half of the present century. For my mother has told me that when she had committed some act of childish naughtiness, her aunt would say, looking gravely over her spectacles at the small culprit, "Emily, your conduct is unworthy of the descendant of the seven kings of France." And Emily, with her sweet grey Irish eyes and her curling masses of raven black hair, would cry in penitent shame over her unworthiness, with some vague idea that those royal,

3

and to her very real, ancestors would despise her small, sweet, rosebud self, so wholly unworthy of their disreputable majesties.

Thus those shadowy forms influenced her in childhood, and exercised over her a power that made her shrink from aught that was unworthy, petty or mean. To her the lightest breath of dishonour was to be avoided at any cost of pain, and she wrought into me, her only daughter, that same proud and passionate horror at any taint of shame or merited disgrace. To the world always a brave front was to be kept, and a stainless reputation, for suffering might be borne but dishonour never. A gentlewoman might starve, but she must not run in debt; she might break her heart, but it must be with a smile on her face. I have often thought that the training in this reticence and pride of honour was a strange preparation for my stormy, public, much attacked and slandered life; and certain it is that this inwrought shrinking from all criticism that touched personal purity and personal honour added a keenness of suffering to the fronting of public odium that none can appreciate who has not been trained in some similar school of dignified self-respect. And yet perhaps there was another result from it that in value outweighed the added pain: it was the stubbornly resistant feeling that rose and inwardly asserted its own purity in face of foulest lie, and turning scornful face against the foe, too proud either to justify itself or to defend, said to itself in its own heart, when condemnation was loudest: "I am not what you think me, and your verdict does not change my own self. You cannot make me vile whatever you think of me, and I will never, in my own eyes, be that which you deem me to be now." And the very pride became a shield against degradation, for, however lost my public reputation, I could never bear to become sullied in my own sight—and that is a thing not without its use to a woman cut off, as I was at one time, from home, and friends, and Society. So peace to the maiden aunt's ashes, and to those of her absurd kings, for I owe them something after all. And I keep grateful memory of that unknown grand-aunt, for what she did in training my dear mother, the tenderest, sweetest, proudest, purest of women. It is well to be able to look back to a mother who served as ideal of all that was noblest and dearest during childhood and girlhood, whose face made the beauty of home, and whose love was both sun and shield. No other experience in life could quite make up for missing the perfect tie between mother and child—a tie that in our case never relaxed and never weakened. Though her grief at my change of faith and consequent social ostracism did much to hasten her death-hour, it never brought a cloud between our hearts; though her pleading was the hardest of all to face in later days, and brought the bitterest agony, it made no gulf between us, it cast no chill upon our mutual love. And I look back at her to-day with the same loving gratitude as ever encircled her to me in her earthly life. I have never met a woman more selflessly devoted to those she loved, more passionately contemptuous of all that was mean or base, more keenly sensitive on every question of honour, more iron in will, more sweet in tenderness, than the mother who made my girlhood sunny as dreamland, who guarded me, until my marriage, from every touch of pain that she could ward off or bear for me, who suffered more in every trouble that touched me in later life than I did myself, and who died in the little house I had taken for our new home in Norwood, worn out, ere old age touched her, by sorrow, poverty, and pain, in May, 1874.

My earliest personal recollections are of a house and garden that we lived in when I was three and four years of age, situated in Grove Road, St. John's Wood. I can remember my mother hovering round the dinner-table to see that all was bright for the home-coming husband; my brother—two years older than myself—and I watching "for papa"; the loving welcome, the game of romps that always preceded the dinner of the elder folks. I can remember on the 1st of October, 1851, jumping up in my little cot, and shouting out triumphantly: "Papa! mamma! I am four years old!" and the grave demand of my brother, conscious of superior age, at dinner-time: "May not Annie have a knife to-day, as she is four years old?"

It was a sore grievance during that same year, 1851, that I was not judged old enough to go to the Great Exhibition, and I have a faint memory of my brother consolingly bringing me home one of those folding pictured strips that are sold in the streets, on which were imaged glories that I longed only the more to see. Far-away, dusky, trivial memories, these. What a pity it is that a baby cannot notice, cannot observe, cannot remember, and so throw light on the fashion of the dawning of the external world on the human consciousness. If only we could remember how things looked when they were first imaged on the retinae; what we felt when first we became conscious of the outer world; what the feeling was as faces of father and mother grew out of the surrounding chaos and became familiar things, greeted with a smile, lost with a cry; if only memory would not become a mist when in later years we strive to throw our glances backward into the darkness of our infancy, what lessons we might learn to help our stumbling psychology, how many questions might be solved whose answers we are groping for in the West in vain.

The next scene that stands out clearly against the background of the past is that of my father's death-bed. The events which led to his death I know from my dear mother. He had never lost his fondness for the profession for which he had been trained, and having many medical friends, he would now and then accompany them on their hospital rounds, or share with them the labours of the dissecting-room. It chanced that during the dissection of the body of a person who had died of rapid consumption, my father cut his finger against the edge of the breast-bone. The cut did not heal easily, and the finger became swollen and inflamed. "I would have that finger off, Wood, if I were you," said one of the surgeons, a day or two afterwards, on seeing the state of the wound. But the others laughed at the suggestion, and my father, at first inclined to submit to the amputation, was persuaded to "leave Nature alone."

About the middle of August, 1852, he got wet through, riding on the top of an omnibus, and the wetting resulted in a severe cold, which "settled on his chest." One of the most eminent doctors of the day, as able as he was rough in manner, was called to see him. He examined him carefully, sounded his lungs, and left the room followed by my mother. "Well?" she asked, scarcely anxious as to the answer, save as it might worry her husband to be kept idly at home. "You must keep up his spirits," was the thoughtless answer. "He is in a galloping consumption; you will not have him with you six weeks longer." The wife staggered back, and fell like a stone on the floor. But love triumphed over agony, and half an hour later she was again at her husband's side, never to leave it again for ten minutes at a time, night or day, till he was lying with closed eyes asleep in death.

I was lifted on to the bed to "say good-bye to dear papa" on the day before his death, and I remember being frightened at his eyes which looked so large, and his voice which sounded so strange, as he made me promise always to be "a very good girl to darling mamma, as papa was going right away." I remember insisting that "papa should kiss Cherry," a doll given me on my birthday, three days before, by his direction, and being removed, crying and struggling, from the room. He died on the following day, October 5th, and I do not think that my elder brother and I—who were staying at our maternal grandfather's—went to the house again until the day of the funeral. With the death, my mother broke down, and when all was over they carried her senseless from the room. I remember hearing afterwards how, when she recovered her senses, she passionately insisted on being left alone, and locked herself into her room for the night; and how on the following morning her mother, at last persuading her to open the door, started back at the face she saw with the cry: "Good God, Emily! your hair is white!" It was even so; her hair, black, glossy and abundant, which, contrasting with her large grey eyes, had made her face so strangely attractive, had turned grey in that night of agony, and to me my mother's face is ever framed in exquisite silver bands of hair as white as the driven unsullied snow.

I have heard that the love between my father and mother was a very beautiful thing, and it most certainly stamped her character for life. He was keenly intellectual and splendidly educated; a mathematician and a good classical scholar, thoroughly master of French, German, Italian, Spanish, and Portuguese, with a smattering of Hebrew and Gaelic, the treasures of ancient and of modern literature were his daily household delight. Nothing pleased him so well as to sit with his wife, reading aloud to her while she worked; now translating from some foreign poet, now rolling forth melodiously the exquisite cadences of "Queen Mab." Student of philosophy as he was, he was deeply and steadily sceptical; and a very religious relative has told me that he often drove her from the room by his light, playful mockery of the tenets of the Christian faith. His mother and sister were strict Roman Catholics, and near the end forced a priest into his room, but the priest was promptly ejected by the wrath of the dying man, and by the almost fierce resolve of the wife that no messenger of the creed he detested should trouble her darling at the last.

Deeply read in philosophy, he had outgrown the orthodox beliefs of his day, and his wife, who loved him too much to criticise, was wont to reconcile her own piety and his scepticism by holding that "women ought to be religious," while men had a right to read everything and think as they would, provided that they were upright and honourable in their lives. But the result of his liberal and unorthodox thought was to insensibly modify and partially rationalise her own beliefs, and she put on one side as errors the doctrines of eternal punishment, the vicarious atonement, the infallibility of the Bible, the equality of the Son with the Father in the Trinity, and other orthodox beliefs, and rejoiced in her later years in the writings of such men as Jowett, Colenso, and Stanley. The last named, indeed, was her ideal Christian gentleman, suave, polished, broad-minded, devout in a stately way. The baldness of a typical Evangelical service outraged her taste as much as the crudity of Evangelical dogmas outraged her intellect; she liked to feel herself a Christian in a dignified and artistic manner, and to be surrounded by solemn music and splendid architecture when she "attended Divine service." Familiarity with celestial personages was detestable to her, and she did her duty of saluting them in a courtly and reverent fashion. Westminster Abbey was her favourite church, with its dim light and shadowy distances; there in a carven stall, with choristers chanting in solemn rhythm, with the many-coloured glories of the painted windows repeating themselves on upspringing arch and clustering pillars, with the rich harmonies of the pealing organ throbbing up against screen and monument, with the ashes of the mighty dead around, and all the stately memories of the past inwrought into the very masonry, there Religion appeared to her to be intellectually dignified and emotionally satisfactory.

To me, who took my religion in strenuous fashion, this dainty and well-bred piety seemed perilously like Laodicean lukewarmness, while my headlong vigour of conviction and practice often jarred on her as alien from the delicate balance and absence of extremes that should characterise the gentlewoman. She was of the old *régime*; I of the stuff from which fanatics are made: and I have often thought, in looking back, that she must have had on her lips many a time unspoken a phrase that dropped from them when she lay a-dying: "My little one, you have never made me sad or sorry except for your own sake; you have always been too religious." And then she murmured to herself: "Yes, it has been darling Annie's only fault; she has always been too religious." Methinks that, as the world judges, the dying voice spoke truly, and the dying eyes saw with a real insight. For though I was then kneeling beside her bed, heretic and outcast, the heart of me was religious in its very fervour of repudiation of a religion, and in its rebellious uprising against dogmas that crushed the reason and did not satisfy the soul. I went out into the darkness alone, not because religion was too good for me, but because it was not good enough; it was too meagre, too commonplace, too little exacting, too bound up with earthly interests, too calculating in its accommodations to social conventionalities. The Roman Catholic Church, had it captured me, as it nearly did, would have sent me on some mission of danger and sacrifice and utilised me as a martyr; the Church established by law transformed me into an unbeliever and an antagonist.

For as a child I was mystical and imaginative religious to the very finger-tips, and with a certain faculty for seeing visions and dreaming dreams. This faculty is not uncommon with the Keltic races, and makes them seem "superstitious" to more solidly-built peoples. Thus, on the day of my father's funeral, my mother sat with vacant eyes and fixed pallid face—the picture comes back to me yet, it so impressed my childish imagination—following the funeral service, stage after stage, and suddenly, with the words, "It is all over!" fell back fainting. She said afterwards that she had followed the hearse, had attended the service, had walked behind the coffin to the grave. Certain it is that a few weeks later she determined to go to the Kensal Green Cemetery, where the body of her husband had been laid, and went thither with a relative; he failed to find the grave, and while another of the party went in search of an official to identify the spot, my mother said, "If you will take me to the chapel where the first part of the service was read, I will find the grave." The idea seemed to her friend, of course, to be absurd; but he would not cross the newly-made widow, so took her to the chapel. She looked round, left the chapel door, and followed the path along which the corpse had been borne till she reached the grave, where she was quietly standing when the caretaker arrived to point it out. The grave is at some distance from the chapel, and is not on one of the main roads; it had nothing on it to mark it, save the wooden peg with the number, and this would be no help to identification at a distance since all the graves are thus marked, and at a little way off these pegs are not visible. How she found the grave remained a mystery in the family, as no one believed her straightforward story that she had been present at the funeral. With my present knowledge the matter is simple enough, for I now know that the consciousness can leave the body, take part in events going onat a distance, and, returning, impress on the physical brain what it has experienced. The very fact that she asked to be taken to the chapel is significant, showing that she was picking up a memory of a previous going from that spot to the grave; she could only find the grave if she started from *the place from which she had started before.* Another proof of this ultra-physical capacity was given a few months later, when her infant son, who had been pining himself ill for "papa," was lying one night in her arms. On the next morning she said to her sister: "Alf is going to die." The child had no definite disease, but was wasting away, and it was argued to her that the returning spring would restore the health lost during the winter. "No," was her answer. "He was lying asleep in my arms last night, and William" (her husband) "came to me and said that he wanted Alf with him, but that I might keep the other two." In vain she was assured that she had been dreaming, that it was quite natural that she should dream about her husband, and that her anxiety for the child had given the dream its shape. Nothing would persuade her that she had not seen her husband, or that the information he had given her was not true. So it was no matter of surprise to her when in the following March her arms were empty, and a waxen form lay lifeless in the baby's cot.

My brother and I were allowed to see him just before he was placed in his coffin; I can see him still, so white and beautiful, with a black spot in the middle of the fair, waxen forehead, and I remember the deadly cold which startled me when I was told to kiss my little brother. It was the first time that I had touched Death. That black spot made a curious impression on me, and long afterwards, asking what had caused it, I was told that at the moment after his death my mother had passionately kissed the baby brow. Pathetic thought, that the mother's kiss of farewell should have been marked by the first sign of corruption on the child's face!

I do not mention these stories because they are in any fashion remarkable or out of the way, but only to show that the sensitiveness to impressions other than physical ones, that was a marked feature in my own childhood, was present also in the family to which I belonged. For the physical nature is inherited from parents, and sensitiveness to psychic impressions is a property of the physical body; in our family, as in so many Irish ones, belief in "ghosts" of all descriptions was general, and my mother has told me of the banshee that she had heard wailing when the death-hour of one of the family was near. To me in my childhood, elves and fairies of all sorts were very real things, and my dolls were as really children as I was myself a child. Punch and Judy were living entities, and the tragedy in which they bore part cost me many an agony of tears; to this day I can remember running away when I heard the squawk of the coming Punch, and burying my head in the pillows that I might shut out the sound of the blows and the cry of the ill-used baby. All the objects about me were to me alive, the flowers that I kissed as much as the kitten I petted, and I used to have a splendid time "making believe" and living out all sorts of lovely stories among my treasured and so-called inanimate playthings. But there was a more serious side to this dreamful fancy when it joined hands with religion.

CHAPTER II

Early Childhood

And now began my mother's time of struggle and of anxiety. Hitherto, since her marriage, she had known no money troubles, for her husband was earning a good income; he was apparently vigorous and well: no thought of anxiety clouded their future. When he died, he believed that he left his wife and children safe, at least, from pecuniary distress. It was not so. I know nothing of the details, but the outcome of all was that nothing was left for the widow and children, save a trifle of ready money. The resolve to which my mother came was characteristic. Two of her husband's relatives, Western and Sir William Wood, offered to educate her son at a good city school, and to start him in commercial life, using their great city influence to push him forward. But the young lad's father and mother had talked of a different future for their eldest boy; he was to go to a public school, and then to the University, and was to enter one of the "learned professions"—to take orders, the mother wished; to go to the Bar, the father hoped. On his death-bed there was nothing more earnestly urged by my father than that Harry should receive the best possible education, and the widow was resolute to fulfil that last wish. In her eyes, a city school was not "the best possible education," and the Irish pride rebelled against the idea of her son not being "a University man." Many were the lectures poured out on the young widow's head about her "foolish pride," especially by the female members of the Wood family; and her persistence in her own way caused a considerable alienation between herself and them. But Western and William, though half-disapproving, remained her friends, and lent many a helping hand to her in her first difficult struggles. After much cogitation, she resolved that the boy should be educated at Harrow, where the fees are comparatively low to lads living in the town, and that he should go thence to Cambridge or to Oxford, as his tastes should direct. A bold scheme for a penniless widow, but carried out to the letter; for never dwelt in a delicate body a more resolute mind and will than that of my dear mother.

In a few months' time—during which we lived, poorly enough, in Richmond Terrace, Clapham, close to her father and mother—to Harrow, then, she betook herself, into lodgings over a grocer's shop, and set herself to look for a house. This grocer was a very pompous man, fond of long words, and patronised the young widow exceedingly, and one day my mother related with much amusement how he had told her that she was sure to get on if she worked hard. "Look at me!" he said, swelling visibly with importance; "I was once a poor boy, without a penny of my own, and now I am a comfortable man, and have my submarine villa to go to every evening." That "submarine villa" was an object of amusement when we passed it in our walks for many a long day.

"There is Mr. ——'s submarine villa," some one would say, laughing: and I, too, used to laugh merrily, because my elders did, though my understanding of the difference between suburban and submarine was on a par with that of the honest grocer.

My mother had fortunately found a boy, whose parents were glad to place him in her charge, of about the age of her own son, to educate with him; and by this means she was able to pay for a tutor, to prepare the two boys for school. The tutor had a cork leg, which was a source of serious trouble to me, for it stuck out straight behind when we knelt down to family prayers—conduct which struck me as irreverent and unbecoming, but which I always felt a desire to imitate. After about a year my mother found a house which she thought would suit her scheme, namely, to obtain permission from Dr. Vaughan, the then head-master of Harrow, to take some boys into her house, and so gain means of education for her own son. Dr. Vaughan, who must have been won by the gentle, strong, little woman, from that time forth became her earnest friend and helper; and to the counsel and active assistance both of himself and of his wife, was due much of the success that crowned her toil. He made only one condition in granting the permission she asked, and that was, that she should also have in her house one of the masters of the school, so that the boys should not suffer from the want of a house-tutor. This condition, of course, she readily accepted, and the arrangement lasted for ten years, until after her son had left school for Cambridge.

The house she took is now, I am sorry to say, pulled down, and replaced by a hideous red-brick structure. It was very old and rambling, rose-covered in front, ivy-covered behind; it stood on the top of Harrow Hill, between the church and the school, and had once been the vicarage of the parish, but the vicar had left it because it was so far removed from the part of the village where all his work lay. The drawing-room opened by an old-fashioned half-window, half-door—which proved a constant source of grief to me, for whenever I had on a new frock I always tore it on the bolt as I flew through—into a large garden which sloped down one side of the hill, and was filled with the most delightful old trees, fir and laurel, may, mulberry, hazel, apple, pear, and damson, not to mention currant and gooseberry bushes innumerable, and large strawberry beds spreading down the sunny slopes. There was not a tree there that I did not climb, and one, a widespreading Portugal laurel, was my private country house. I had there my bedroom and my sitting-rooms, my study, and my larder. The larder was supplied by the fruit-trees, from which I was free to pick as I would, and in the study I would sit for hours with some favourite book—Milton's "Paradise Lost" the chief favourite of all. The birds must often have felt startled, when from the small swinging form perching on a branch, came out in childish tones the "Thrones, dominations, princedoms, virtues, powers," of Milton's stately and sonorous verse. I liked to personify Satan, and to declaim the grand speeches of the hero-rebel, and many a happy hour did I pass in Milton's heaven and hell, with for companions Satan and "the Son," Gabriel and Abdiel. Then there was a terrace running by the side of the churchyard, always dry in the wettest weather, and bordered by an old wooden fence, over which clambered roses of every shade; never was such a garden for roses as that of the Old Vicarage. At the end of the terrace was a little summer-house, and in this a trap-door in the fence, which swung open and displayed one of the fairest views in England. Sheer from your feet downwards went the hill, and then far below stretched the wooded country till your eye reached the towers of Windsor Castle, far away on the horizon. It was the view at which Byron was never tired of gazing, as he lay on the flat tombstone close by—Byron's tomb, as it is still called—of which he wrote:—

> "Again I behold where for hours I have pondered,
> As reclining, at eve, on yon tombstone I lay,
> Or round the steep brow of the churchyard I wandered,
> To catch the last gleam of the sun's setting ray."

Reader mine, if ever you go to Harrow, ask permission to enter the old garden, and try the effect of that sudden burst of beauty, as you swing back the small trap-door at the terrace end.

Into this house we moved on my eighth birthday, and for eleven years it was "home" to me, left always with regret, returned to always with joy.

Almost immediately afterwards I left my mother for the first time; for one day, visiting a family who lived close by, I found a stranger sitting in the drawing-room, a lame lady with a strong face, which softened marvellously as she smiled at the child who came dancing in; she called me to her presently, and took me on her lap and talked to me, and on the following day our friend came to see my mother, to ask if she would let me go away and be educated with this lady's niece, coming home for the holidays regularly, but leaving my education in her hands. At first my mother would not hear of it, for she and I scarcely ever left each other; my love for her was an idolatry, hers for me a devotion. (A foolish little story, about which I was unmercifully teased for years, marked that absolute idolatry of her, which has not yet faded from my heart. In tenderest rallying one day of the child who trotted after her everywhere, content to sit, or stand, or wait, if only she might touch hand or dress of "mamma," she said: "Little one" (the name by which she always called me), "if you cling to mamma in this way, I must really get a string and tie you to my apron, and how will you like that?" "O mamma, darling," came the fervent answer, "do let it be in a knot." And, indeed, the tie of love between us was so tightly knotted that nothing ever loosened it till the sword of Death cut that which pain and trouble never availed to slacken in the slightest degree.) But it was urged upon her that the advantages of education offered were such as no money could purchase for me; that it would be a disadvantage for me to grow up in a houseful of boys—and, in truth, I was as good a cricketer and climber as the best of them—that my mother would soon be obliged to send me to school, unless she accepted an offer which gave me every advantage of school without its disadvantages. At last she yielded, and it was decided that Miss Marryat, on returning home, should take me with her.

Miss Marryat—the favourite sister of Captain Marryat, the famous novelist—was a maiden lady of large means. She had nursed her brother through the illness that ended in his death, and had been living with her mother at Wimbledon Park. On her mother's death she looked round for work which would make her useful in the world, and finding that one of her brothers had a large family of girls, she offered to take charge of one of them, and to educate her thoroughly. Chancing to come to Harrow, my good fortune threw me in her way, and she took a fancy to me and thought she would like to teach two little girls rather than one. Hence her offer to my mother.

Miss Marryat had a perfect genius for teaching, and took in it the greatest delight. From time to time she added another child to our party, sometimes a boy, sometimes a girl. At first, with Amy Marryat and myself, there was a little boy, Walter Powys, son of a clergyman with a large family, and him she trained for some years, and then sent him on to school admirably prepared. She chose "her children"—as she loved to call us—in very definite fashion. Each must be gently born and gently trained, but in such position that the education freely given should be a relief and aid to a slender parental purse. It was her delight to seek out and aid those on whom poverty presses most heavily, when the need for education for the children weighs on the proud and the poor. "Auntie" we all called her, for she thought "Miss Marryat" seemed too cold and stiff. She taught us everything herself except music, and for this she had a master, practising us in composition, in recitation, in reading aloud English and French, and later, German, devoting herself to training us in the soundest, most thorough fashion. No words of mine can tell how much I owe her, not only of knowledge, but of that love of knowledge which has remained with me ever since as a constant spur to study.

Her method of teaching may be of interest to some, who desire to train children with least pain, and the most enjoyment to the little ones themselves. First, we never used a spelling-book— that torment of the small child—nor an English grammar. But we wrote letters, telling of the things we had seen in our walks, or told again some story we had read; these childish compositions she would read over with us, correcting all faults of spelling, of grammar, of style, of cadence; a clumsy sentence would be read aloud, that we might hear how unmusical it sounded, an error in observation or expression pointed out. Then, as the letters recorded what we had seen the day before, the faculty of observation was drawn out and trained. "Oh, dear! I have nothing to say!" would come from a small child, hanging over a slate. "Did you not go out for a walk yesterday?" Auntie would question. "Yes," would be sighed out; "but there's nothing to say about it." "Nothing to say! And you walked in the lanes for an hour and saw nothing, little No-eyes? You must use your eyes better to-day." Then there was a very favourite "lesson," which proved an excellent way of teaching spelling. We used to write out lists of all the words we could think of which sounded the same but were differently spelt. Thus: "key, quay," "knight, night," and so on, and great was the glory of

16

the child who found the largest number. Our French lessons—as the German later—included reading from the very first. On the day on which we began German we began reading Schiller's "Wilhelm Tell," and the verbs given to us to copy out were those that had occurred in the reading. We learned much by heart, but always things that in themselves were worthy to be learned. We were never given the dry questions and answers which lazy teachers so much affect. We were taught history by one reading aloud while the others worked—the boys as well as the girls learning the use of the needle. "It's like a girl to sew," said a little fellow, indignantly, one day. "It is like a baby to have to run after a girl if you want a button sewn on," quoth Auntie. Geography was learned by painting skeleton maps—an exercise much delighted in by small fingers—and by putting together puzzle maps, in which countries in the map of a continent, or counties in the map of a country, were always cut out in their proper shapes. I liked big empires in those days; there was a solid satisfaction in putting down Russia, and seeing what a large part of the map was filled up thereby.

The only grammar that we ever learned as grammar was the Latin, and that not until composition had made us familiar with the use of the rules therein given. Auntie had a great horror of children learning by rote things they did not understand, and then fancying they knew them. "What do you mean by that expression, Annie?" she would ask me. After feeble attempts to explain, I would answer: "Indeed, Auntie, I know in my own head, but I can't explain." "Then, indeed, Annie, you do not know in your own head, or you could explain, so that I might know in my own head." And so a healthy habit was fostered of clearness of thought and of expression. The Latin grammar was used because it was more perfect than the modern grammars, and served as a solid foundation for modern languages.

Miss Marryat took a beautiful place, Fern Hill, near Charmouth, in Dorsetshire, on the borders of Devon, and there she lived for some five years, a centre of beneficence in the district. She started a Sunday School, and a Bible Class after awhile for the lads too old for the school, who clamoured for admission to her class in it. She visited the poor, taking help wherever she went, and sending food from her own table to the sick. It was characteristic of her that she would never give "scraps" to the poor, but would have a basin brought in at dinner, and would cut the best slice to tempt the invalid appetite. Money she rarely, if ever, gave, but she would find a day's work, or busy herself to seek permanent employment for any one seeking aid. Stern in rectitude herself, and iron to the fawning or the dishonest, her influence, whether she was feared or loved, was always for good. Of the strictest sect of the Evangelicals, she was an Evangelical. On the Sunday no books were allowed save the Bible or the "Sunday at Home"; but she would try to make the day bright by various little devices; by a walk with her in the garden; by the singing of hymns, always attractive to children; by telling us wonderful missionary stories of Moffat and Livingstone, whose adventures with savages and wild beasts were as exciting as any tale of Mayne Reid's. We used to learn passages from the Bible and hymns for repetition; a favourite amusement was a "Bible puzzle," such as a description of some Bible scene, which was to be recognised by the description. Then we taught in the Sunday School, for Auntie would tell us that it was useless for us to learn if we did not try to help those who had no one to teach them. The Sunday-school lessons had to be carefully prepared on the Saturday, for we were always taught that work given to the poor should be work that cost something to the giver. This principle, regarded by her as an illustration of the text, "Shall I give unto the Lord my God that which has cost me nothing?" ran through all her precept and her practice. When in some public distress we children went to her crying, and asking whether we could not help the little children who were starving, her prompt reply was, "What will you give up for them?" And then she said that if we liked to give up the use of sugar, we might thus each save sixpence a week to give away. I doubt if a healthier lesson can be given to children than that of personal self-denial for the good of others.

Daily, when our lessons were over, we had plenty of fun; long walks and rides, rides on a lovely pony, who found small children most amusing, and on which the coachman taught us to stick firmly, whatever his eccentricities of the moment; delightful all-day picnics in the lovely country round Charmouth, Auntie our merriest playfellow. Never was a healthier home, physically and mentally, made for young things than in that quiet village. And then the delight of the holidays! The pride of my mother at the good report of her darling's progress, and the renewal of acquaintance with every nook and corner in the dear old house and garden.

The dreamy tendency in the child, that on its worldly side is fancy, imagination, on its religious side is the germ of mysticism, and I believe it to be far more common than many people think. But the remorseless materialism of the day—not the philosophic materialism of the few, but the religious materialism of the many—crushes out all the delicate buddings forth of the childish thought, and bandages the eyes that might otherwise see. At first the child does not distinguish between what it "sees" and what it "fancies"; the one is as real, as objective, to it as the other, and it will talk to and play with its dream-comrades as merrily as with children like itself. As a child, I myself very much preferred the former, and never knew what it was to be lonely. But clumsy grown-ups come along and tramp right through the dream-garden, and crush the dream-flowers, and push the dream-children aside, and then say, in their loud, harsh voices— not soft and singable like the dream-voices—"You must not tell such naughty stories, Miss Annie; you give me the shivers, and your mamma will be very vexed with you." But this tendency in me was too strong to be stifled, and it found its food in the fairy tales I loved, and in the religious allegories that I found yet more entrancing. How or when I learned to read, I do not know, for I cannot remember the time when a book was not a delight. At five years of age I must have read easily, for I remember being often unswathed from a delightful curtain, in which I used to roll myself with a book, and told to "go and play," while I was still a five-years'-old dot. And I had a habit of losing myself so completely in the book that my name might be called in the room where I was, and I never hear it, so that I used to be blamed for wilfully hiding myself, when I had simply been away in fairyland, or lying trembling beneath some friendly cabbage-leaf as a giant went by.

I was between seven and eight years of age when I first came across some children's allegories of a religious kind, and a very little later came "Pilgrim's Progress," and Milton's "Paradise Lost." Thenceforth my busy fancies carried me ever into the fascinating world where boy-soldiers kept some outpost for their absent Prince, bearing a shield with his sign of a red cross on it; where devils shaped as dragons came swooping down on the pilgrim, but were driven away defeated after hard struggle; where angels came and talked with little children, and gave them some talisman which warned them of coming danger, and lost its light if they were leaving the right path. What a dull, tire-some world it was that I had to live in, I used to think to myself, when I was told to be a good child, and not to lose my temper, and to be tidy, and not mess my pinafore at dinner. How much easier to be a Christian if one could have a red-cross shield and a white banner, and have a real devil to fight with, and a beautiful Divine Prince to smile at you when the battle was over. How much more exciting to struggle with a winged and clawed dragon, that you knew meant mischief, than to look after your temper, that you never remembered you ought to keep until you had lost it. If I had been Eve in the garden, that old serpent would never have got the better of me; but how was a little girl to know that she might not pick out the rosiest, prettiest apple from a tree that had no serpent to show it was a forbidden one? And as I grew older the dreams and fancies grew less fantastic, but more tinged with real enthusiasm. I read tales of the early Christian martyrs, and passionately regretted I was born so late when no suffering for religion was practicable; I would spend many an hour in daydreams, in which I stood before Roman judges, before Dominican Inquisitors, was flung to lions, tortured on the rack, burned at the stake; one day I saw myself preaching some great new faith to a vast crowd of people, and they listened and were converted, and I became a great religious leader. But always, with a shock, I was brought back to earth, where there were no heroic deeds to do, no lions to face, no judges to defy, but only some dull duty to be performed. And I used to fret that I was born so late, when all the grand things had been done, and when there was no chance of preaching and suffering for a new religion.

From the age of eight my education accented the religious side of my character. Under Miss Marryat's training my religious feeling received a strongly Evangelical bent, but it was a subject of some distress to me that I could never look back to an hour of "conversion"; when others gave their experiences, and spoke of the sudden change they had felt, I used to be sadly conscious that no such change had occurred in me, and I felt that my dreamy longings were very poor things compared with the vigorous "sense of sin" spoken of by the preachers, and used dolefully to wonder if I were "saved." Then I had an uneasy sense that I was often praised for my piety when emulation and vanity were more to the front than religion; as when I learned by heart the Epistle of James, far more to distinguish myself for my good memory than from any love of the text itself; the sonorous cadences of many parts of the Old and New Testaments pleased my ear, and I took a dreamy pleasure in repeating them aloud, just as I would recite for my own amusement hundreds of lines of Milton's "Paradise Lost," as I sat swinging on some branch of a tree, lying back often on some swaying bough and gazing into the unfathomable blue of the sky, till I lost myself in an ecstasy of sound and colour, half chanting the melodious sentences and peopling all the blue with misty forms. This facility of learning by heart, and the habit of dreamy recitation, made me very familiar with the Bible and very apt with its phrases. This stood me in good stead at the prayer-meetings dear to the Evangelical, in which we all took part; in turn we were called on to pray aloud—a terrible ordeal to me, for I was painfully shy when attention was called to me; I used to suffer agonies while I waited for the dreaded words, "Now, Annie dear, will you speak to our Lord." But when my trembling lips had forced themselves into speech, all the nervousness used to vanish and I was swept away by an enthusiasm that readily clothed itself in balanced sentences, and alack! at the end, I too often hoped that God and Auntie had noticed that I prayed very nicely—a vanity certainly not intended to be fostered by the pious exercise. On the whole, the somewhat Calvinistic teaching tended, I think, to make me a little morbid, especially as I always fretted silently after my mother. I remember she was surprised on one of my home-comings, when Miss Marryat noted "cheerfulness" as a want in my character, for at home I was ever the blithest of children, despite my love of solitude; but away, there was always an aching for home, and the stern religion cast somewhat of a shadow over me, though, strangely enough, hell never came into my dreamings except in the interesting shape it took in "Paradise Lost." After reading that, the devil was to me no horned and hoofed horror, but the beautiful shadowed archangel, and I always hoped that Jesus, my ideal Prince, would save him in the end. The things that really frightened me were vague, misty presences that I felt were near, but could not see; they were so real that I knew just where they were in the room, and the peculiar terror they excited lay largely in the feeling that I was just going to see them. If by chance I came across a ghost story it haunted me for months, for I saw whatever unpleasant spectre was described; and there was one horrid old woman in a tale by Sir Walter Scott, who glided up to the foot of your bed and sprang on it in some eerie fashion and glared at you, and who made my going to bed a terror to me for many weeks. I can still recall the feeling so vividly that it almost frightens me now!

CHAPTER III

Girlhood

In the spring of 1861 Miss Marryat announced her intention of going abroad, and asked my dear mother to let me accompany her. A little nephew whom she had adopted was suffering from cataract, and she desired to place him under the care of the famous Düsseldorf oculist. Amy Marryat had been recalled home soon after the death of her mother, who had died in giving birth to the child adopted by Miss Marryat, and named at her desire after her favourite brother Frederick (Captain Marryat). Her place had been taken by a girl a few months older than myself, Emma Mann, one of the daughters of a clergyman, who had married Miss Stanley, closely related, indeed, if I remember rightly, a sister of the Miss Mary Stanley who did such noble work in nursing in the Crimea.

For some months we had been diligently studying German, for Miss Marryat thought it wise that we should know a language fairly well before we visited the country of which it was the native tongue. We had been trained also to talk French daily during dinner, so we were not quite "helpless foreigners" when we steamed away from St. Catherine's Docks, and found ourselves on the following day in Antwerp, amid what seemed to us a very Babel of conflicting tongues. Alas for our carefully spoken French, articulated laboriously! We were lost in that swirl of disputing luggage-porters, and could not understand a word! But Miss Marryat was quite equal to the occasion, being by no means new to travelling, and her French stood the test triumphantly, and steered us safely to a hotel. On the morrow we started again through Aix-la-Chapelle to Bonn, the town which lies on the borders of the exquisite scenery of which the Siebengebirge and Rolandseck serve as the magic portal. Our experiences in Bonn were not wholly satisfactory. Dear Auntie was a maiden lady, looking on all young men as wolves to be kept far from her growing lambs. Bonn was a university town, and there was a mania just then prevailing there for all things English. Emma was a plump, rosy, fair-haired typical English maiden, full of frolic and harmless fun; I a very slight, pale, black-haired girl, alternating between wild fun and extreme pensiveness. In the boarding-house to which we went at first—

the "Château du Rhin," a beautiful place overhanging the broad, blue Rhine—there chanced to be staying the two sons of the late Duke of Hamilton, the Marquis of Douglas and Lord Charles, with their tutor. They had the whole drawing-room floor: we a sitting-room on the ground floor and bedrooms above. The lads discovered that Miss Marryat did not like her "children" to be on speaking terms with any of the "male sect."

Here was a fine source of amusement. They would make their horses caracole on the gravel in front of our window; they would be just starting for their ride as we went for walk or drive, and would salute us with doffed hat and low bow; they would waylay us on our way downstairs with demure "Good morning"; they would go to church and post themselves so that they could survey our pew, and Lord Charles—who possessed the power of moving at will the whole skin of the scalp—would wriggle his hair up and down till we were choking with laughter, to our own imminent risk. After a month of this Auntie was literally driven out of the pretty château, and took refuge in a girls' school, much to our disgust; but still she was not allowed to be at rest. Mischievous students would pursue us wherever we went; sentimental Germans, with gashed cheeks, would whisper complimentary phrases as we passed; mere boyish nonsense of most harmless kind, but the rather stern English lady thought it "not proper," and after three months of Bonn we were sent home for the holidays, somewhat in disgrace. But we had some lovely excursions during those months; such clambering up mountains, such rows on the swift-flowing Rhine, such wanderings in exquisite valleys. I have a long picture-gallery to retire into when I want to think of something fair, in recalling the moon as it silvered the Rhine at the foot of Drachenfels, or the soft, mist-veiled island where dwelt the lady who is consecrated for ever by Roland's love.

A couple of months later we rejoined Miss Marryat in Paris, where we spent seven happy, workful months. On Wednesdays and Saturdays we were free from lessons, and many a long afternoon was passed in the galleries of the Louvre, till we became familiar with the masterpieces of art gathered there from all lands. I doubt if there was a beautiful church in Paris that we did not visit during those weekly wanderings; that of St. Germain de l'Auxerrois was my favourite—the church whose bell gave the signal for the massacre of St. Bartholomew—for it contained such marvellous stained glass, deepest, purest glory of colour that I had ever seen. The solemn beauty of Notre Dame, the somewhat gaudy magnificence of La Sainte Chapelle, the stateliness of La Madeleine, the impressive gloom of St. Roch, were all familiar to us. Other delights were found in mingling with the bright crowds which passed along the Champs Elysees and sauntered in the Bois de Boulogne, in strolling in the garden of the Tuileries, in climbing to the top of every monument whence view of Paris could be gained. The Empire was then in its heyday of glitter, and we much enjoyed seeing the brilliant escort of the imperial carriage, with plumes and gold and silver dancing and glistening in the sunlight, while in the carriage sat the exquisitely lovely empress, with the little boy beside her, touching his cap shyly, but with something of her own grace, in answer to a greeting—the boy who was thought to be born to an imperial crown, but whose brief career was to find an ending from the spears of savages in a quarrel in which he had no concern.

In the spring of 1862 it chanced that the Bishop of Ohio visited Paris, and Mr. Forbes, then English chaplain at the Church of the Rue d'Aguesseau, arranged to have a confirmation. As said above, I was under deep "religious impressions," and, in fact, with the exception of that little aberration in Germany, I was decidedly a pious girl. I looked on theatres (never having been to one) as traps set by Satan for the destruction of foolish souls; I was quite determined never to go to a ball, and was prepared to "suffer for conscience' sake "—little prig that I was—if I was desired to go to one. I was consequently quite prepared to take upon myself the vows made in my name at my baptism, and to renounce the world, the flesh, and the devil, with a heartiness and sincerity only equalled by my profound ignorance of the things I so readily resigned. That confirmation was to me a very solemn matter; the careful preparation, the prolonged prayers, the wondering awe as to the "seven-fold gifts of the Spirit," which were to be given by "the laying on of hands," all tended to excitement. I could scarcely control myself as I knelt at the altar rails, and felt as though the gentle touch of the aged bishop, which fluttered for an instant on my bowed head, were the very touch of the wing of that "Holy Spirit, heavenly Dove," whose presence had been so earnestly invoked. Is there anything easier,

I wonder, than to make a young and sensitive girl "intensely religious"? This stay in Paris roused into activity an aspect of my religious nature that had hitherto been latent. I discovered the sensuous enjoyment that lay in introducing colour and fragrance and pomp into religious services, so that the gratification of the aesthetic emotions became dignified with the garb of piety. The picture-galleries of the Louvre, crowded with Madonnas and saints, the Roman Catholic churches with their incense-laden air and exquisite music, brought a new joy into my life, a more vivid colour to my dreams. Insensibly, the colder, cruder Evangelicalism that I had never thoroughly assimilated, grew warmer and more brilliant, and the ideal Divine Prince of my childhood took on the more pathetic lineaments of the Man of Sorrows, the deeper attractiveness of the suffering Saviour of Men. Keble's "Christian Year" took the place of "Paradise Lost," and as my girlhood began to bud towards womanhood, all its deeper currents set in the direction of religious devotion. My mother did not allow me to read love stories, and my daydreams of the future were scarcely touched by any of the ordinary hopes and fears of a girl lifting her eyes towards the world she is shortly to enter. They were filled with broodings over the days when girl-martyrs were blessed with visions of the King of Martyrs, when sweet St. Agnes saw her celestial Bridegroom, and angels stooped to whisper melodies in St. Cecilia's raptured ear. "Why then and not now?" my heart would question, and I would lose myself in these fancies, never happier than when alone.

The summer of 1862 was spent with Miss Marryat at Sidmouth, and, wise woman that she was, she now carefully directed our studies with a view to our coming enfranchisement from the "schoolroom." More and more were we trained to work alone; our leading-strings were slackened, so that we never felt them save when we blundered; and I remember that when I once complained, in loving fashion, that she was "teaching me so little," she told me that I was getting old enough to be trusted to work by myself, and that I must not expect to "have Auntie for a crutch all through life." And I venture to say that this gentle withdrawal of constant supervision and teaching was one of the wisest and kindest things that this noble-hearted woman ever did for us. It is the usual custom to keep girls in the schoolroom until they "come out"; then, suddenly, they are left to their own devices, and, bewildered by their unaccustomed freedom, they waste time that might be priceless for their intellectual growth. Lately, the opening of universities to women has removed this danger for the more ambitious; but at the time of which I am writing no one dreamed of the changes soon to be made in the direction of the "higher education of women."

During the winter of 1862-63 Miss Marryat was in London, and for a few months I remained there with her, attending the admirable French classes of M. Roche. In the spring I returned home to Harrow, going up each week to the classes; and when these were over, Auntie told me that she thought all she could usefully do was done, and that it was time that I should try my wings alone. So well, however, had she succeeded in her aims, that my emancipation from the schoolroom was but the starting-point of more eager study, though now the study turned into the lines of thought towards which my personal tendencies most attracted me. German I continued to read with a master, and music, under the marvellously able teaching of Mr. John Farmer, musical director of Harrow School, took up much of my time. My dear mother had a passion for music, and Beethoven and Bach were her favourite composers. There was scarcely a sonata of Beethoven's that I did not learn, scarcely a fugue of Bach's that I did not master. Mendelssohn's "Lieder" gave a lighter recreation, and many a happy evening did we spend, my mother and I, over the stately strains of the blind Titan, and the sweet melodies of the German wordless orator. Musical "At Homes," too, were favourite amusements at Harrow, and at these my facile fingers made me a welcome guest.

Thus set free from the schoolroom at 16½, an only daughter, I could do with my time as I would, save for the couple of hours a day given to music, for the satisfaction of my mother. From then till I became engaged, just before I was 19, my life flowed on smoothly, one current visible to all and dancing in the sunlight, the other running underground, but full and deep and strong. As regards my outer life, no girl had a brighter, happier life than mine; studying all the mornings and most of the afternoons in my own way, and spending the latter part of the day in games and walks and rides—varied with parties at which I was one of the merriest of guests. I practised archery so zealously that I carried up triumphantly as prize for the best score the first ring I ever possessed, while croquet found me a most eager devotee.

My darling mother certainly "spoiled" me, so far as were concerned all the small roughnesses of life. She never allowed a trouble of any kind to touch me, and cared only that all worries should fall on her, all joys on me. I know now what I never dreamed then, that her life was one of serious anxiety. The heavy burden of my brother's school and college life pressed on her constantly, and her need of money was often serious. A lawyer whom she trusted absolutely cheated her systematically, using for his own purposes the remittances she made for payment of liabilities, thus keeping upon her a constant drain. Yet for me all that was wanted was ever there. Was it a ball to which we were going? I need never think of what I would wear till the time for dressing arrived, and there laid out ready for me was all I wanted, every detail complete from top to toe. No hand but hers must dress my hair, which, loosed, fell in dense curly masses nearly to my knees; no hand but hers must fasten dress and deck with flowers, and if I sometimes would coaxingly ask if I might not help by sewing in laces, or by doing some trifle in aid, she would kiss me and bid me run to my books or my play, telling me that her only pleasure in life was caring for her "treasure." Alas! how lightly we take the self-denying labour that makes life so easy, ere yet we have known what life means when the protecting motherwing is withdrawn. So guarded and shielded had been my childhood and youth from every touch of pain and anxiety that love could bear for me, that I never dreamed that life might be a heavy burden, save as I saw it in the poor I was sent to help; all the joy of those happy years I took, not ungratefully I hope, but certainly with as glad unconsciousness of anything rare in it as I took the sunlight. Passionate love, indeed, I gave to my darling, but I never knew all I owed her till I passed out of her tender guardianship, till I left my mother's home. Is such training wise? I am not sure. It makes the ordinary roughnesses of life come with so stunning a shock, when one goes out into the world, that one is apt to question whether some earlier initiation into life's sterner mysteries would not be wiser for the young. Yet it is a fair thing to have that joyous youth to look back upon, and at least it is a treasury of memory that no thief can steal in the struggles of later life. "Sunshine" they called me in those bright days of merry play and earnest study. But that study showed the bent of my thought and linked itself to the hidden life; for the Fathers of the early Christian Church now became my chief companions, and I pored over the Shepherd of Hernias, the Epistles of Polycarp, Barnabas, Ignatius, and Clement, the commentaries of Chrysostom, the confessions of Augustine. With these I studied the writings of Pusey, Liddon, and Keble, with many another smaller light, joying in the great conception of a Catholic Church, lasting through the centuries, built on the foundations of apostles and of martyrs, stretching from the days of Christ Himself down to our own—"One Lord, one Faith one Baptism," and I myself a child of that Holy Church. The hidden life grew stronger, constantly fed by these streams of study; weekly communion became the centre round which my devotional life revolved, with its ecstatic meditation, its growing intensity of conscious contact with the Divine; I fasted, according to the ordinances of the Church; occasionally flagellated myself to see if I could bear physical pain, should I be fortunate enough ever to tread the pathway trodden by the saints; and ever the Christ was the figure round which clustered all my hopes and longings, till I often felt that the very passion of, my devotion would draw Him down from His throne in heaven, present visibly in form as I felt Him invisibly in spirit. To serve Him through His Church became more and more a definite ideal in my life, and my thoughts began to turn towards some kind of "religious life," in which I might prove my love by sacrifice and turn my passionate gratitude into active service.

Looking back to-day over my life, I see that its keynote—through all the blunders, and the blind mistakes, and clumsy follies—has been this longing for sacrifice to something felt as greater than the self. It has been so strong and so persistent that I recognise it now as a tendency brought over from a previous life and dominating the present one; and this is shown by the fact that to follow it is not the act of a deliberate and conscious will, forcing self into submission and giving up with pain something the heart desires, but the following it is a joyous springing forward along the easiest path, the "sacrifice" being the supremely attractive thing, not to make which would be to deny the deepest longings of the soul, and to feel oneself polluted and dishonoured. And it is here that the misjudgment comes in of many generous hearts who have spoken sometimes lately so strongly in my praise. For the efforts to serve have not been painful acts of self-denial, but the yielding to an overmastering desire. We do not praise the mother who, impelled by her protecting love, feeds her crying infant and stills its wailings at her breast; rather should we blame her if she turned aside from its weeping to play with some toy. And so with all those whose ears are opened to the wailings of the great orphan Humanity; they are less to be praised for helping than they would be to be blamed if they stood aside. I now know that it is those wailings that have stirred my heart through life, and that I brought with me the ears open to hear them from previous lives of service paid to men. It was those lives that drew for the child the alluring pictures of martyrdom, breathed into the girl the passion of devotion, sent the woman out to face scoff and odium, and drove her finally into the Theosophy that rationalises sacrifice, while opening up possibilities of service beside which all other hopes grow pale.

The Easter of 1866 was a memorable date in my life. I was introduced to the clergyman I married, and I met and conquered my first religious doubt. A little mission church had been opened the preceding Christmas in a very poor district of Clapham. My grandfather's house was near at hand, In Albert Square, and a favourite aunt and myself devoted ourselves a good deal to this little church, as enthusiastic girls and women will. At Easter we decorated it with spring flowers, with dewy primroses and fragrant violets, and with the yellow bells of the wild daffodil, to the huge delight of the poor who crowded in, and of the little London children who had, many of them, never seen a flower. Here I met the Rev. Frank Besant, a young Cambridge man, who had just taken orders, and was serving the little mission church as deacon; strange that at the same time I should meet the man I was to marry, and the doubts which were to break the marriage tie. For in the Holy Week preceding that Easter Eve, I had been—as English and Roman Catholics are wont to do—trying to throw the mind back to the time when the commemorated events occurred, and to follow, step by step, the last days of the Son of Man, living, as it were, through those last hours, so that I might be ready to kneel before the cross on Good Friday, to stand beside the sepulchre on Easter Day. In order to facilitate the realisation of those last sacred days of God incarnate on earth, working out man's salvation, I resolved to write a brief history of that week, compiled from the Four Gospels, meaning them to try and realise each day the occurrences that had happened on the corresponding date in A.D. 33, and so to follow those "blessed feet" step by step, till they were

" nailed for our advantage to the bitter cross."

With the fearlessness which springs from ignorance I sat down to my task. My method was as follows:—

MATTHEW.	MARK.	LUKE.	JOHN.
PALM SUNDAY.	PALM SUNDAY.	PALM SUNDAY.	PALM SUNDAY.
Rode into Jerusalem. Purified the Temple. Returned to Bethany.	Rode into Jerusalem. Returned to Bethany.	Rode into Jerusalem. Purified the Temple. Note: "Taught daily in the temple."	Rode into Jerusalem. Spoke in the Temple.
MONDAY.	MONDAY.	MONDAY.	MONDAY.
Cursed the fig-tree. Taught in the Temple, and spake many parables. No breaks shown, but the fig-tree (xxi.19) did not wither till Tuesday (see Mark).	Cursed the fig-tree. Purified the Temple. Went out of city.	Like Matthew.	——
TUESDAY.	TUESDAY.	TUESDAY.	TUESDAY.
All chaps, xxi. 20, xxii-xxv., spoken on Tuesday, for xxvi. 2 gives Passover as "after two days."	Saw fig-tree withered up. Then discourses.	Discourses. No date shown.	——
WEDNESDAY.	WEDNESDAY.	WEDNESDAY.	WEDNESDAY.

Blank. (Possibly remained in Bethany, the alabaster box of

ointment.)

THURSDAY.	THURSDAY.	THURSDAY.	THURSDAY.
Preparation of Passover. Eating of Passover, and institution of the Holy Eucharist. Gethsemane. Betrayal by Judas. Led captive to Caiaphas. Denied by St. Peter.	Same as Matt.	Same as Matt.	Discourses with disciples, but *before* the Passover. Washes the disciples' feet. Nothing said of Holy Eucharist, nor of agony in Gethsemane. Malchus' ear. Led captives to Annas first. Then to Caiaphas. Denied by St. Peter.
FRIDAY.	**FRIDAY.**	**FRIDAY.**	**FRIDAY.**
Led to Pilate. Judas hangs himself. Tried. Condemned to death. Scourged and mocked. Led to crucifixion. Darkness from 12 to 3. Died at 3.	As Matthew, but hour of crucifixion given, 9 a.m.	Led to Pilate. Sent to Herod. Sent back to Pilate. Rest as in Matthew; but *one* malefactor repents.	Taken to Pilate. Jews would not enter, that they might eat the Passover. Scourged by Pilate before condemnation, and mocked. Shown by Pilate to Jews at 12.

I became uneasy as I proceeded with my task, for discrepancies leaped at me from my four columns; the uneasiness grew as the contradictions increased, until I saw with a shock of horror that my "harmony" was a discord, and a doubt of the veracity of the story sprang up like a serpent hissing in my face. It was struck down in a moment, for to me to doubt was sin, and to have doubted on the very eve of the Passion was an added crime. Quickly I assured myself that these apparent contradictions were necessary as tests of faith, and I forced myself to repeat Tertullian's famous "Credo quia impossible," till, from a wooden recital, it became a triumphant affirmation. I reminded myself that St. Peter had said of the Pauline Epistles that in them were "some things hard to be understood, which they that are unlearned and unstable wrest unto their own destruction." I shudderingly recognised that I must be very unlearned and unstable to find discord among the Holy Evangelists, and imposed on myself an extra fast as penance for my ignorance and lack of firmness in the faith. For my mental position was one to which doubt was one of the worst of sins. I knew that there were people like Colenso, who questioned the infallibility of the Bible, but I remembered how the Apostle John had fled from the Baths when Cerinthus entered them, lest the roof should fall on the heretic, and crush any one in his neighbourhood, and I looked on all heretics with holy horror. Pusey had indoctrinated me with his stern hatred of all heresy, and I was content to rest with him on that faith, "which must be old because it is eternal, and must be unchangeable because it is true." I would not even read the works of my mothers favourite Stanley, because he was "unsound," and because Pusey had condemned his "variegated use of words which destroys all definiteness of meaning"—a clever and pointed description, be it said in passing, of the Dean's exquisite phrases, capable of so many readings. It can then be imagined with what a stab of pain this first doubt struck me, and with what haste I smothered it up, buried it, and smoothed the turf over its grave. *But it had been there*, and it left its mark.

CHAPTER IV

Marriage

The last year of my girlish freedom was drawing to its close; how shall I hope to make commonsense readers understand how I became betrothed maiden ere yet nineteen, girl-wife when twenty years had struck? Looking back over twenty-five years, I feel a profound pity for the girl standing at that critical point of life, so utterly, hopelessly ignorant of all that marriage meant, so filled with impossible dreams, so unfitted for the *rôle* of wife. As I have said, my day-dreams held little place for love, partly from the absence of love novels from my reading, partly from the mystic fancies that twined themselves round the figure of the Christ. Catholic books of devotion—English or Roman, it matters not, for to a large extent they are translations of the same hymns and prayers—are exceedingly glowing in their language, and the dawning feelings of womanhood unconsciously lend to them a passionate fervour. I longed to spend my time in worshipping Jesus, and was, as far as my inner life was concerned, absorbed in that passionate love of "the Saviour" which, among emotional Catholics, really is the human passion of love transferred to an ideal—for women to Jesus, for men to the Virgin Mary. In order to show that I am not here exaggerating, I subjoin a few of the prayers in which I found daily delight, and I do this in order to show how an emotional girl may be attracted by these so-called devotional exercises:—

"O crucified Love, raise in me fresh ardours of love and consolation, that it may henceforth be the greatest torment I can endure ever to offend Thee; that it may be my greatest delight to please Thee."

"Let the remembrance of Thy death, O Lord Jesu, make me to desire and pant after Thee, that I may delight in Thy gracious presence."

"O most sweet Jesu Christ, I, unworthy sinner, yet redeemed by Thy precious blood. Thine I am and will be, in life and in death."

"O Jesu, beloved, fairer than the sons of men, draw me after Thee with the cords of Thy love."

"Blessed are Thou, O most merciful God, who didst vouchsafe to espouse me to the heavenly Bridegroom in the waters of baptism, and hast imparted Thy body and blood as a new gift of espousal and the meet consummation of Thy love."

"O most sweet Lord Jesu, transfix the affections of my inmost soul with that most joyous and most healthful wound of Thy love, with true, serene, most holy, apostolical charity; that my soul may ever languish and melt with entire love and longing for Thee. Let it desire Thee and faint for Thy courts; long to be dissolved and be with Thee."

"Oh, that I could embrace Thee with that most burning love of angels."

"Let Him kiss me with the kisses of His mouth; for Thy love is better than wine. Draw me, we will run after Thee. The king hath brought me into his chambers. Let my soul, O Lord, feel the sweetness of Thy presence. May it taste how sweet Thou art. May the sweet and burning power of Thy love, I beseech Thee, absorb my soul."

All girls have in them the germ of passion, and the line of its development depends on the character brought into the world, and the surrounding influences of education. I had but two ideals in my childhood and youth, round whom twined these budding tendrils of passion; they were my mother and the Christ. I know this may seem strange, but I am trying to state things as they were in this life-story, and not give mere conventionalisms, and so it was. I had men friends, but no lovers—at least, to my knowledge, for I have since heard that my mother received two or three offers of marriage for me, but declined them on account of my youth and my childishness—friends with whom I liked to talk, because they knew more than I did; but they had no place in my day-dreams. These were more and more filled with the one Ideal Man, and my hopes turned towards the life of the Sister of Mercy, who ever worships the Christ, and devotes her life to the service of His poor. I knew my dear mother would set herself against this idea, but it nestled warm at my heart, for ever that idea of escaping from the humdrum of ordinary life by some complete sacrifice lured me onwards with its overmastering fascination.

Now one unlucky result of this view of religion is the idealisation of the clergyman, the special messenger and chosen servant of the Lord. Far more lofty than any title bestowed by earthly monarch is that patent of nobility straight from the hand of the "King of kings," that seems to give to the mortal something of the authority of the immortal, and to crown the head of the priest with the diadem that belongs to those who are "kings and priests unto God." Viewed in this way, the position of the priest's wife seems second only to that of the nun, and has, therefore, a wonderful attractiveness, an attractiveness in which the particular clergyman affected plays a very subordinate part; it is the "sacred office," the nearness to "holy things," the consecration which seems to include the wife—it is these things that shed a glamour over the clerical life which attracts most those who are most apt to self-devotion, most swayed by imagination. And the saddest pity of all this is that the glamour is most over those whose brains are quick, whose hearts are pure, who are responsive to all forms of noble emotions, all suggestions of personal self-sacrifice; if such in later life rise to the higher emotions whose shadows have attracted them, and to that higher self-sacrifice whose whispers reached them in their early youth, then the false prophet's veil is raised, the poverty of the conception seen, and the life is either wrecked, or through storm-wind and surge of battling billows, with loss of mast and sail, is steered by firm hand into the port of a nobler faith.

That summer of 1866 saw me engaged to the young clergyman I had met at the mission church in the spring, our knowledge of each other being an almost negligeable quantity. We were thrown together for a week, the only two young ones in a small party of holiday-makers, and in our walks, rides, and drives we were naturally companions; an hour or two before he left he asked me to marry him, taking my consent for granted as I had allowed him such full companionship—a perfectly fair assumption with girls accustomed to look on all men as possible husbands, but wholly mistaken as regarded myself, whose thoughts were in quite other directions. Startled, and my sensitive pride touched by what seemed to my strict views an assumption that I had been flirting, I hesitated, did not follow my first impulse of refusal, but took refuge in silence; my suitor had to catch his train, and bound me over to silence till he could himself speak to my mother, urging authoritatively that it would be dishonourable of me to break his confidence, and left me—the most upset and distressed little person on the Sussex coast. The fortnight that followed was the first unhappy one of my life, for I had a secret from my mother, a secret which I passionately longed to tell her, but dared not speak at the risk of doing a dishonourable thing. On meeting my suitor on our return to town I positively refused to keep silence any longer, and then out of sheer weakness and fear of inflicting pain I drifted into an engagement with a man I did not pretend to love. "Drifted" is the right word, for two or three months passed, on the ground that I was so much of a child, before my mother would consent to a definite engagement; my dislike of the thought of marriage faded before the idea of becoming the wife of a priest, working ever in the Church and among the poor. I had no outlet for my growing desire for usefulness in my happy and peaceful home-life, where all religious enthusiasm was regarded as unbalanced and unbecoming; all that was deepest and truest in my nature chafed against my easy, useless days, longed for work, yearned to devote itself, as I had read women saints had done, to the service of the Church and of the poor, to the battling against sin and misery—what empty names sin and misery then were to me! "You will have more opportunities for doing good as a clergyman's wife than as anything else," was one of the pleas urged on my reluctance.

In the autumn I was definitely betrothed, and I married fourteen months later. Once, in the interval, I tried to break the engagement, but, on my broaching the subject to my mother, all her pride rose up in revolt. Would I, her daughter, break my word, would I dishonour myself by jilting a man I had pledged myself to marry? She could be stern where honour was involved, that sweet mother of mine, and I yielded to her wish as I had been ever wont to do, for a look or a word from her had ever been my law, save where religion was concerned. So I married in the winter of 1867 with no more idea of the marriage relation than if I had been four years old instead of twenty. My dreamy life, into which no knowledge of evil had been allowed to penetrate, in which I had been guarded from all pain, shielded from all anxiety, kept, innocent on all questions of sex, was no preparation for married existence, and left me defenceless to face a rude awakening. Looking back on it all, I deliberately say that no more fatal blunder can be made than to train a girl to womanhood in ignorance of all life's duties and burdens, and then to let her face them for the first time away from all the old associations, the old helps, the old refuge on the mother's breast. That "perfect innocence" may be very beautiful, but it is a perilous possession, and Eve should have the knowledge of good and evil ere she wanders forth from the paradise of a mother's love. Many an unhappy marriage dates from its very beginning, from the terrible shock to a young girl's sensitive modesty and pride, her helpless bewilderment and fear. Men, with their public school and college education, or the knowledge that comes by living in the outside world, may find it hard to realise the possibility of such infantile ignorance in many girls. None the less, such ignorance is a fact in the case of some girls at least, and no mother should let her daughter, blindfold, slip her neck under the marriage yoke.

Before leaving the harbourage of girlhood to set sail on the troublous sea of life, there is an occurrence of which I must make mention, as it marks my first awakening of interest in the outer world of political struggle. In the autumn of 1867 my mother and I were staying with some dear friends of ours, the Robertses, at Pendleton, near Manchester. Mr. Roberts was "the poor man's lawyer," in the affectionate phrase used of him by many a hundred men. He was a close friend of Ernest Jones, and was always ready to fight a poor man's battle without fee. He worked hard in the agitation which saved women from working in the mines, and I have heard him tell how he had seen them toiling, naked to the waist, with short petticoats barely reaching to their knees, rough, foul-tongued, brutalised out of all womanly decency and grace; and how he had seen little children working there too, babies of three and four set to watch a door, and falling asleep at their work to be roused by curse and kick to the unfair toil. The old man's eye would begin to flash and his voice to rise as he told of these horrors, and then his face would soften as he added that, after it was all over and the slavery was put an end to, as he went through a coal district the women standing at their doors would lift up their children to see "Lawyer Roberts" go by, and would bid "God bless him" for what he had done. This dear old man was my first tutor in Radicalism, and I was an apt pupil. I had taken no interest in politics, but had unconsciously reflected more or less the decorous Whiggism which had always surrounded me. I regarded "the poor" as folk to be educated, looked after, charitably dealt with, and always treated with most perfect courtesy, the courtesy being due from me, as a lady, to all equally, whether they were rich or poor. But to Mr. Roberts "the poor" were the working-bees, the wealth producers, with a right to self-rule not to looking after, with a right to justice, not to charity, and he preached his doctrines to me in season and out of season. I was a pet of his, and used often to drive him to his office in the morning, glorying much in the fact that my skill was trusted in guiding a horse through the crowded Manchester streets. During these drives, and on all other available occasions, Mr. Roberts would preach to me the cause of the people. "What do you think of John Bright?" he demanded suddenly one day, looking at me with fiery eyes from under heavy brows. "I have never thought of him at all," was the careless answer. "Isn't he a rather rough sort of man, who goes about making rows?" "There, I thought so!" he thundered at me fiercely. "That's just what I say. I believe some of you fine ladies would not go to heaven if you had to rub shoulders with John Bright, the noblest man God ever gave to the cause of the poor."

This was the hot-tempered and lovable "demagogue," as he was called, with whom we were staying when Colonel Kelly and Captain Deasy, two Fenian leaders, were arrested in Manchester and put on their trial. The whole Irish population became seething with excitement, and on September 18th the police van carrying them to Salford Gaol was stopped at the Bellevue Railway Arch by the sudden fall of one of the horses, shot from the side of the road. In a moment the van was surrounded, and crowbars were wrenching at the van door. It resisted; a body of police was rapidly approaching, and if the rescue was to be effective the door must be opened. The rescuers shouted to Brett, the constable inside, to pass out his keys; he refused, and some one exclaimed, "Blow off the lock!" In a moment the muzzle of a revolver was against the lock, and it was blown off; but Brett, stooping down to look through the keyhole, received the bullet in his head, and fell dying as the door flew open. Another moment, and Allen, a lad of seventeen, had wrenched open the doors of the compartments occupied by Kelly and Deasy, dragged them out, and while two or three hurried them off to a place of safety, the others threw themselves between the fugitives and the police, and with levelled revolvers guarded their flight. The Fenian leaders once safe, they scattered, and young William Allen, whose one thought had been for his chiefs, seeing them safe, fired his revolver in the air, for he would not shed blood in his own defence. Disarmed by his own act, he was set on by the police, brutally struck down, kicked and stoned, and was dragged off to gaol, faint and bleeding, to meet there some of his comrades in much the same plight as himself. Then Manchester went mad, and race-passions flared up into flame; no Irish workman was safe in a crowd of Englishmen, no Englishman safe in the Irish quarter. The friends of the prisoners besieged "Lawyer Roberts's" house, praying his aid, and he threw his whole fiery soul into their defence. The man who had fired the accidentally fatal shot was safely out of the way, and none of the others had hurt a human being. A Special Commission was issued, with Mr. Justice Blackburn at its head—"the hanging judge," groaned Mr. Roberts—and it was soon in Manchester, for all Mr. Roberts's efforts to get the venue of the trial changed were futile, though of fair trial then in Manchester there was no chance. On October 25th the prisoners were actually brought up before the magistrates in irons, and Mr. Ernest Jones, their counsel, failing in his protest against this outrage, threw down his brief and left the court. So great was the haste with which the trial was hurried on that on the 29th Allen, Larkin, Gould (O'Brien), Maguire, and Condon were standing in the dock before the Commission charged with murder.

My first experience of an angry crowd was on that day as we drove to the court; the streets were barricaded, the soldiers were under arms, every approach to the court crowded with surging throngs. At last our carriage was stopped as we were passing at a foot's pace through an Irish section of the crowd, and various vehement fists came through the window, with hearty curses at the "d——d English who were going to see the boys murdered." The situation was critical, for we were two women and three girls, when I bethought myself that we were unknown, and gently touched the nearest fist: "Friends, these are Mr. Roberts' wife and daughters." "Roberts! Lawyer Roberts! God bless Roberts! Let his carriage through." And all the scowling faces became smile-wreathen, and curses changed to cheers, as a road to the court steps was cleared for us.

Alas! if there was passion on behalf of the prisoners outside, there was passion against them within, and the very opening of the trial showed the spirit that animated the prosecution and the bench. Digby Seymour, Q.C., and Ernest Jones, were briefed for the defence, and Mr. Roberts did not think that they exercised sufficiently their right of challenge; he knew, as we all did, that many on the panel had loudly proclaimed their hostility to the Irish, and Mr. Roberts persisted in challenging them as his counsel would not. In vain Judge Blackburn threatened to commit the rebellious solicitor: "These men's lives are at stake, my lord," was his indignant plea. "Remove that man!" cried the angry judge, but as the officers of the court came forward very slowly—for all poor men loved and honoured the sturdy fighter—he changed his mind and let him stay. Despite all his efforts, the jury contained a man who had declared that he "didn't care what the evidence was, he would hang every d——d Irishman of the lot." And the result showed that he was not alone in his view, for evidence of the most disreputable kind was admitted; women of the lowest type were put into the box as witnesses, and their word taken as unchallengeable; thus was destroyed an *alibi* for Maguire, afterwards accepted by the Crown, a free pardon being issued on the strength of it. Nothing could save the doomed men from the determined verdict, and I could see from where I was sitting into a little room behind the bench, where an official was quietly preparing the black caps before the verdict had been delivered. The foregone "Guilty" was duly repeated as verdict on each of the five cases, and the prisoners asked if they had anything to say why sentence of death should not be passed on them. Allen, boy as he was, made a very brave and manly speech; he had not fired, save in the air—if he had done so he might have escaped; he had helped to free Kelly and Deasy, and did not regret it; he was willing to die for Ireland. Maguire and Condon (he also was reprieved) declared they were not present, but, like Allen, were ready to die for their country. Sentence of death was passed, and, as echo to the sardonic "The Lord have mercy on your souls," rang back from the dock in five clear voices, with never a quiver of fear in them, "God save Ireland!" and the men passed one by one from the sight of my tear-dimmed eyes.

It was a sorrowful time that followed; the despair of the heart-broken girl who was Allen's sweetheart, and who cried to us on her knees, "Save my William!" was hard to see; nothing we or any one could do availed to avert the doom, and on November 23rd Allen, Larkin, and O'Brien were hanged outside Salford Gaol. Had they striven for freedom in Italy England would have honoured them; here she buried them as common murderers in quicklime in the prison yard.

I have found, with a keen sense of pleasure, that Mr. Bradlaugh and myself were in 1867 to some extent co-workers, although we knew not of each other's existence, and although he was doing much, and I only giving such poor sympathy as a young girl might, who was only just awakening to the duty of political work. I read in the *National Reformer* for November 24, 1867, that in the preceding week he was pleading on Clerkenwell Green for these men's lives:—"According to the evidence at the trial, Deasy and Kelly were illegally arrested. They had been arrested for vagrancy of which no evidence was given, and apparently remanded for felony without a shadow of justification. He had yet to learn that in England the same state of things existed as in Ireland; he had yet to learn that an illegal arrest was sufficient ground to detain any of the citizens of any country in the prisons of this one. If he were illegally held, he was justified in using enough force to procure his release. Wearing a policeman's coat gave no authority when the officer exceeded his jurisdiction. He had argued this before Lord Chief Justice Erie in the Court of Common Pleas, and that learned judge did not venture to contradict the argument which he submitted. There was another reason why they should spare these men, although he hardly expected the Government to listen, because the Government sent down one of the judges who was predetermined to convict the prisoners; it was that the offence was purely a political one. The death of Brett was a sad mischance, but no one who read the evidence could regard the killing of Brett as an intentional murder. Legally, it was murder; morally, it was homicide in the rescue of a political captive. If it were a question of the rescue of the political captives of Varignano, or of political captives in Bourbon, in Naples, or in Poland, or in Paris, even earls might be found so to argue. Wherein is our sister Ireland less than these? In executing these men, they would throw down the gauntlet for terrible reprisals. It was a grave and solemn question. It had been said by a previous speaker that they were prepared to go to any lengths to save these Irishmen. They were not. He wished they were. If they were, if the men of England, from one end to the other, were prepared to say, 'These men shall not be executed,' they would not be. He was afraid they had not pluck enough for that. Their moral courage was not equal to their physical strength. Therefore he would not say that they were prepared to do so. They must plead *ad misericordiam*. He appealed to the press, which represented the power of England; to that press which in its panic-stricken moments had done much harm, and which ought now to save these four doomed men. If the press demanded it, no Government would be mad enough to resist. The memory of the blood which was shed in 1798 rose up like a bloody ghost against them to-day. He only feared that what they said upon the subject might do the poor men more harm than good. If it were not so, he would coin words that should speak in words of fire. As it was, he could only say to the Government: You are strong to-day; you hold these men's lives in your hands; but if you want to reconcile their country to you, if you want to win back Ireland, if you want to make her children love you—then do not embitter their hearts still more by taking the lives of these men. Temper your strength with mercy; do not use the sword of justice like one of vengeance, for the day may come when it shall be broken in your hands, and you yourselves brained by the hilt of the weapon you have so wickedly wielded." In October he had printed a plea for Ireland, strong and earnest, asking:—

"Where is our boasted English freedom when you cross to Kingstown pier? Where has it been for near two years? The Habeas Corpus Act suspended, the gaols crowded, the steamers searched, spies listening at shebeen shops for sedition, and the end of it a Fenian panic in England. Oh, before it be too late, before more blood stain the pages of our present history, before we exasperate and arouse bitter animosities, let us try and do justice to our sister land. Abolish once and for all the land laws, which in their iniquitous operation have ruined her peasantry. Sweep away the leech-like Church which has sucked her vitality, and has given her back no word even of comfort in her degradation. Turn her barracks into flax mills, encourage a spirit of independence in her citizens, restore to her people the protection of the law, so that they may speak without fear of arrest, and beg them to plainly and boldly state their grievances. Let a commission of the best and wisest amongst Irishmen, with some of our highest English judges added, sit solemnly to hear all complaints, and then let us honestly legislate, not for the punishment of the discontented, but to remove the causes of the discontent. It is not the Fenians who have depopulated Ireland's strength and increased her misery. It is not the Fenians who have evicted tenants by the score. It is not the Fenians who have checked cultivation. Those who have caused the wrong at least should frame the remedy."

In December, 1867, I sailed out of the safe harbour of my happy and peaceful girlhood on to the wide sea of life, and the waves broke roughly as soon as the bar was crossed. We were an ill-matched pair, my husband and I, from the very outset; he, with very high ideas of a husband's authority and a wife's submission, holding strongly to the "master-in-my-own-house theory," thinking much of the details of home arrangements, precise, methodical, easily angered and with difficulty appeased. I, accustomed to freedom, indifferent to home details, impulsive, very hot-tempered, and proud as Lucifer. I had never had a harsh word spoken to me, never been ordered to do anything, had had my way smoothed for my feet, and never a worry had touched me. Harshness roused first incredulous wonder, then a storm of indignant tears, and after a time a proud, defiant resistance, cold and hard as iron. The easy-going, sunshiny, enthusiastic girl changed—and changed pretty rapidly—into a grave, proud, reticent woman, burying deep in her own heart all her hopes, her fears, and her disillusions. I must have been a very unsatisfactory wife from the beginning, though I think other treatment might gradually have turned me into a fair imitation of the proper conventional article. Beginning with the ignorance before alluded to, and so scared and outraged at heart from the very first; knowing nothing of household management or economical use of money—I had never had an allowance or even bought myself a pair of gloves—though eager to perform my new duties creditably; unwilling to potter over little things, and liking to do swiftly what I had to do, and then turn to my beloved books; at heart fretting for my mother but rarely speaking of her, as I found my longing for her presence raised jealous vexation; with strangers about me with whom I had no sympathy; visited by ladies who talked to me only about babies and servants—troubles of which I knew nothing and which bored me unutterably—and who were as uninterested in all that had filled my life, in theology, in politics, in science, as I was uninterested in the discussions on the housemaid's young man and on the cook's extravagance in using "butter, when dripping would have done perfectly well, my dear"; was it wonderful that I became timid, dull, and depressed?

All my eager, passionate enthusiasm, so attractive to men in a young girl, were doubtless incompatible with "the solid comfort of a wife," and I must have been inexpressibly tiring to the Rev. Frank Besant. And, in truth, I ought never to have married, for under the soft, loving, pliable girl there lay hidden, as much unknown to herself as to her surroundings, a woman of strong dominant will, strength that panted for expression and rebelled against restraint, fiery and passionate emotions that were seething under compression—a most undesirable partner to sit in the lady's arm-chair on the domestic rug before the fire. [*Que le diable faisait-elle dans cette galère,*] I have often thought, looking back at my past self, and asking, Why did that foolish girl make her bed so foolishly? But self-analysis shows the contradictories in my nature that led me into so mistaken a course. I have ever been the queerest mixture of weakness and strength, and have paid heavily for the weakness. As a child I used to suffer tortures of shyness, and if my shoe-lace was untied would feel shamefacedly that every eye was fixed on the unlucky string; as a girl I would shrink away from strangers and think myself unwanted and unliked, so that I was full of eager gratitude to any one who noticed me kindly; as the young mistress of a house, I was afraid of my servants, and would let careless work pass rather than bear the pain of reproving the ill-doer; when I have been lecturing and debating with no lack of spirit on the platform, I have preferred to go without what I wanted at the hotel rather than to ring and make the waiter fetch it; combative on the platform in defence of any cause I cared for, I shrink from quarrel or disapproval in the home, and am a coward at heart in private while a good fighter in public. How often have I passed unhappy quarters of an hour screwing up my courage to find fault with some subordinate whom my duty compelled me to reprove, and how often have I jeered at myself for a fraud as the doughty platform combatant, when shrinking from blaming some lad or lass for doing their work badly! An unkind look or word has availed to make me shrink into myself as a snail into its shell, while on the platform opposition makes me speak my best. So I slid into marriage blindly and stupidly, fearing to give pain; fretted my heart out for a year; then, roused by harshness and injustice, stiffened and hardened, and lived with a wall of ice round me within which I waged mental conflicts that nearly killed me; and learned at last how to live and work in armour that turned the edge of the weapons that struck it, and left the flesh beneath unwounded, armour laid aside, but in the presence of a very few.

My first serious attempts at writing were made in 1868, and I took up two very different lines of composition; I wrote some short stories of a very flimsy type, and also a work of a much more ambitious character, "The Lives of the Black Letter Saints." For the sake of the unecclesiastically trained it may be as well to mention that in the Calendar of the Church of England there are a number of Saints' Days; some of these are printed in red, and are Red Letter Days, for which services are appointed by the Church; others are printed in black, and are Black Letter Days, and have no special services fixed for them. It seemed to me that it would be interesting to take each of these days and write a sketch of the life of the saint belonging to it, and accordingly I set to work to do so, and gathered various books of history and legend where-from to collect my "facts." I do not in the least know what became of that valuable book; I tried Macmillans with it, and it was sent on by them to some one who was preparing a series of Church books for the young; later I had a letter from a Church brotherhood offering to publish it, if I would give it as "an act of iety" to their order; its ultimate fate is to me unknown.

The short stories were more fortunate. I sent the first to the *Family Herald*, and some weeks afterwards received a letter from which dropped a cheque as I opened it. Dear me! I have earned a good deal of money since by my pen, but never any that gave me the intense delight of that first thirty shillings. It was the first money I had ever earned, and the pride of the earning was added to the pride of authorship. In my childish delight and practical religion, I went down on my knees and thanked God for sending it to me, and I saw myself earning heaps of golden guineas, and becoming quite a support of the household. Besides, it was "my very own," I thought, and a delightful sense of independence came over me. I had not then realised the beauty of the English law, and the dignified position in which it placed the married woman; I did not understand that all a married woman earned by law belonged to her owner, and that she could have nothing that belonged to her of right.[1] I did not want the money: I was only so glad to have something of my own to give, and it was rather a shock to learn that it was not really mine at all.

From time to time after that I earned a few pounds for stories in the same journal; and the *Family Herald*, let me say, has one peculiarity which should render it beloved by poor authors; it pays its contributor when it accepts the paper, whether it prints it immediately or not; thus my first story was not printed for some weeks after I received the cheque, and it was the same with all the others accepted by the same journal. Encouraged by these small successes, I began writing a novel! It took a long time to do, but was at last finished, and sent off to the *Family Herald*. The poor thing came back, but with a kind note, telling me that it was too political for their pages, but that if I would write one of "purely domestic interest," and up to the same level, it would probably be accepted. But by that time I was in the full struggle of theological doubt, and that novel of "purely domestic interest" never got itself written.

I contributed further to the literature of my country a theological pamphlet, of which I forget the exact title, but it dealt with the

---

[1] This odious law has now been altered, and a married woman is a person, not a chattel.

duty of fasting incumbent on all faithful Christians, and was very patristic in its tone.

In January, 1869, my little son was born, and as I was very ill for some months before, and was far too much interested in the tiny creature afterwards, to devote myself to pen and paper, my literary career was checked for a while. The baby gave a new interest and a new pleasure to life, and as we could not afford a nurse I had plenty to do in looking after his small majesty. My energy in reading became less feverish when it was done by the side of the baby's cradle, and the little one's presence almost healed the abiding pain of my mother's loss.

From a photograph by Dighton's Art Studio, Cheltenham.

ANNIE BESANT 1869.

I may pass very quickly over the next two years. In August, 1870, a little sister was born to my son, and the recovery was slow and tedious, for my general health had been failing for some time.

The boy was a bright, healthy little fellow, but the girl was delicate from birth, suffering from her mother's unhappiness, and born somewhat prematurely in consequence of a shock.

When, in the spring of 1871, the two children caught the whooping cough, my Mabel's delicacy made the ordeal well-nigh fatal to her. She was very young for so trying a disease, and after a while bronchitis set in and was followed by congestion of the lungs. For weeks she lay in hourly peril of death We arranged a screen round the fire like a tent, and kept it full of steam to ease the panting breath; and there I sat, day and night, all through those weary weeks, the tortured baby on my knees. I loved my little ones passionately, for their clinging love soothed the aching at my heart, and their baby eyes could not critically scan the unhappiness that grew deeper month by month; and that steam-filled tent became my world, and there, alone, I fought with Death for my child. The doctor said that recovery was impossible, and that in one of the paroxysms of coughing she must die; the most distressing thing was that, at last, even a drop or two of milk would bring on the terrible convulsive choking, and it seemed cruel to add to the pain of the apparently dying child. At length, one morning the doctor said she could not last through the day; I had sent for him hurriedly, for the body had suddenly swollen up as a result of the perforation of one of the pleurae, and the consequent escape of air into the cavity of the chest. While he was there one of the fits of coughing came on, and it seemed as though it must be the last. He took a small bottle of chloroform out of his pocket, and putting a drop on a handkerchief held it near the child's face, till the drug soothed the convulsive struggle. "It can't do any harm at this stage," he said, "and it checks the suffering." He went away, saying that he feared he would never see the child alive again. One of the kindest friends I had in my married life was that same doctor, Mr. Lauriston Winterbotham; he was as good as he was clever, and, like so many of his noble profession, he had the merits of discretion and silence. He never breathed a word as to my unhappiness, until in 1878 he came up to town to give evidence as to cruelty which—had the deed of separation not been held as condonation—would have secured me a divorce *a mensa et thoro.*

The child, however, recovered, and her recovery was due, I think, to that chance thought of Mr. Winterbotham's about the chloroform, for I used it whenever the first sign of a fit of coughing appeared, and so warded off the convulsive attack and the profound exhaustion that followed, in which a mere flicker of breath at the top of the throat was the only sign of life, and sometimes even that disappeared, and I thought her gone. For years the child remained ailing and delicate, requiring the tenderest care, but those weeks of anguish left a deeper trace on mother than on child. Once she was out of danger I collapsed physically, and lay in bed for a week unmoving, and then rose to face a struggle which lasted for three years and two months, and nearly cost me my life, the struggle which transformed me from a Christian into an Atheist. The agony of the struggle was in the first nineteen months—a time to be looked back upon with shrinking, as it was a hell to live through at the time. For no one who has not felt it knows the fearful anguish inflicted by doubt on the earnestly religious soul. There is in life no other pain so horrible, so keen in its torture, so crushing in its weight. It seems to shipwreck everything, to destroy the one steady gleam of happiness "on the other side" that no earthly storm could obscure; to make all life gloomy with a horror of despair, a darkness that verily may be felt. Nothing but an imperious intellectual and moral necessity can drive into doubt a religious mind, for it is as though an earthquake shook the foundations of the soul, and the very being quivers and sways under the shock. No life in the empty sky; no gleam in the blackness of the night; no voice to break the deadly silence; no hand outstretched to save. Empty-brained triflers who have never tried to think, who take their creed as they take their fashions, speak of Atheism as the outcome of foul life and vicious desires. In their shallow heartlessness and shallower thought they cannot even dimly imagine the anguish of entering the mere penumbra of the Eclipse of Faith, much less the horror of that great darkness in which the orphaned soul cries out into the infinite emptiness: "Is it a Devil that has made the world? Is the echo, 'Children, ye have no Father,' true? Is all blind chance, is all the clash of unconscious forces, or are we the sentient toys of an Almighty Power that sports with our agony, whose peals of awful mockery of laughter ring back answer to the wailings of our despair?"

How true are the noble words of Mrs. Hamilton King:—

"For some may follow Truth from dawn to dark,
As a child follows by his mother's hand,
Knowing no fear, rejoicing all the way;
And unto some her face is as a Star
Set through an avenue of thorns and fires,
And waving branches black without a leaf;
And still It draws them, though the feet must bleed,
Though garments must be rent, and eyes be scorched:
And if the valley of the shadow of death
Be passed, and to the level road they come,

Still with their faces to the polar star,
It is not with the same looks, the same limbs,
But halt, and maimed, and of infirmity.
And for the rest of the way they have to go
It is not day but night, and oftentimes

A night of clouds wherein the stars are lost."[2]

Aye! but never lost is the Star of Truth to which the face is set, and while that shines all lesser lights may go. It was the long months of suffering through which I had been passing, with the seemingly purposeless torturing of my little one as a climax, that struck the first stunning blow at my belief in God as a merciful Father of men. I had been visiting the poor a good deal, and had marked the patient suffering of their lives; my idolised mother had been defrauded by a lawyer she had trusted, and was plunged into debt by his non-payment of the sums that should have passed through his hands to others; my own bright life had been enshrouded by pain and rendered to me degraded by an intolerable sense of bondage; and here was my helpless, sinless babe tortured for weeks and left frail and suffering. The smooth brightness of my previous life made all the disillusionment more startling, and the sudden plunge into conditions so new and so unfavourable dazed and stunned me. My religious past became the worst enemy of the suffering present. All my personal belief in Christ, all my intense faith in His constant direction of affairs, all my habit of continual prayer and of realisation of His Presence—all were against me now. The very height of my trust was the measure of the shock when the trust gave way. To me He was no abstract idea, but a living reality, and all my heart rose up against this Person in whom I believed, and whose individual finger I saw in my baby's agony, my own misery, the breaking of my mother's proud heart under a load of debt, and all the bitter suffering of the poor. The presence of pain and evil in a world made by a good God; the pain falling on the innocent, as on my seven months' old babe; the pain begun here reaching on into eternity unhealed; a sorrow-laden world; a lurid, hopeless hell; all these, while I still believed, drove me desperate, and instead of like the devils believing and trembling, I believed and hated. All the hitherto dormant and unsuspected strength of my nature rose up in rebellion; I did not yet dream of denial, but I would no longer kneel.

---

[2] "The Disciples,"

As the first stirrings of this hot rebellion moved in my heart I met a clergyman of a very noble type, who did much to help me by his ready and wise sympathy. Mr. Besant brought him to see me during the crisis of the child's illness; he said little, but on the following day I received from him the following note:—

"*April* 21, 1871.

"My Dear Mrs. Besant,—I am painfully conscious that I gave you but little help in your trouble yesterday. It is needless to say that it was not from want of sympathy. Perhaps it would be nearer the truth to say that it was from excess of sympathy. I shrink intensely from meddling with the sorrow of any one whom I feel to be of a sensitive nature. 'The heart hath its own bitterness, and the stranger meddleth not therewith.' It is to me a positively fearful thought that I might awaken such a reflection as

"'And common was the commonplace,
And vacant chaff well meant for grain.'

Conventional consolations, conventional verses out of the Bible, and conventional prayers are, it seems to me, an intolerable aggravation of suffering. And so I acted on a principle that I mentioned to your husband that 'there is no power so great as that of one human faith looking upon another human faith.' The promises of God, the love of Christ for little children, and all that has been given to us of hope and comfort, are as deeply planted in your heart as in mine, and I did not care to quote them. But when I talk face to face with one who is in sore need of them, my faith in them suddenly becomes so vast and heart-stirring that I think I must help most by talking naturally, and letting the faith find its own way from soul to soul. Indeed, I could not find words for it if I tried. And yet I am compelled, as a messenger of the glad tidings of God, to solemnly assure you that all is well. We have no key to the 'mystery of pain' excepting the Cross of Christ. But there is another and a deeper solution in the hands of our Father; and it will be ours when we can understand it. There is—in the place to which we travelsome blessed explanation of your baby's pain and your grief, which will fill with light the darkest heart. Now you must believe without having seen; that is true faith. You must

"'Reach a hand through time to catch
The far-off interest of tears.'

That you may have strength so to do is part of your share in the prayers of

"Yours very faithfully,

"W. D——."

A noble letter, but the storm was beating too fiercely to be stilled, and one night in that summer of 1871 stands out clearly before me. Mr. Besant was away, and there had been a fierce quarrel before he left. I was outraged, desperate, with no door of escape from a life that, losing its hope in God, had not yet learned to live for hope for man. No door of escape? The thought came like a flash: "There is one!" And before me there swung open, with lure of peace and of safety, the gateway into silence and security, the gateway of the tomb. I was standing by the drawing-room window, staring hopelessly at the evening sky; with the thought came the remembrance that the means was at hand—the chloroform that had soothed my baby's pain, and that I had locked away upstairs. I ran up to my room, took out the bottle, and carried it downstairs, standing again at the window in the summer twilight, glad that the struggle was over and peace at hand. I uncorked the bottle, and was raising it to my lips, when, as though the words were spoken softly and clearly, I heard: "O coward, coward, who used to dream of martyrdom, and cannot bear a few short years of pain!" A rush of shame swept over me, and I flung the bottle far away among the shrubs in the garden at my feet, and for a moment I felt strong as for a struggle, and then fell fainting on the floor. Only once again in all the strifes of my career did the thought of suicide recur, and then it was but for a moment, to be put aside as unworthy a strong soul.

My new friend, Mr. D——, proved a very real help. The endless torture of hell, the vicarious sacrifice of Christ, the trustworthiness of revelation, doubts on all these hitherto accepted doctrines grew and heaped themselves on my bewildered soul. My questionings were neither shirked nor discouraged by Mr. D——; he was not horrified nor was he sanctimoniously rebukeful, but met them all with a wide comprehension inexpressibly soothing to one writhing in the first agonies of doubt. He left Cheltenham in the early autumn of 1871, but the following extracts from a letter written in November will show the kind of net in which I was struggling (I had been reading M'Leod Campbell's work "On the Atonement"):—

"You forget one great principle—that God is impassive, cannot suffer. Christ, *quâ* God, did not suffer, but as Son of *Man* and in His humanity. Still, it may be correctly stated that He felt to sin and sinners 'as God eternally feels'—*i.e., abhorrence of sin, and love of the sinner.* But to infer from that that the Father in His Godhead feels the sufferings which Christ experienced solely in humanity, and because incarnate is, I think, wrong.

"(2) I felt strongly inclined to blow you up for the last part of your letter. You assume, I think quite gratuitously, that God condemns the major part of His children to objectless future suffering. You say that if He does not, He places a book in their hands which threatens what He does not mean to inflict. But how utterly this seems to me opposed to the gospel of Christ! All Christ's references to eternal punishment may be resolved into references to the Valley of Hinnom, by way of imagery; with the exception of the Dives parable, where is distinctly inferred a moral amendment beyond the grave. I speak of the unselfish desire of Dives to save his brothers. The more I see of the controversy, the more baseless does the eternal punishment theory appear. It seems then, to me, that instead of feeling aggrieved and shaken, you ought to feel encouraged and thankful that God is so much better than you were taught to believe Him. You will have discovered by this time in Maurice's 'What is Revelation?' (I suppose you have the 'Sequel,' too?), that God's truth is our truth, and His love is our love, only more perfect and full. There is no position more utterly defeated in modern philosophy and theology than Dean Mansel's attempt to show that God's love, justice, &c., are different in kind from ours. Mill and Maurice, from totally alien points of view, have shown up the preposterous nature of the notion.

"(3) A good deal of what you have thought is, I fancy, based on a strange forgetfulness of your former experience. If you have known Christ—(whom to know is eternal life)—and that you have known Him I am certain—can you really say that a few intellectual difficulties, nay, a few moral difficulties if you will, are able at once to obliterate the testimony of that higher state of being?

"Why, the keynote of all my theology is that Christ is lovable because, and *just* because, He is the perfection of all that I know to be noble and generous, and loving, and tender, and true. If an angel from heaven brought me a gospel which contained doctrines that would not stand the test of such perfect lovableness—doctrines hard, or cruel, or unjust—I should reject him and his trumpery gospel with scorn, knowing that neither could be Christ's. Know Christ and judge religions by Him; don't judge Him by religions, and then complain because they find yourself looking at Him through a blood-coloured glass."

"I am saturating myself with Maurice, who is the antidote given by God to this age against all dreary doublings and temptings of the devil to despair."

Many a one, in this age of controversy over all things once held sacred, has found peace and new light on this line of thought, and has succeeded in thus reconciling theological doctrines with the demands of the conscience for love and justice in a world made by a just and loving God. I could not do so. The awakening to what the world was, to the facts of human misery, to the ruthless tramp of nature and of events over the human heart, making no difference between innocent and guilty—the shock had been too great for the equilibrium to be restored by arguments that appealed to the emotions and left the intellect unconvinced. Months of this long-drawn-out mental anguish wrought their natural effects on physical health, and at last I broke down completely, and lay for weeks helpless and prostrate, in raging and unceasing head-pain, unable to sleep, unable to bear the light, lying like a log on the bed, not unconscious, but indifferent to everything, consciousness centred, as it were, in the ceaseless pain. The doctor tried every form of relief, but, entrenched in its citadel, the pain defied his puny efforts. He covered my head with ice, he gave me opium— which only drove me mad—he did all that skill and kindness could do, but all in vain. Finally the pain wore itself out, and the moment he dared to do so, he tried mental diversion; he brought me books on anatomy, on science, and persuaded me to study them; and out of his busy life would steal an hour to explain to me knotty points on physiology. He saw that if I were to be brought back to reasonable life, it could only be by diverting thought from the channels in which the current had been running to a dangerous extent. I have often felt that I owed life and sanity to that good man, who felt for the helpless, bewildered child-woman, beaten down by the cyclone of doubt and misery.

So it will easily be understood that my religious wretchedness only increased the unhappiness of homelife, for how absurd it was that any reasonable human being should be so tossed with anguish over intellectual and moral difficulties on religious matters, and should make herself ill over these unsubstantial troubles. Surely it was a woman's business to attend to her husband's comforts and to see after her children, and not to break her heart over misery here and hell hereafter, and distract her brain with questions that had puzzled the greatest thinkers and still remained unsolved! And, truly, women or men who get themselves concerned about the universe at large, would do well not to plunge hastily into marriage, for they do not run smoothly in the double-harness of that honourable estate. *Sturm und Drang* should be faced alone, and the soul should go out alone into the wilderness to be tempted of the devil, and not bring his majesty and all his imps into the placid circle of the home. Unhappy they who go into marriage with the glamour of youth upon them and the destiny of conflict imprinted on their nature, for they make misery for their partner in marriage as well as for themselves. And if that partner, strong in traditional authority and conventional habits, seeks to "break in" the turbulent and storm-tossed creature—well, it comes to a mere trial of strength and endurance, whether that driven creature will fall panting and crushed, or whether it will turn in its despair, assert its Divine right to intellectual liberty, rend its fetters in pieces, and, discovering its own strength in its extremity, speak at all risks its "No" when bidden to live a lie.

When that physical crisis was over I decided on my line of action. I resolved to take Christianity as it had been taught in the Churches, and carefully and thoroughly examine its dogmas one by one, so that I should never again say "I believe" where I had not proved, and that, however diminished my area of belief, what was left of it might at least be firm under my feet. I found that four chief problems were pressing for solution, and to these I addressed myself. How many are to-day the souls facing just these problems, and disputing every inch of their old ground of faith with the steadily advancing waves of historical and scientific criticism! Alas! for the many Canutes, as the waves wash over their feet. These problems were:—

(1) The eternity of punishment after death.

(2) The meaning of "goodness" and "love," as applied to a God who had made this world, with all its sin and misery.

54

(3) The nature of the atonement of Christ, and the "justice" of God in accepting a vicarious suffering from Christ, and a vicarious righteousness from the sinner.

(4) The meaning of "inspiration" as applied to the Bible, and the reconciliation of the perfections of the author with the blunders and immoralities of the work.

It will be seen that the deeper problems of religion—the deity of Christ, the existence of God, the immortality of the soul—were not yet brought into question, and, looking back, I cannot but see how orderly was the progression of thought, how steady the growth, after that first terrible earthquake, and the first wild swirl of agony. The points that I set myself to study were those which would naturally be first faced by any one whose first rebellion against the dogmas of the Churches was a rebellion of the moral nature rather than of the intellectual, a protest of the conscience rather than of the brain. It was not a desire for moral licence which gave me the impulse that finally landed me in Atheism; it was the sense of outraged justice and insulted right. I was a wife and mother, blameless in moral life, with a deep sense of duty and a proud self-respect; it was while I was this that doubt struck me, and while I was in the guarded circle of the home, with no dream of outside work or outside liberty, that I lost all faith in Christianity. My education, my mother's example, my inner timidity and self-distrust, all fenced me in from temptations from without. It was the uprising of an outraged conscience that made me a rebel against the Churches and finally an unbeliever in God. And I place this on record, because the progress of Materialism will never be checked by diatribes against unbelievers, as though they became unbelievers from desire for vice and for licence to do evil. What Religion has to face in the controversies of to-day is not the unbelief of the sty, but the unbelief of the educated conscience and of the soaring intellect; and unless it can arm itself with a loftier ethic and a grander philosophy than its opponent, it will lose its hold over the purest and the strongest of the younger generation.

CHAPTER V

The Storm of Doubt

My reading of heretical and Broad Church works on one side, and of orthodox ones on the other, now occupied a large part of my time, and our removal to Sibsey, in Lincolnshire, an agricultural village with a scattered population, increased my leisure. I read the works of Robertson, Stopford Brooke, Stanley, Greg, Matthew Arnold, Liddon, Mansel, and many another, and my scepticism grew deeper and deeper as I read. The Broad Church arguments appeared to me to be of the nature of special pleading, skilful evasions of difficulties rather than the real meeting and solving of them. For the problem was: Given a good God, how can He have created mankind, knowing beforehand that the vast majority of those whom He created were to be tortured for ever? Given a just God, how can He punish people for being sinful, when they have inherited a sinful nature without their own choice and of necessity? Given a righteous God, how can He allow sin to exist for ever, so that evil shall be as eternal as good, and Satan shall reign in hell as long as Christ in heaven? Worst of all puzzles, perhaps, was that of the existence of evil and of misery, and the racking doubt whether God *could* be good, and yet look on the evil and the misery of the world unmoved and untouched. It seemed so impossible to believe that a Creator could be either cruel enough to be indifferent to the misery, or weak enough to be unable to stop it. The old dilemma faced me incessantly: "If He can prevent it and does not, He is not good; if He wishes to prevent it and cannot, He is not almighty." I racked my brains for an answer. I searched writings of believers for a clue, but I found no way of escape. Not yet had any doubt of the existence of God crossed my mind.

Mr. D—— continued to write me, striving to guide me along the path which had led his own soul to contentment, but I can only find room here for two brief extracts, which will show how to himself he solved the problem. He thought me mistaken in my view

"Of the nature of the *sin* and *error* which is supposed to grieve God. I take it that sin is an absolutely necessary factor in the production of the perfect man. It was foreseen and allowed as means to an end—as, in fact, an education. The view of all the sin and misery in the world cannot grieve God any more than it can grieve you to see Digby fail in his first attempt to build a card-castle or a rabbit-hutch. All is part of the training. God looks at the ideal man to which all tends. "No, Mrs. Besant; I never feel at all inclined to give up the search, or to suppose that the other side may be right. I claim no merit for it, but I have an invincible faith in the morality of God and the moral order of the world. I have no more doubt about the falsehood of the popular theology than I have about the unreality of six robbers who attacked me three nights ago in a horrid dream. I exult and rejoice in the grandeur and freedom of the little bit of truth it has been given me to see. I am told that 'Present-day Papers,' by Bishop Ewing (edited), are a wonderful help, many of them, to puzzled people; I mean to get them. But I am sure you will find that the truth will (even so little as we may be able to find out) grow on you, make you free, light your path, and dispel, at no distant time, your *painful* difficulties and doubts. I should say on no account give up your reading. I think with you that you could not do without it. It will be a wonderful source of help and peace to you. For there are struggles far more fearful than those of intellectual doubt. I am keenly alive to the gathered-up sadness of which your last two pages are an expression. I was sorrier than I can say to read them. They reminded me of a long and very dark time in my own life, when I thought the light never would come. Thank God it came, or I think I could not have held out much longer. But you have evidently strength to bear it now. The more dangerous time, I should fancy, has passed. You will have to mind that the fermentation leaves clear spiritual wine, and not (as too often) vinegar. I wish I could write something more helpful to you in this great matter. But as I sit in front of my large bay window and see the shadows on the grass and the sunlight on the leaves, and the soft glimmer of the rosebuds left by the storms, I can but believe that all will be very well. 'Trust in the Lord, wait patiently for Him'—they are trite words. But He made the grass, the leaves, the rosebuds, and the sunshine, and He is the Father of our Lord Jesus Christ. And now the trite words have swelled into a mighty argument."

I found more help in Theistic writers like Grey, and Agnostic like Arnold, than I did in the Broad Church teachers, but these, of course, served to make return to the old faith more and more impossible. The Church services were a weekly torture, but feeling as I did that I was only a doubter, I kept my doubts to myself. It was possible, I felt, that all my difficulties might be cleared up, and I had no right to shake the faith of others while in uncertainty myself. Others had doubted and had afterwards recovered their faith; for the doubter silence was a duty; the blinded had better keep their misery to themselves.

During these weary months of anxiety and torment I found some relief from the mental strain in practical parish work, nursing the sick, trying to brighten the lot of the poor. I learned then some of the lessons as to the agricultural labourer and the land that I was able in after-years to teach from the platform. The movement among the agricultural labourers, due to the energy and devotion of Joseph Arch, was beginning to be discussed in the fens, and my sympathies went strongly with the claims of the labourers, for I knew their life-conditions. In one cottage I had found four generations sleeping in one room—the great-grandfather and his wife, the unmarried grandmother, the unmarried mother, the little child; three men lodgers completed the tale of eight human beings crowded into that narrow, ill-ventilated garret. Other cottages were hovels, through the broken roofs of which poured the rain, and wherein rheumatism and ague lived with the human dwellers. How could I do aught but sympathise with any combination that aimed at the raising of these poor? But the Agricultural Labourers' Union was bitterly opposed by the farmers, and they would give no work to a "Union man." One example may serve for all. There was a young married man with two small children, who was sinful enough to go to a Union meeting and sinful enough to talk of it on his return home. No farmer would employ him in all the district round. He tramped about vainly looking for work, grew reckless, and took to drink. Visiting his cottage, consisting of one room and a "lean-to," I found his wife ill with fever, a fever-stricken babe in her arms, the second child lying dead on the bed. In answer to my soft-spoken questions: Yes, she was pining (starving), there was no work. Why did she leave the dead child on the bed? Because she had no other place for it till the coffin came. And at night the unhappy, driven man, the fever-stricken wife, the fever-stricken child, the dead child, all lay in the one bed. The farmers hated the Union because its success meant higher wages for the men, and it never struck them that they might well pay less rent to the absent landlord and higher wage to the men who tilled their fields. They had only civil words for the burden that crushed them, hard words for the mowers of their harvests and the builders-up of their ricks; they made common cause with their enemies instead of with their friends, and instead of leaguing themselves together with the labourers as forming together the true agricultural interest, they leagued themselves with the landlords against the labourers, and so made ruinous fratricidal strife instead of easy victory over the common foe. And, seeing all this, I learned some useful lessons, and the political education progressed while the theological strife went on within.

In the early autumn a ray of light broke the darkness. I was in London with my mother, and wandered one Sunday morning into St. George's Hall, where the Rev. Charles Voysey was preaching. There to my delight I found, on listening to the sermon and buying some literature on sale in the ante-room, that there were people who had passed through my own difficulties, and had given up the dogmas that I found so revolting. I went again on the following Sunday, and when the service was over I noticed that the outgoing stream of people were passing by Mr. and Mrs. Voysey, and that many who were evidently strangers spoke a word of thanks to him as they went on. Moved by a strong desire, after the long months of lonely striving, to speak to one who had struggled out of Christian difficulties, I said to Mr. Voysey, as I passed in my turn, "I must thank you for very great help in what you said this morning," for in truth, never having yet doubted the existence of God, the teaching of Mr. Voysey that He was "loving unto *every* man, and His tender mercy over *all* His works," came like a gleam of light across the stormy sea of doubt and distress on which I had so long been tossing. The next Sunday saw me again at the Hall, and Mrs. Voysey gave me a cordial invitation to visit them in their Dulwich home. I found their Theism was free from the defects that had revolted me in Christianity, and they opened up to me new views of religion. I read Theodore Parker's "Discourse on Religion," Francis Newman's works, those of Miss Frances Power Cobbe, and of others; the anguish of the tension relaxed; the nightmare of an Almighty Evil passed away; my belief in God, not yet touched, was cleared from all the dark spots that had sullied it, and I no longer doubted whether the dogmas that had shocked my conscience were true or false. I shook them off, once for all, with all their pain and horror and darkness, and felt, with joy and relief inexpressible, that they were delusions of the ignorance of man, not the revelations of a God.

But there was one belief that had not been definitely challenged, but of which the *rationale* was gone with the orthodox dogmas now definitely renounced—the doctrine of the Deity of Christ. The whole teaching of the Broad Church school tends, of course, to emphasise the humanity of Christ at the expense of His Deity, and when eternal punishment and the substitutionary atonement had gone there seemed no reason remaining sufficient to account for so tremendous a miracle as the incarnation of the Deity. In the course of my reading I had become familiar with the idea of Avatâras in Eastern creeds, and I saw that the incarnate God was put forward as a fact by all ancient religions, and thus the way was paved for challenging the especially Christian teaching, when the doctrines morally repulsive were cleared away. But I shrank from the thought of placing in the crucible a doctrine so dear from all the associations of the past; there was so much that was soothing and ennobling in the idea of a union between Man and God, between a perfect man and a Divine life, between a human heart and an almighty strength. Jesus as God was interwoven with all art and all beauty in religion; to break with the Deity of Jesus was to break with music, with painting, with literature; the Divine Babe in His Mother's arms; the Divine Man in His Passion and His Triumph; the Friend of Man encircled with the majesty of the Godhead. Did inexorable Truth demand that this ideal Figure, with all its pathos, its beauty, its human love, should pass away into the Pantheon of the dead Gods of the Past?

Nor was this all. If I gave up belief in Christ as God, I must give up Christianity as creed. Once challenge the unique position of the Christ, and the name Christian seemed to me to be a hypocrisy, and its renouncement a duty binding on the upright mind. I was a clergyman's wife; what would be the effect of such a step? Hitherto mental pain alone had been the price demanded inexorably from the searcher after truth; but with the renouncing of Christ outer warfare would be added to the inner, and who might guess the result upon my life? The struggle was keen but short; I decided to carefully review the evidence for and against the Deity of Christ, with the result that that belief followed the others, and I stood, no longer Christian, face to face with a dim future in which I sensed the coming conflict.

One effort I made to escape it; I appealed to Dr. Pusey, thinking that if he could not answer my questionings, no answer to them could be reasonably hoped for. I had a brief correspondence with him, but was referred only to lines of argument familiar to me— as those of Liddon in his "Bampton Lectures"—and finally, on his invitation, went down to Oxford to see him. I found a short, stout gentleman, dressed in a cassock, looking like a comfortable monk; but keen eyes, steadfastly gazing straight into mine, told of the force and subtlety enshrined in the fine, impressive head. But the learned doctor took the wrong line of treatment; he probably saw I was anxious, shy, and nervous, and he treated me as a penitent going to confession and seeking the advice of a director, instead of as an inquirer struggling after truth, and resolute to obtain some firm standing-ground in the sea of doubt. He would not deal with the question of the Deity of Jesus as a question for argument. "You are speaking of your Judge," he retorted sternly, when I pressed a difficulty. The mere suggestion of an imperfection in the character of Jesus made him shudder, and he checked me with raised hand. "You are blaspheming. The very thought is a terrible sin." Would he recommend me any books that might throw light on the subject? "No, no; you have read too much already. You must pray; you must pray." When I urged that I could not believe without proof, I was told, "Blessed are they that have not seen and yet have believed"; and my further questioning was checked by the murmur, "O my child, how undisciplined! how impatient!" Truly, he must have found in me—hot, eager, passionate in my determination to *know*, resolute not to profess belief while belief was absent—nothing of the meek, chastened, submissive spirit with which he was wont to deal in penitents seeking his counsel as their spiritual guide. In vain did he bid me pray as though I believed; in vain did he urge the duty of blind submission to the authority of the Church, of blind, unreasoning faith that questioned not. I had not trodden the thorny path of doubt to come to the point from which I had started; I needed, and would have, solid grounds ere I believed. He had no conception of the struggles of a sceptical spirit; he had evidently never felt the pangs of doubt; his own faith was solid as a rock, firm, satisfied, unshakable; he would as soon have committed suicide as have doubted of the infallibility of the "Universal Church."

"It is not your duty to ascertain the truth," he told me, sternly. "It is your duty to accept and believe the truth as laid down by the Church. At your peril you reject it. The responsibility is not yours so long as you dutifully accept that which the Church has laid down for your acceptance. Did not the Lord promise that the presence of the Spirit should be ever with His Church, to guide her into all truth?"

"But the fact of the promise and its value are just the very points on which I am doubtful," I answered.

He shuddered. "Pray, pray," he said. "Father, forgive her, for she knows not what she says."

It was in vain that I urged on him the sincerity of my seeking, pointing out that I had everything to gain by following his directions, everything to lose by going my own way, but that it seemed to me untruthful to pretend to accept what was not really believed.

"Everything to lose? Yes, indeed. You will be lost for time and lost for eternity."

"Lost or not," I rejoined, "I must and will try to find out what is true, and I will not believe till I am sure."

"You have no right to make terms with God," he retorted, "as to what you will believe or what you will not believe. You are full of intellectual pride."

I sighed hopelessly. Little feeling of pride was there in me just then, but only a despairful feeling that in this rigid, unyielding dogmatism there was no comprehension of my difficulties, no help for me in my strugglings. I rose, and, thanking him for his courtesy, said that I would not waste his time further, that I must go home and face the difficulties, openly leaving the Church and taking the consequences. Then for the first time his serenity was ruffled.

"I forbid you to speak of your disbelief," he cried. "I forbid you to lead into your own lost state the souls for whom Christ died."

THOMAS SCOTT

Slowly and sadly I took my way back to the station, knowing that my last chance of escape had failed me. I recognised in this famous divine the spirit of priest-craft, that could be tender and pitiful to the sinner, repentant, humble, submissive; but that was iron to the doubter, the heretic, and would crush out all questionings of "revealed truth," silencing by force, not by argument, all challenge of the traditions of the Church. Out of such men were made the Inquisitors of the Middle Ages, perfectly conscientious, perfectly rigid, perfectly merciless to the heretic. To them heretics are centres of infectious disease, and charity to the heretic is "the worst cruelty to the souls of men." Certain that they hold, "by no merit of our own, but by the mercy of our God, the one truth which He has revealed," they can permit no questionings, they can accept nought but the most complete submission. But while man aspires after truth, while his mind yearns after knowledge, while his intellect soars upward into the empyrean of speculation and "beats the air with tireless wing," so long shall those who demand faith from him be met by challenge for proof, and those who would blind him shall be defeated by his resolve to gaze unblenching on the face of Truth, even though her eyes should turn him into stone. It was during this same autumn of 1872 that I first met Mr. and Mrs. Scott, introduced to them by Mr. Voysey. At that time Thomas Scott was an old man, with beautiful white hair, and eyes like those of a hawk gleaming from under shaggy eyebrows. He had been a man of magnificent physique, and, though his frame was then enfeebled, the splendid lion-like head kept its impressive strength and beauty, and told of a unique personality. Well born and wealthy, he had spent his earlier life in adventure in all parts of the world, and after his marriage he had settled down at Ramsgate, and had made his home a centre of heretical thought. His wife, "his right hand," as he justly called her, was young enough to be his daughter—a sweet, strong, gentle, noble woman, worthy of her husband, and than that no higher praise could be spoken. Mr. Scott for many years issued monthly a series of pamphlets, all heretical, though very varying in their shades of thought; all were well written, cultured, and polished in tone, and to this rule Mr. Scott made no exception; his writers might say what they liked, but they must have something to say, and must say it in good English. His correspondence was enormous, from Prime Ministers downwards. At his house met people of the most varied opinions; it was a veritable heretical *salon*. Colenso of Natal, Edward Maitland, E. Vansittart Neale, Charles Bray, Sarah Hennell, and hundreds more, clerics and laymen, scholars and thinkers, all coming to this one house, to which the *entrée* was gained only by love of Truth and desire to spread Freedom among men. For Thomas Scott my first Freethought essay was written a few months after, "On the Deity of Jesus of Nazareth," by the wife of a benefited clergyman. My name was not mine to use, so it was agreed that any essays from my pen should be anonymous.

And now came the return to Sibsey, and with it the need for definite steps as to the Church. For now I no longer doubted, I had rejected, and the time for silence was past. I was willing to attend the Church services, taking no part in any not directed to God Himself, but I could no longer attend the Holy Communion, for in that service, full of recognition of Jesus as Deity and of His atoning sacrifice, I could no longer take part without hypocrisy. This was agreed to, and well do I remember the pain and trembling wherewith on the first "Sacrament Sunday" after my return I rose and left the church. That the vicar's wife should "communicate" was as much a matter of course as that the vicar should "administer"; I had never done anything in public that would draw attention to me, and a feeling of deadly sickness nearly overcame me as I made my exit, conscious that every eye was on me, and that my non-participation would be the cause of unending comment. As a matter of fact, every one naturally thought I was taken suddenly ill, and I was overwhelmed with calls and inquiries. To any direct question I answered quietly that I was unable to take part in the profession of faith required by an honest communicant, but the statement was rarely necessary, as the idea of heresy in a vicar's wife is slow to suggest itself to the ordinary bucolic mind, and I proffered no information where no question was asked.

It happened that, shortly after that (to me) memorable Christmas of 1872, a sharp epidemic of typhoid fever broke out in the village of Sibsey. The drainage there was of the most primitive type, and the contagion spread rapidly. Naturally fond of nursing, I found in this epidemic work just fitted to my hand, and I was fortunate enough to be able to lend personal help that made me welcome in the homes of the stricken poor. The mothers who slept exhausted while I watched beside their darlings' bedsides will never, I like to fancy, think over-harshly of the heretic whose hand was as tender and often more skilful than their own. I think Mother Nature meant me for a nurse, for I take a sheer delight in nursing any one, provided only that there is peril in the sickness, so that there is the strange and solemn feeling of the struggle between the human skill one wields and the supreme enemy, Death. There is a strange fascination in fighting Death, step by step, and this is of course felt to the full where one fights for life as life, and not for a life one loves. When the patient is beloved the struggle is touched with agony, but where one fights with Death over the body of a stranger there is a weird enchantment in the contest without personal pain, and as one forces back the hated foe there is a curious triumph in the feeling which marks the death-grip yielding up its prey, as one snatches back to earth the life which had well-nigh perished.

The spring of 1873 brought me knowledge of a power that was to mould much of my future life. I delivered my first lecture, but delivered it to rows of empty pews in Sibsey Church. A queer whim took me that I would like to know how "it felt" to preach, and vague fancies stirred in me that I could speak if I had the chance. I saw no platform in the distance, nor had any idea of possible speaking in the future dawned upon me. But the longing to find outlet in words came upon me, and I felt as though I had something to say and was able to say it. So locked alone in the great, silent church, whither I had gone to practise some organ exercises, I ascended the pulpit steps and delivered my first lecture on the Inspiration of the Bible. I shall never forget the feeling of power and delight—but especially of power—that came upon me as I sent my voice ringing down the aisles, and the passion in me broke into balanced sentences and never paused for musical cadence or for rhythmical expression. All I wanted then was to see the church full of upturned faces, alive with throbbing sympathy, instead of the dreary emptiness of silent pews. And as though in a dream the solitude was peopled, and I saw the listening faces and the eager eyes, and as the sentences flowed unbidden from my lips and my own tones echoed back to me from the pillars of the ancient church, I knew of a verity that the gift of speech was mine, and that if ever—and then it seemed so impossible!—if ever the chance came to me of public work, this power of melodious utterance should at least win hearing for any message I had to bring.

But the knowledge remained a secret all to my own self for many a long month, for I quickly felt ashamed of that foolish speechifying in an empty church; but, foolish as it was, I note it here, as it was the first effort of that expression in spoken words which later became to me one of the deepest delights of life. And, indeed, none can know, save they who have felt it, what joy there is in the full rush of language that moves and sways; to feel a crowd respond to the lightest touch; to see the faces brighten or darken at your bidding; to know that the sources of human emotion and human passion gush forth at the word of the speaker as the stream from the riven rock; to feel that the thought which thrills through a thousand hearers has its impulse from you, and throbs back to you the fuller from a thousand heart-beats. Is there any emotional joy in life more brilliant than this, fuller of passionate triumph, and of the very essence of intellectual delight?

In 1873 my marriage tie was broken. I took no new step, but my absence from the Communion led to some gossip, and a relative of Mr. Besant pressed on him highly-coloured views of the social and professional dangers which would accrue if my heresy became known. My health, never really restored since the autumn of 1871, grew worse and worse, serious heart trouble having arisen from the constant strain under which I lived. At last, in July or August, 1873, the crisis came. I was told that I must conform to the outward observances of the Church, and attend the Communion; I refused. Then came the distinct alternative; conformity or exclusion from home—in other words, hypocrisy or expulsion. I chose the latter.

A bitterly sad time followed. My dear mother was heart-broken. To her, with her wide and vague form of Christianity, loosely held, the intensity of my feeling that where I did not believe I would not pretend belief, was incomprehensible. She recognised far more fully than I did all that a separation from my home meant for me, and the difficulties that would surround a young woman, not yet twenty-six, living alone. She knew how brutally the world judges, and how the mere fact that a woman was young and alone justified any coarseness of slander. Then I did not guess how cruel men and women could be, how venomous their tongues; now, knowing it, having faced slander and lived it down, I deliberately say that were the choice again before me I would choose as I chose then; I would rather go through it all again than live "in Society" under the burden of an acted lie.

The hardest struggle was against my mother's tears and pleading; to cause her pain was tenfold pain to me. Against harshness I had been rigid as steel, but it was hard to remain steadfast when my darling mother, whom I loved as I loved nothing else on earth, threw herself on her knees before me, imploring me to yield. It seemed like a crime to bring such anguish on her; and I felt as a murderer as the snowy head was pressed against my knees. And yet—to live a lie? Not even for her was that shame possible; in that worst crisis of blinding agony my will clung fast to Truth. And it is true now as it ever was that he who loves father or mother better than Truth is not worthy of her, and the flint-strewn path of honesty is the way to Light and Peace.

Then there were the children, the two little ones who worshipped me, who was to them mother, nurse, and playfellow. Were they, too, demanded at my hands? Not wholly—for a time. Facts which I need not touch on here enabled my brother to obtain for me a legal separation, and when everything was arranged, I found myself guardian of my little daughter, and possessor of a small monthly income sufficient for respectable starvation. With a great price I had obtained my freedom, but—I was free. Home, friends, social position, were the price demanded and paid, and, being free, I wondered what to do with my freedom. I could have had a home with my brother if I would give up my heretical friends and keep quiet, but I had no mind to put my limbs into fetters again, and in my youthful inexperience I determined to find something to do. The difficulty was the "something," and I spent various shillings in agencies, with a quite wonderful unanimity of failures. I tried fancy needle-work, offered to "ladies in reduced circumstances," and earned 4s. 6d. by some weeks of stitching. I experimented with a Birmingham firm, who generously offered every one the opportunity of adding to their incomes, and on sending the small fee demanded, received a pencil-case, with an explanation that I was to sell little articles of that description, going as far as cruet-stands, to my friends. I did not feel equal to springing pencil-cases and cruet-stands on my acquaintances, so did not enter on that line of business, and similar failures in numerous efforts made me feel, as so many others have found, that the world-oyster is hard to open. However, I was resolute to build a nest for my wee daughter, my mother, and myself, and the first thing to do was to save my monthly pittance to buy furniture. I found a tiny house in Colby Road, Upper Norwood, near the Scotts, who were more than good to me, and arranged to take it in the spring, and then accepted a loving invitation to Folkestone, where my grandmother and two aunts were living, to look for work there. And found it. The vicar wanted a governess, and one of my aunts suggested me as a stop-gap, and thither I went with my little Mabel, our board and lodging being payment for my work. I became head cook, governess, and nurse, glad enough to have found "something to do" that enabled me to save my little income. But I do not think I will ever take to cooking for a permanence; broiling and frying are all right, and making pie-crust is rather pleasant; but saucepans and kettles blister your hands. There is a charm in making a stew, to the unaccustomed cook, from the excitement of wondering what the result will be, and whether any flavour save that of onions will survive the competition in the mixture. On the whole, my cooking (strictly by cookery book) was a success, but my sweeping was bad, for I lacked muscle. This curious episode came to an abrupt end, for one of my little pupils fell ill with diphtheria, and I was transformed from cook to nurse. Mabel I despatched to her grandmother, who adored her with a love condescendingly returned by the little fairy of three, and never was there a prettier picture than the red-gold curls nestled against the white, the baby-grace in exquisite contrast with the worn stateliness of her tender nurse. Scarcely was my little patient out of danger when the youngest boy fell ill of scarlet fever; we decided to isolate him on the top floor, and I cleared away carpets and curtains, hung sheets over the doorways and kept them wet with chloride of lime, shut myself up there with the boy, having my meals left on the landing; and when all risk was over, proudly handed back my charge, the disease touching no one else in the house.

And now the spring of 1874 had come, and in a few weeks my mother and I were to set up house together. How we had planned all, and had knitted on the new life together we anticipated to the old one we remembered! How we had discussed Mabel's education, and the share which should fall to each! Day-dreams; day-dreams! never to be realised.

My mother went up to town, and in a week or two I received a telegram, saying she was dangerously ill, and as fast as express train would take me I was beside her. Dying, the doctor said; three days she might live—no more. I told her the death-sentence, but she said resolutely, "I do not feel that I am going to die just yet," and she was right. There was an attack of fearful prostration—the valves of the heart had failed—a very wrestling with Death, and then the grim shadow drew backwards. I nursed her day and night with a very desperation of tenderness, for now Fate had touched the thing dearest to me in life. A second horrible crisis came, and for the second time her tenacity and my love beat back the death-stroke. She did not wish to die, the love of life was strong in her; I would not let her die; between us we kept the foe at bay. Then dropsy supervened, and the end loomed slowly sure.

It was then, after eighteen months' abstention, that I took the Sacrament for the last time. My mother had an intense longing to communicate before she died, but absolutely refused to do so unless I took it with her. "If it be necessary to salvation," she persisted, doggedly, "I will not take it if darling Annie is to be shut out. I would rather be lost with her than saved without her." I went to a clergyman I knew well, and laid the case before him; as I expected, he refused to allow me to communicate. I tried a second, with the same result. At last a thought struck me. There was Dean Stanley, my mother's favourite, a man known to be of the broadest school within the Church of England; suppose I asked him? I did not know him, and I felt the request would be an impertinence; but there was just the chance that he might consent, and what would I not do to make my darling's death-bed easier? I said nothing to any one, but set out to the Deanery, Westminster, timidly asked for the Dean, and followed the servant upstairs with a sinking heart. I was left for a moment alone in the library, and then the Dean came in. I don't think I ever in my life felt more intensely uncomfortable than I did in that minute's interval as he stood waiting for me to speak, his clear, grave, piercing eyes gazing questioningly into mine. Very falteringly—it must have been very clumsily—I preferred my request, stating boldly, with abrupt honesty, that I was not a Christian, that my mother was dying, that she was fretting to take the Sacrament, that she would not take it unless I took it with her, that two clergymen had refused to allow me to take part in the service, that I had come to him in despair, feeling how great was the intrusion, but—she was dying.

His face changed to a great softness. "You were quite right to come to me," he answered, in that low, musical voice of his, his keen gaze having altered into one no less direct, but marvellously gentle. "Of course I will go and see your mother, and I have little doubt that, if you will not mind talking over your position with me, we may see our way clear to doing as your mother wishes."

I could barely speak my thanks, so much did the kindly sympathy move me; the revulsion from the anxiety and fear of rebuff was strong enough to be almost pain. But Dean Stanley did more than I asked. He suggested that he should call that afternoon, and have a quiet chat with my mother, and then come again on the following day to administer the Sacrament.

"A stranger's presence is always trying to a sick person," he said, with rare delicacy of thought, "and, joined to the excitement of the service, it might be too much for your dear mother. If I spend half an hour with her to-day, and administer the Sacrament to-morrow, it will, I think, be better for her."

So Dean Stanley came that afternoon, all the way to Brompton, and remained talking with my mother for about half an hour, and then set himself to understand my own position. He finally told me that conduct was far more important than theory, and that he regarded all as "Christians" who recognised and tried to follow the moral law of Christ. On the question of the absolute Deity of Jesus he laid but little stress; Jesus was "in a special sense the Son of God," but it was folly to quarrel over words with only human meanings when dealing with the mystery of the Divine existence, and, above all, it was folly to make such words into dividing walls between earnest souls. The one important matter was the recognition of "duty to God and man," and all who were one in that recognition might rightfully join in an act of worship, the essence of which was not acceptance of dogma, but love of God and self-sacrifice for man. "The Holy Communion," he concluded, in his soft tones, "was never meant to divide from each other hearts that are searching after the one true God. It was meant by its founder as a symbol of unity, not of strife."

On the following day Dean Stanley celebrated the Holy Communion by the bedside of my dear mother, and well was I repaid for the struggle it had cost me to ask so great a kindness from a stranger, when I saw the comfort that gentle, noble heart had given to her. He soothed away all her anxiety about my heresy with tactful wisdom, bidding her have no fear of differences of opinion where the heart was set on truth. "Remember," she told me he said to her—"remember that our God is the God of truth, and that therefore the honest search for truth can never be displeasing in His eyes." Once again after that he came, and after his visit to my mother we had another long talk. I ventured to ask him, the conversation having turned that way, how, with views so broad as his, he found it possible to remain in communion with the Church of England. "I think," he answered, gently, "that I am of more service to true religion by remaining in the Church and striving to widen its boundaries from within, than if I left it and worked from without." And he went on to explain how, as Dean of Westminster, he was in a rarely independent position, and could make the Abbey of a wider national service than would otherwise be possible. In all he said on this his love for and his pride in the glorious Abbey were manifest, and it was easy to see that old historical associations, love of music, of painting, of stately architecture, were the bonds that held him bound to the "old historic Church of England." His emotions, not his intellect, kept him Churchman, and he shrank, with the over-sensitiveness of the cultured scholar, from the idea of allowing the old traditions to be handled roughly by inartistic hands. Naturally of a refined and delicate nature, he had been rendered yet more exquisitely sensitive by the training of the college and the court; the polished courtesy of his manners was but the natural expression of a noble and lofty mind—a mind whose very gentleness sometimes veiled its strength. I have often heard Dean Stanley harshly spoken of, I have heard his honesty roughly challenged; but never has he been attacked in my presence that I have not uttered my protest against the injustice done him, and thus striven to repay some small fraction of that great debt of gratitude which I shall ever owe his memory.

And now the end came swiftly. I had hurriedly furnished a couple of rooms in the little house, now ours, that I might take my mother into the purer air of Norwood, and permission was given to drive her down in an invalid carriage. The following evening she was suddenly taken worse; we lifted her into bed, and telegraphed for the doctor. But he could do nothing, and she herself felt that the hand of Death had gripped her. Selfless to the last, she thought but for my loneliness. "I am leaving you alone," she sighed from time to time; and truly I felt, with an anguish I did not dare to realise, that when she died I should indeed be alone on earth.

For two days longer she was with me, my beloved, and I never left her side for five minutes. On May 10th the weakness passed into gentle delirium, but even then the faithful eyes followed me about the room, until at length they closed for ever, and as the sun sank low in the heavens, the breath came slower and slower, till the silence of Death came down upon us and she was gone.

Stunned and dazed with the loss, I went mechanically through the next few days. I would have none touch my dead save myself and her favourite sister, who was with us at the last. Cold and dry-eyed I remained, even when they hid her from me with the coffin-lid, even all the dreary way to Kensal Green where her husband and her baby-son were sleeping, and when we left her alone in the chill earth, damp with the rains of spring. I could not believe that our day-dream was dead and buried, and the home in ruins ere yet it was fairly built. Truly, my "house was left unto me desolate," and the rooms, filled with sunshine but unlighted by her presence, seemed to echo from their bare walls, "You are all alone."

But my little daughter was there, and her sweet face and dancing feet broke the solitude, while her imperious claims for love and tendance forced me into attention to the daily needs of life. And life was hard in those days of spring and summer, resources small, and work difficult to find. In truth, the two months after my mother's death were the dreariest my life has known, and they were months of tolerably hard struggle. The little house in Colby Road taxed my slender resources heavily, and the search for work was not yet successful. I do not know how I should have managed but for the help ever at hand, of Mr. and Mrs. Thomas Scott. During this time I wrote for Mr. Scott pamphlets on Inspiration, Atonement, Mediation and Salvation, Eternal Torture, Religious Education of Children, Natural *v.* Revealed Religion, and the few guineas thus earned were very valuable. Their house, too, was always open to me, and this was no small help, for often in those days the little money I had was enough to buy food for two but not enough to buy it for three, and I would go out and study all day at the British Museum, so as to "have my dinner in town," the said dinner being conspicuous by its absence. If I was away for two evenings running from the hospitable house in the terrace, Mrs. Scott would come down to see what had happened, and many a time the supper there was of real physical value to me. Well might I write, in 1879, when Thomas Scott lay dead: "It was Thomas Scott whose house was open to me when my need was sorest, and he never knew, this generous, noble heart, how sometimes, when I went in, weary and overdone, from a long day's study in the British Museum, with scarce food to struggle through the day—he never knew how his genial, 'Well, little lady,' in welcoming tone, cheered the then utter loneliness of my life. To no living man—save one—do I owe the debt of gratitude that I owe to Thomas Scott."

The small amount of jewellery I possessed, and all my superfluous clothes, were turned into more necessary articles, and the child, at least, never suffered a solitary touch of want. My servant Mary was a wonderful contriver, and kept house on the very slenderest funds that could be put into a servant's hands, and she also made the little place so bright and fresh-looking that it was always a pleasure to go into it. Recalling those days of "hard living," I can now look on them without regret. More, I am glad to have passed through them, for they have taught me how to sympathise with those who are struggling as I struggled then, and I never can hear the words fall from pale lips, "I am hungry," without remembering how painful a thing hunger is, and without curing that pain, at least for the moment.

The presence of the child was good for me, keeping alive my aching, lonely heart: she would play contentedly for hours while I was working, a word now and again being enough for happiness; when I had to go out without her, she would run to the door with me, and the "good-bye" would come from down-curved lips; she was ever watching at the window for my return, and the sunny face was always the first to welcome me home. Many and many a time have I been coming home, weary, hungry, and heart-sick, and the glimpse of the little face watching has reminded me that I must not carry in a grave face to sadden my darling, and the effort to throw off the depression for her sake threw it off altogether, and brought back the sunshine. She was the sweetness and joy of my life, my curly-headed darling, with her red-gold hair and glorious eyes, and passionate, wilful, loving nature. The torn, bruised tendrils of my heart gradually twined round this little life; she gave something to love and to tend, and thus gratified one of the strongest impulses of my nature.

CHAPTER VI

Charles Bradlaugh

During all these months the intellectual life had not stood still; I was slowly, cautiously feeling my way onward. And in the intellectual and social side of my life I found a delight unknown in the old days of bondage. First, there was the joy of freedom, the joy of speaking out frankly and honestly each thought. Truly, I had a right to say: "With a great price obtained I this freedom," and having paid the price, I revelled in the liberty I had bought. Mr. Scott's valuable library was at my service; his keen brain challenged my opinions, probed my assertions, and suggested phases of thought hitherto untouched. I studied harder than ever, and the study now was unchecked by any fear of possible consequences. I had nothing left of the old faith save belief in "a God," and that began slowly to melt away. The Theistic axiom: "If there be a God at all He must be at least as good as His highest creature," began with an "if," and to that "if" I turned my attention. "Of all impossible things," writes Miss Frances Power Cobbe, "the most impossible must surely be that a man should dream something of the good and the noble, and that it should prove at last that his Creator was less good and less noble than he had dreamed." But, I questioned, are we sure that there is a Creator? Granted that, if there is, He must be above His highest creature, but—is there such a being? "The ground," says the Rev. Charles Voysey, "on which our belief in God rests is man. Man, parent of Bibles and Churches, inspirer of all good thoughts and good deeds. Man, the masterpiece of God's thought on earth. Man, the text-book of all spiritual knowledge. Neither miraculous nor infallible, man is nevertheless the only trustworthy record of the Divine mind in things pertaining to God. Man's reason, conscience, and affections are the only true revelation of his Maker." But what if God were only man's own image reflected in the mirror of man's mind? What if man were the creator, not the revelation of his God?

It was inevitable that such thoughts should arise after the more palpably indefensible doctrines of Christianity had been discarded. Once encourage the human mind to think, and bounds to the thinking can never again be set by authority. Once challenge traditional beliefs, and the challenge will ring on every shield which is hanging in the intellectual arena. Around me was the atmosphere of conflict, and, freed from its long repression, my mind leapt up to share in the strife with a joy in the intellectual tumult, the intellectual strain.

I often attended South Place Chapel, where Moncure D. Conway was then preaching, and discussion with him did something towards widening my views on the deeper religious problems; I re-read Dean Mansel's "Bampton Lectures," and they did much towards turning me in the direction of Atheism; I re-read Mill's "Examination of Sir William Hamilton's Philosophy," and studied carefully Comte's "Philosophie Positive." Gradually I recognised the limitations of human intelligence and its incapacity for understanding the nature of God, presented as infinite and absolute; I had given up the use of prayer as a blasphemous absurdity, since an all-wise God could not need my suggestions, nor an all-good God require my promptings. But God fades out of the daily life of those who never pray; a personal God who is not a Providence is a superfluity; when from the heaven does not smile a listening Father, it soon becomes an empty space, whence resounds no echo of man's cry. I could then reach no loftier conception of the Divine than that offered by the orthodox, and that broke hopelessly away as I analysed it.

At last I said to Mr. Scott, "Mr. Scott, may I write a tract on the nature and existence of God?"

He glanced at me keenly. "Ah, little lady, you are facing, then, that problem at last? I thought it must come. Write away."

While this pamphlet was in MS. an event occurred which coloured all my succeeding life. I met Charles Bradlaugh. One day in the late spring, talking with Mrs. Conway—one of the sweetest and steadiest natures whom it has been my lot to meet, and to whom, as to her husband, I owe much for kindness generously shown when I was poor and had but few friends—she asked me if I had been to the Hall of Science, Old Street. I answered, with the stupid, ignorant reflection of other people's prejudices so sadly common, "No, I have never been there. Mr. Bradlaugh is rather a rough sort of speaker, is he not?"

"He is the finest speaker of Saxon-English that I have ever heard," she answered, "except, perhaps, John Bright, and his power over a crowd is something marvellous. Whether you agree with him or not, you should hear him."

CHARLES BRADLAUGH M.P.

In the following July I went into the shop of Mr. Edward Truelove, 256, High Holborn, in search of some Comtist publications, having come across his name as a publisher in the course of my study at the British Museum. On the counter was a copy of the *National Reformer*, and, attracted by the title, I bought it. I read it placidly in the omnibus on my way to Victoria Station, and found it excellent, and was sent into convulsions of inward merriment when, glancing up, I saw an old gentleman gazing at me, with horror speaking from every line of his countenance. To see a young woman, respectably dressed in crape, reading an Atheistic journal, had evidently upset his peace of mind, and he looked so hard at the paper that I was tempted to offer it to him, but repressed the mischievous inclination.

This first copy of the paper with which I was to be so closely connected bore date July 19, 1874, and contained two long letters from a Mr. Arnold of Northampton, attacking Mr. Bradlaugh, and a brief and singularly self-restrained answer from the latter. There was also an article on the National Secular Society, which made me aware that there was an organisation devoted to the propagandism of Free Thought. I felt that if such a society existed, I ought to belong to it, and I consequently wrote a short note to the editor of the *National Reformer*, asking whether it was necessary for a person to profess Atheism before being admitted to the Society. The answer appeared in the *National*

Reformer:—

"S.E.—To be a member of the National Secular Society it is only necessary to be able honestly to accept the four principles, as given in the *National Reformer* of June 14th. This any person may do without being required to avow himself an Atheist. Candidly, we can see no logical resting-place between the entire acceptance of authority, as in the Roman Catholic Church, and the most extreme Rationalism. If, on again looking to the Principles of the Society, you can accept them, we repeat to you our invitation."

I sent my name in as an active member, and find it is recorded in the *National Reformer* of August 9th. Having received an Intlmatlon that Londoners could receive their certificates at the Hall of Science from Mr. Bradlaugh on any Sunday evening, I betook myself thither, and it was on August 2, 1874, that I first set foot in a Freethought hall. The Hall was crowded to suffocation, and, at the very moment announced for the lecture, a roar of cheering burst forth, a tall figure passed swiftly up the Hall to the platform, and, with a slight bow in answer to the voluminous greeting, Charles Bradlaugh took his seat. I looked at him with interest, impressed and surprised. The grave, quiet, stern, strong face, the massive head, the keen eyes, the magnificent breadth and height of forehead—was this the man I had heard described as a blatant agitator, an ignorant demagogue?

He began quietly and simply, tracing out the resemblances between the Krishna and the Christ myths, and as he went from point to point his voice grew in force and resonance, till it rang round the hall like a trumpet. Familiar with the subject, I could test the value of his treatment of it, and saw that his knowledge was as sound as his language was splendid. Eloquence, fire, sarcasm, pathos, passion, all in turn were bent against Christian superstition, till the great audience, carried away by the torrent of the orator's force, hung silent, breathing soft, as he went on, till the silence that followed a magnificent peroration broke the spell, and a hurricane ofcheers relieved the tension.

He came down the Hall with some certificates in his hand, glanced round, and handed me mine with a questioning "Mrs. Besant?" Then he said, referring to my question as to a profession of Atheism, that he would willingly talk over the subject of Atheism with me if I would make an appointment, and offered me a book he had been using in his lecture. Long afterwards I asked him how he knew me, whom he had never seen, that he came straight to me in such fashion. He laughed and said he did not know, but, glancing over the faces, he felt sure that I was Annie Besant.

From that first meeting in the Hall of Science dated a friendship that lasted unbroken till Death severed the earthly bond, and that to me stretches through Death's gateway and links us together still. As friends, not as strangers, we met—swift recognition, as it were, leaping from eye to eye; and I know now that the instinctive friendliness was in very truth an outgrowth of strong friendship in other lives, and that on that August day we took up again an ancient tie, we did not begin a new one. And so in lives to come we shall meet again, and help each other as we helped each other in this. And let me here place on record, as I have done before, some word of what I owe him for his true friendship; though, indeed, how great is my debt to him I can never tell. Some of his wise phrases have ever remained in my memory. "You should never say you have an opinion on a subject until you have tried to study the strongest things said against the view to which you are inclined." "You must not think you know a subject until you are acquainted with all that the best minds have said about it." "No steady work can be done in public unless the worker study at home far more than he talks outside." "Be your own harshest judge, listen to your own speech and criticise it; read abuse of yourself and see what grains of truth are in it." "Do not waste time by reading opinions that are mere echoes of your own; read opinions you disagree with, and you will catch aspects of truth you do not readily see." Through our long comradeship he was my sternest as well as gentlest critic, pointing out to me that in a party like ours, where our own education and knowledge were above those whom we led, it was very easy to gain indiscriminate praise and unstinted admiration; on the other hand, we received from Christians equally indiscriminate abuse and hatred. It was, therefore, needful that we should be our own harshest judges, and that we should be sure that we knew thoroughly every subject that we taught. He saved me from the superficiality that my "fatal facility" of speech might so easily have induced; and when I began to taste the intoxication of easily won applause, his criticism of weak points, his challenge of weak arguments, his trained judgment, were of priceless service to me, and what of value there is in my work is very largely due to his influence, which at once stimulated and restrained.

One very charming characteristic of his was his extreme courtesy in private life, especially to women. This outward polish, which sat so gracefully on his massive frame and stately presence, was foreign rather than English—for the English, as a rule, save such as go to Court, are a singularly unpolished people—and it gave his manner a peculiar charm. I asked him once where he had learned his gracious fashions that were so un-English—he would stand with uplifted hat as he asked a question of a maidservant, or handed a woman into a carriage—and he answered, with a half-smile, half-scoff, that it was only in England he was an outcast from society. In France, in Spain, in Italy, he was always welcomed among men and women of the highest social rank, and he supposed that he had unconsciously caught the foreign tricks of manner. Moreover, he was absolutely indifferent to all questions of social position; peer or artisan, it was to him exactly the same; he never seemed conscious of the distinctions of which men make so much.

Our first conversation, after the meeting at the Hall of Science, took place a day or two later in his little study in 29, Turner Street, Commercial Road, a wee room overflowing with books, in which he looked singularly out of place. Later I learned that he had failed in business in consequence of Christian persecution, and, resolute to avoid bankruptcy, he had sold everything he possessed, save his books, had sent his wife and daughters to live in the country with his father-in-law, had taken two tiny rooms in Turner Street, where he could live for a mere trifle, and had bent himself to the task of paying off the liabilities he had incurred—incurred in consequence of his battling for political and religious liberty. I took with me my MS. essay "On the Nature and Existence of God," and it served as the basis for our conversation; we found there was little difference in our views. "You have thought yourself into Atheism without knowing it," he said, and all that I changed in the essay was the correction of the vulgar error that the Atheist says "there is no God," by the insertion of a passage disclaiming this position from an essay pointed out to me by Mr. Bradlaugh. And at this stage of my life-story, it is necessary to put very clearly the position I took up and held so many years as Atheist, because otherwise the further evolution into Theosophist will be wholly incomprehensible. It will lead me into metaphysics, and to some readers these are dry, but if any one would understand the evolution of a Soul he must be willing to face the questions which the Soul faces in its growth. And the position of the philosophic Atheist is so misunderstood that it is the more necessary to put it plainly, and Theosophists, at least, in reading it, will see how Theosophy stepped in finally as a further evolution towards knowledge, rendering rational, and therefore acceptable, the loftiest spirituality that the human mind can as yet conceive.

In order that I may not colour my past thinkings by my present thought, I take my statements from pamphlets written when I adopted the Atheistic philosophy and while I continued an adherent thereof. No charge can then be made that I have softened my old opinions for the sake of reconciling them with those now held.

CHAPTER VII

Atheism as I Knew and Taught It

The first step which leaves behind the idea of a limited and personal God, an extra-cosmic Creator, and leads the student to the point whence Atheism and Pantheism diverge, is the recognition that a profound unity of substance underlies the infinite diversities of natural phenomena, the discernment of the One beneath the Many. This was the step I had taken ere my first meeting with Charles Bradlaugh, and I had written:—

"It is manifest to all who will take the trouble to think steadily, that there can be only one eternal and underived substance, and that matter and spirit must, therefore, only be varying manifestations of this one substance. The distinction made between matter and spirit is, then, simply made for the sake of convenience and clearness, just as we may distinguish perception from judgment, both of which, however, are alike processes of thought. Matter is, in its constituent elements, the same as spirit; existence is *one*, however manifold in its phenomena; life is one, however multiform in its evolution. As the heat of the coal differs from the coal itself, so do memory, perception, judgment, emotion, and will differ from the brain which is the instrument of thought. But nevertheless they are all equally products of the one sole substance, varying only in their conditions. I find myself, then, compelled to believe that one only substance exists in all around me; that the universe is eternal, or at least eternal so far as our faculties are concerned, since we cannot, as some one has quaintly put it, 'get to the outside of everywhere'; that a Deity cannot be conceived of as apart from the universe; that the Worker and the Work are inextricably interwoven, and in some sense eternally and indissolubly combined. Having got so far, we will proceed to examine into the possibility of proving the existence of that one essence popularly called by the name of *God*, under the conditions strictly defined by the orthodox. Having demonstrated, as I hope to do, that the orthodox idea of God is unreasonable and absurd, we will endeavour to ascertain whether *any* idea of God, worthy to be called an idea, is attainable in the present state of our faculties." "The Deity must of necessity be that one and only substance out of which all things are evolved, under the uncreated conditions and eternal laws of the universe; He must be, as Theodore Parker somewhat oddly puts it, 'the materiality of matter as well as the spirituality of spirit'—*i.e.*, these must both be products of this one substance; a truth which is readily accepted as soon as spirit and matter are seen to be but different modes of one essence. Thus we identify substance with the all-comprehending and vivifying force of nature, and in so doing we simply reduce to a physical impossibility the existence of the Being described by the orthodox as a God possessing the attributes of personality. The Deity becomes identified with nature, co-extensive with the universe, but the *God* of the orthodox no longer exists; we may change the signification of God, and use the word to express a different idea, but we can no longer mean by it a Personal Being in the orthodox sense, possessing an individuality which divides Him from the rest of the universe."[3]

Proceeding to search whether *any* idea of God was attainable, I came to the conclusion that evidence of the existence of a conscious Power was lacking, and that the ordinary proofs offered were inconclusive; that we could grasp phenomena and no more. "There appears, also, to be a possibility of a mind in nature, though we have seen that intelligence is, strictly speaking, impossible. There cannot be perception, memory, comparison, or judgment, but may there not be a perfect mind, unchanging, calm, and still? Our faculties fail us when we try to estimate the Deity, and we are betrayed into contradictions and absurdities; but does it therefore follow that He *is* not? It seems to me that to deny His existence is to overstep the boundaries of our thought-power almost as much as to try and define it. We pretend to know the Unknown if we declare Him to be the Unknowable. Unknowable to us at present, yes! Unknowable for ever, in other possible stages of existence? We have reached a region into which we cannot penetrate; here all human faculties fail us; we bow our heads on 'the threshold of the unknown.'

"'And the ear of man cannot hear, and the eye of man cannot see,
But if we could see and hear, this vision—were it not He?'

---

[3] "On the Nature and Existence of God." 1874.

Thus sings Alfred Tennyson, the poet of metaphysics: '*if* we could see and hear.' Alas! it is always an 'if!'[4]

This refusal to believe without evidence, and the declaration that anything "behind phenomena" is unknowable to man as at present constituted—these are the two chief planks of the Atheistic platform, as Atheism was held by Charles Bradlaugh and myself. In 1876 this position was clearly reaffirmed. "It is necessary to put briefly the Atheistic position, for no position is more continuously and more persistently misrepresented. Atheism is *without* God. It does not assert *no* God. 'The Atheist does not say "There is no God," but he says, "I know not what you mean by God; I am without idea of God; the word God is to me a sound conveying no clear or distinct affirmation. I do not deny God, because I cannot deny that of which I have no conception, and the conception of which, by its affirmer, is so imperfect that he is unable to define it to me.'" (Charles Bradlaugh, "Freethinker's Text-book," p. 118.) The Atheist neither affirms nor denies the possibility of phenomena differing from those recognised by human experience. As his knowledge of the universe is extremely limited and very imperfect, the Atheist declines either to deny or to affirm anything with regard to modes of existence of which he knows nothing. Further, he refuses to believe anything concerning that of which he knows nothing, and affirms that that which can never be the subject of knowledge ought never to be the object of belief. While the Atheist, then, neither affirms nor denies the unknown, he *does* deny all which conflicts with the knowledge to which he has already attained. For example, he *knows* that one is one, and that three times one are three; he *denies* that three times one are, or can be, one. The position of the Atheist is a clear and a reasonable one: I know nothing about 'God,' and therefore I do not believe in Him or in it; what you tell me about your God is self-contradictory, and is therefore incredible. I do not deny 'God,' which is an unknown tongue to me; I do deny your God, who is an impossibility. I am without God."[5] Up to 1887 I find myself writing on the same lines: "No man can rationally affirm 'There is no God,' until the word 'God' has for him a definite meaning, and until everything that exists is known to him, and known with what Leibnitz calls 'perfect knowledge.' The Atheist's denial of the Gods begins only when these Gods are defined or described. Never yet has a God been defined in terms which were

[4] "On the Nature and Existence of God." 1874.
[5] "The Gospel of Atheism." 1876.

not palpably self-contradictory and absurd; never yet has a God been described so that a concept of Him was made possible to human thought—Nor is anything gained by the assertors of Deity when they allege that He is incomprehensible. If 'God' exists and is incomprehensible, His incomprehensibility is an admirable reason for being silent about Him, but can never justify the affirmation of self-contradictory propositions, and the threatening of people with damnation if they do not accept them."[6] "The belief of the Atheist stops where his evidence stops. He believes in the existence of the universe, judging the accessible proof thereof to be adequate, and he finds in this universe sufficient cause for the happening of all phenomena. He finds no intellectual satisfaction in placing a gigantic conundrum behind the universe, which only adds its own unintelligibility to the already sufficiently difficult problem of existence. Our lungs are not fitted to breathe beyond the atmosphere which surrounds our globe, and our faculties cannot breathe outside the atmosphere of the phenomenal."[7] And I summed up this essay with the words: "I do not believe in God. My mind finds no grounds on which to build up a reasonable faith. My heart revolts against the spectre of an Almighty Indifference to the pain of sentient beings. My conscience rebels against the injustice, the cruelty, the inequality, which surround me on every side. But I believe in Man. In man's redeeming power; in man's remoulding energy; in man's approaching triumph, through knowledge, love, and work."[8]

These views of existence naturally colour all views of life and of the existence of the Soul. And here steps in the profound difference between Atheism and Pantheism; both posit an Existence at present inscrutable by human faculties, of which all phenomena are modes; but to the Atheist that Existence manifests as Force-Matter, unconscious, unintelligent, while to the Pantheist it manifests as Life-Matter, conscious, intelligent. To the one, life and consciousness are attributes, properties, dependent upon arrangements of matter; to the other they are fundamental, essential, and only limited in their manifestation by arrangements of matter. Despite the attraction held for me in Spinoza's luminous arguments, the over-mastering sway which Science was beginning to exercise over me drove me to seek for the explanation of all problems of life and mind at the

---

[6] "Why I do not Believe in God." 1887.
[7] Ibid.
[8] Ibid.

hands of the biologist and the chemist. They had done so much, explained so much, could they not explain all? Surely, I thought, the one safe ground is that of experiment, and the remembered agony of doubt made me very slow to believe where I could not prove. So I was fain to regard life as an attribute, and this again strengthened the Atheistic position. "Scientifically regarded, life is not an entity but a property; it is not a mode of existence, but a characteristic of certain modes. Life is the result of an arrangement of matter, and when rearrangement occurs the former result can no longer be present; we call the result of the changed arrangement death. Life and death are two convenient words for expressing the general outcome of two arrangements of matter, one of which is always found to precede the other."[9]And then, having resorted to chemistry for one illustration, I took another from one of those striking and easily grasped analogies, facility for seeing and presenting which has ever been one of the secrets of my success as a propagandist. Like pictures, they impress the mind of the hearer with a vivid sense of reality. "Every one knows the exquisite iridiscence of mother-of-pearl, the tender, delicate hues which melt into each other, glowing with soft radiance. How different is the dull, dead surface of a piece of wax. Yet take that dull, black wax and mould it so closely to the surface of the mother-of-pearl that it shall take every delicate marking of the shell, and when you raise it the seven-hued glory shall smile at you from the erstwhile colourless surface. For, though it be to the naked eye imperceptible, all the surface of the mother-of-pearl is in delicate ridges and furrows, like the surface of a newly-ploughed field; and when the waves of light come dashing up against the ridged surface, they are broken like the waves on a shingly shore, and are flung backwards, so that they cross each other and the oncoming waves; and, as every ray of white light is made up of waves of seven colours, and these waves differ in length each from the others, the fairy ridges fling them backward separately, and each ray reaches the eye by itself; so that the colour of the mother-of-pearl is really the spray of the light waves, and comes from arrangement of matter once again. Give the dull, black wax the same ridges and furrows, and its glory shall differ in nothing from that of the shell. To apply our illustration: as the colour belongs to one arrangement of matter and the dead surface to another, so life belongs to some arrangements of matter and is

---

[9] "Life, Death, and Immortality." 1886.

their resultant, while the resultant of other arrangements is death."[10]

The same line of reasoning naturally was applied to the existence of "spirit" in man, and it was argued that mental activity, the domain of the "spirit," was dependent on bodily organisation. "When the babe is born it shows no sign of mind. For a brief space hunger and repletion, cold and warmth are its only sensations. Slowly the specialised senses begin to function; still more slowly muscular movements, at first aimless and reflex, become co-ordinated and consciously directed. There is no sign here of an intelligent spirit controlling a mechanism; there is every sign of a learning and developing intelligence, developing *pari passu* with the organism of which it is a function. As the body grows, the mind grows with it, and the childish mind of the child develops into the hasty, quickly-judging, half-informed, unbalanced youthful mind of the youth; with maturity of years comes maturity of mind, and body and mind are vigorous and in their prime. As old age comes on and the bodily functions decay, the mind decays also, until age passes into senility, and body and mind sink into second childhood. Has the immortal spirit decayed with the organisation, or is it dwelling in sorrow, bound in its 'house of clay'? If this be so, the 'spirit' must be unconscious, or else separate from the very individual whose essence it is supposed to be, for the old man does not suffer when his mind is senile, but is contented as a little child. And not only is this constant, simultaneous growth and decay of body and mind to be observed, but we know that mental functions are disordered and suspended by various physical conditions. Alcohol, many drugs, fever, disorder the mind; a blow on the cranium suspends its functions, and the 'spirit' returns with the surgeon's trepanning. Does the 'spirit' take part in dreams? Is it absent from the idiot, from the lunatic? Is it guilty of manslaughter when the madman murders, or does it helplessly watch its own instrument performing actions at which it shudders? If it can only work here through an organism, is its nature changed in its independent life, severed from all with which it was identified? Can it, in its 'disembodied state,' have anything in common with its past?"[11]

It will be seen that my unbelief in the existence of the Soul or Spirit was a matter of cold, calm reasoning. As I wrote in 1885: "For many of us evidence must precede belief. I would gladly

[10] "Life, Death, and Immortality." 1886.
[11] "Life, Death, and Immortality." 1886.

believe in a happy immortality for all, as I would gladly believe that all misery and crime and poverty will disappear in 1885—*if I could*. But I am unable to believe an improbable proposition unless convincing evidence is brought in support of it. Immortality is most improbable; no evidence is brought forward in its favour. I cannot believe only because I wish."[12] Such was the philosophy by which I lived from 1874 to 1886, when first some researches that will be dealt with in their proper place, and which led me ultimately to the evidence I had before vainly demanded, began to shake my confidence in its adequacy. Amid outer storm and turmoil and conflict, I found it satisfy my intellect, while lofty ideals of morality fed my emotions. I called myself Atheist, and rightly so, for I was without God, and my horizon was bounded by life on earth; I gloried in the name then, as it is dear to my heart now, for all the associations with which it is connected. "Atheist is one of the grandest titles a man can wear; it is the Order of Merit of the world's heroes. Most great discoverers, most deep-thinking philosophers, most earnest reformers, most toiling pioneers of progress, have in their turn had flung at them the name of Atheist. It was howled over the grave of Copernicus; it was clamoured round the death-pile of Bruno; it was yelled at Vanini, at Spinoza, at Priestley, at Voltaire, at Paine; it has become the laurel-bay of the hero, the halo of the martyr; in the world's history it has meant the pioneer of progress, and where the cry of 'Atheist' is raised there may we be sure that another step is being taken towards the redemption of humanity. The saviours of the world are too often howled at as Atheists, and then worshipped as Deities. The Atheists are the vanguard of the army of Freethought, on whom falls the brunt of the battle, and are shivered the hardest of the blows; their feet trample down the thorns that others may tread unwounded; their bodies fill up the ditch that, by the bridge thus made, others may pass to victory. Honour to the pioneers of progress, honour to the vanguard of Liberty's army, honour to those who to improve earth have forgotten heaven, and who in their zeal for man have forgotten God."[13]

This poor sketch of the conception of the universe, to which I had conquered my way at the cost of so much pain, and which was the inner centre round which my life revolved for twelve years, may perhaps show that the Atheistic Philosophy is misjudged sorely when it is scouted as vile or condemned as intellectually

---

[12] Ibid.
[13] "The Gospel of Atheism." 1876.

87

degraded. It has outgrown anthropomorphic deities, and it leaves us face to face with Nature, open to all her purifying, strengthening inspirations. "There is only one kind of prayer," it says, "which is reasonable, and that is the deep, silent adoration of the greatness and beauty and order around us, as revealed in the realms of non-rational life and in Humanity; as we bow our heads before the laws of the universe, and mould our lives into obedience to their voice, we find a strong, calm peace steal over our hearts, a perfect trust in the ultimate triumph of the right, a quiet determination to 'make our lives sublime.' Before our own high ideals, before those lives which show us 'how high the tides of Divine life have risen in the human world,' we stand with hushed voice and veiled face; from them we draw strength to emulate, and even dare struggle to excel. The contemplation of the ideal is true prayer; it inspires, it strengthens, it ennobles. The other part of prayer is work; from contemplation to labour, from the forest to the street. Study nature's laws, conform to them, work in harmony with them, and work becomes a prayer and a thanksgiving, an adoration of the universal wisdom, and a true obedience to the universal law."[14]

To a woman of my temperament, filled with passionate desire for the bettering of the world, the elevation of humanity, a lofty system of ethics was of even more importance than a logical, intellectual conception of the universe; and the total loss of all faith in a righteous God only made me more strenuously assertive of the binding nature of duty and the overwhelming importance of conduct. In 1874 this conviction found voice in a pamphlet on the "True Basis of Morality," and in all the years of my propaganda on the platform of the National Secular Society no subject was more frequently dealt with in my lectures than that of human ethical growth and the duty of man to man. No thought was more constantly in my mind than that of the importance of morals, and it was voiced at the very outset of my public career. Speaking of the danger lest "in these stirring times of inquiry," old sanctions of right conduct should be cast aside ere new ones were firmly established, I wrote: "It therefore becomes the duty of every one who fights in the ranks of Freethought, and who ventures to attack the dogmas of the Churches, and to strike down the superstitions which enslave men's intellect, to beware how he uproots sanctions of morality which he is too weak to replace, or how, before he is prepared with better ones, he removes the barriers which do yet, however

---

[14] "On the Nature and Existence of God." 1874.

poorly, to some extent check vice and repress crime. That which touches morality touches the heart of society; a high and pure morality is the life-blood of humanity; mistakes in belief are inevitable, and are of little moment; mistakes in life destroy happiness, and their destructive consequences spread far and wide. It is, then, a very important question whether we, who are endeavouring to take away from the world the authority on which has hitherto been based all its morality, can offer a new and firm ground whereupon may safely be built up the fair edifice of a noble life."

I then proceeded to analyse revelation and intuition as a basis for morals, and, discarding both, I asserted: "The true basis of morality is utility; that is, the adaptation of our actions to the promotion of the general welfare and happiness; the endeavour so to rule our lives that we may serve and bless mankind." And I argued for this basis, showing that the effort after virtue was implied in the search for happiness: "Virtue is an indispensable part of all true and solid happiness. But it is, after all, only reasonable that happiness should be the ultimate test of right and wrong, if we live, as we do, in a realm of law. Obedience to law must necessarily result in harmony, and disobedience in discord. But if obedience to law result in harmony it must also result in happiness—all through nature obedience to law results in happiness, and through obedience each living thing fulfils the perfection of its being, and in that perfection finds its true happiness." It seemed to me most important to remove morality from the controversies about religion, and to give it a basis of its own: "As, then, the grave subject of the existence of Deity is a matter of dispute, it is evidently of deep importance to society that morality should not be dragged into this battlefield, to stand or totter with the various theories of the Divine nature which human thought creates and destroys. If we can found morality on a basis apart from theology, we shall do humanity a service which can scarcely be overestimated." A study of the facts of nature, of the consequences of man in society, seemed sufficient for such a basis. "Our faculties do not suffice to tell us about God; they do suffice to study phenomena, and to deduce laws from correlated facts. Surely, then, we should do wisely to concentrate our strength and our energies on the discovery of the attainable, instead of on the search after the unknowable. If we are told that morality consists in obedience to the supposed will of a supposed perfectly moral being, because in so doing we please God, then we are at once placed in a region where our faculties are useless to us, and where our judgment is at fault.

89

But if we are told that we are to lead noble lives, because nobility of life is desirable for itself alone, because in so doing we are acting in harmony with the laws of Nature, because in so doing we spread happiness around our pathway and gladden our fellow-men—then, indeed, motives are appealed to which spring forward to meet the call, and chords are struck in our hearts which respond in music to the touch." It was to the establishment of this secure basis that I bent my energies, this that was to me of supreme moment. "Amid the fervid movement of society, with its wild theories and crude social reforms, with its righteous fury against oppression and its unconsidered notions of wider freedom and gladder life, it is of vital importance that morality should stand on a foundation unshakable; that so through all political and religious revolutions human life may grow purer and nobler, may rise upwards into settled freedom, and not sink downwards into anarchy. Only utility can afford us a sure basis, the reasonableness of which will be accepted alike by thoughtful student and hard-headed artisan. Utility appeals to all alike, and sets in action motives which are found equally in every human heart. Well shall it be for humanity that creeds and dogmas pass away, that superstition vanishes, and the clear light of freedom and science dawns on a regenerated earth—but well only if men draw tighter and closer the links of trustworthiness, of honour, and of truth. Equality before the law is necessary and just; liberty is the birthright of every man and woman; free individual development will elevate and glorify the race. But little worth these priceless jewels, little worth liberty and equality with all their promise for mankind, little worth even wider happiness, if that happiness be selfish, if true fraternity, true brotherhood, do not knit man to man, and heart to heart, in loyal service to the common need, and generous self-sacrifice to the common good."[15]

To the forwarding of this moral growth of man, two things seemed to me necessary—an Ideal which should stir the emotions and impel to action, and a clear understanding of the sources of evil and of the methods by which they might be drained. Into the drawing of the first I threw all the passion of my nature, striving to paint the Ideal in colours which should enthral and fascinate, so that love and desire to realise might stir man to effort. If "morality touched by emotion" be religion, then truly was I the most religious of Atheists, finding in this dwelling on and glorifying of the Ideal full satisfaction for the

[15] "The True Basis of Morality." 1874.

loftiest emotions. To meet the fascination exercised over men's hearts by the Man of Sorrows, I raised the image of man triumphant, man perfected. "Rightly is the ideal Christian type of humanity a Man of Sorrows. Jesus, with worn and wasted body; with sad, thin lips, curved into a mournful droop of penitence for human sin; with weary eyes gazing up to heaven because despairing of earth; bowed down and aged with grief and pain, broken-hearted with long anguish, broken-spirited with unresisted ill-usage—such is the ideal man of the Christian creed. Beautiful with a certain pathetic beauty, telling of the long travail of earth, eloquent of the sufferings of humanity, but not the model type to which men should conform their lives, if they would make humanity glorious. And, therefore, in radiant contrast with this, stands out in the sunshine and under the blue summer sky, far from graveyards and torture of death agony, the fair ideal Humanity of the Atheist. In form strong and fair, perfect in physical development as the Hercules of Grecian art, radiant with love, glorious in self-reliant power; with lips bent firm to resist oppression, and melting into soft curves of passion and of pity; with deep, far-seeing eyes, gazing piercingly into the secrets of the unknown, and resting lovingly on the beauties around him; with hands strong to work in the present; with heart full of hope which the future shall realise; making earth glad with his labour and beautiful with his skill—this, this is the Ideal Man, enshrined in the Atheist's heart. The ideal humanity of the Christian is the humanity of the slave, poor, meek, broken-spirited, humble, submissive to authority, however oppressive and unjust; the ideal humanity of the Atheist is the humanity of the free man who knows no lord, who brooks no tyranny, who relies on his own strength, who makes his brother's quarrel his, proud, true-hearted, loyal, brave."[16]

A one-sided view? Yes. But a very natural outcome of a sunny nature, for years held down by unhappiness and the harshness of an outgrown creed. It was the rebound of such a nature suddenly set free, rejoicing in its liberty and self-conscious strength, and it carried with it a great power of rousing the sympathetic enthusiasm of men and women, deeply conscious of their own restrictions and their own longings. It was the cry of the freed soul that had found articulate expression, and the many inarticulate and prisoned souls answered to it tumultuously, with fluttering of caged wings. With hot insistence I battled for the inspiration to be drawn from the beauty and grandeur of which

[16] "Gospel of Atheism." 1876.

human life was capable. "Will any one exclaim, 'You are taking all beauty out of human life, all hope, all warmth, all inspiration; you give us cold duty for filial obedience, and inexorable law in the place of God'? All beauty from life? Is there, then, no beauty in the idea of forming part of the great life of the universe, no beauty in conscious harmony with Nature, no beauty in faithful service, no beauty in ideals of every virtue? 'All hope'? Why, I give you more than hope, I give you certainty; if I bid you labour for this world, it is with the knowledge that this world will repay you a, thousand-fold, because society will grow purer, freedom more settled, law more honoured, life more full and glad. What is your heaven? A heaven in the clouds! I point to a heaven attainable on earth. 'All warmth'? What! you serve warmly a God unknown and invisible, in a sense the projected shadow of your own imaginings, and can only serve coldly your brother whom you see at your side? There is no warmth in brightening the lot of the sad, in reforming abuses, in establishing equal justice for rich and poor? You find warmth in the church, but none in the home? Warmth in imagining the cloud glories of heaven, but none in creating substantial glories on earth?' All inspiration'? If you want inspiration to feeling, to sentiment, perhaps you had better keep to your Bible and your creeds; if you want inspiration to work, go and walk through the East of London, or the back streets of Manchester. You are inspired to tenderness as you gaze at the wounds of Jesus, dead in Judaea long ago, and find no inspiration in the wounds of men and women, dying in the England of to-day? You 'have tears to shed for Him,' but none for the sufferer at your doors? His passion arouses your sympathies, but you see no pathos in the passion of the poor? Duty is colder than 'filial obedience'? What do you mean by filial obedience? Obedience to your ideal of goodness and love—is it not so? Then how is duty cold? I offer you ideals for your homage: here is Truth for your Mistress, to whose exaltation you shall devote your intellect; here is Freedom for your General, for whose triumph you shall fight; here is Love for your Inspirer, who shall influence your every thought; here is Man for your Master—not in heaven, but on earth—to whose service you shall consecrate every faculty of your being. 'Inexorable law in the place of God'? Yes; a stern certainty that you shall not waste your life, yet gather a rich reward at the close; that you shall not sow misery, yet reap gladness; that you shall not be selfish, yet be crowned with love; nor shall you sin, yet find safety in repentance. True, our creed *is* a stern one, stern with the beautiful sternness of Nature. But if we be in the right, look to yourselves; laws do not check their action for your ignorance; fire will not cease to scorch, because you 'did not know.'"[17]

With equal vigour did I maintain that "virtue was its own reward," and that payment on the other side of the grave was unnecessary as an incentive to right living. "What shall we say to Miss Cobbe's contention that duty will 'grow grey and cold' without God and immortality? Yes, for those with whom duty is a matter of selfish calculation, and who are virtuous only because they look for a 'golden crown' in payment on the other side the grave. Those of us who find joy in right-doing, who work because work is useful to our fellows, who live well because in such living we pay our contribution to the world's wealth, leaving earth richer than we found it—we need no paltry payment after death for our life's labour, for in that labour is its own 'exceeding great reward.'"[18] But did any one yearn for immortality, that "not all of me shall die"? "Is it true that Atheism has no immortality? What is true immortality? Is Beethoven's true immortality in his continued personal consciousness, or in his glorious music deathless while the world endures? Is Shelley's true life in his existence in some far-off heaven, or in the pulsing liberty his lyrics send through men's hearts, when they respond to the strains of his lyre? Music does not die, though one instrument be broken; thought does not die, though one brain be shivered; love does not die, though one heart's strings be rent; and no great thinker dies so long as his thought re-echoes through the ages, its melody the fuller-toned the more human brains send its music on. Not only to the hero and the sage is this immortality given; it belongs to each according to the measure of his deeds; world-wide life for world-wide service; straitened life for straitened work; each reaps as he sows, and the harvest is gathered by each in his rightful order."[19]

This longing to leave behind a name that will live among men by right of service done them, this yearning for human love and approval that springs naturally from the practical and intense realisation of human brotherhood—these will be found as strong motives in the breasts of the most earnest men and women who have in our generation identified themselves with the Freethought cause. They shine through the written and spoken words of Charles Bradlaugh all through his life, and every friend

[17] "On the Nature and Existence of God." 1874.
[18] "A World without God." 1885.
[19] "The Gospel of Atheism." 1876.

of his knows how often he has expressed the longing that "when the grass grows green over my grave, men may love me a little for the work I tried to do."

Needless to say that, in the many controversies in which I took part, it was often urged against me that such motives were insufficient, that they appealed only to natures already ethically developed, and left the average man, and, above all, the man below the average, with no sufficiently constraining motive for right conduct. I resolutely held to my faith in human nature, and the inherent response of the human heart when appealed to from the highest grounds; strange—I often think now—this instinctive certainty I had of man's innate grandeur, that governed all my thought, inconsistent as that certainty was with my belief in his purely animal ancestry. Pressed too hard, I would take refuge in a passionate disdain for all who did not hear the thrilling voice of Virtue and love her for her own sweet sake. "I have myself heard the question asked: 'Why should I seek for truth, and why should I lead a good life, if there be no immortality in which to reap a reward?' To this question the Freethinker has one clear and short answer: 'There is no reason why you should seek Truth, if to you the search has no attracting power. There is no reason why you should lead a noble life, if you find your happiness in leading a poor and a base one.' Friends, no one can enjoy a happiness which is too high for his capabilities; a book may be of intensest interest, but a dog will very much prefer being given a bone. To him whose highest interest is centred in his own miserable self, to him who cares only to gain his own ends, to him who seeks only his own individual comfort, to that man Freethought can have no attraction. Such a man may indeed be made religious by a bribe of heaven; he may be led to seek for truth, because he hopes to gain his reward hereafter by the search; but Truth disdains the service of the self-seeker; she cannot be grasped by a hand that itches for reward. If Truth is not loved for her own pure sake, if to lead a noble life, if to make men happier, if to spread brightness around us, if to leave the world better than we found it—if these aims have no attraction for us, if these thoughts do not inspire us, then we are not worthy to be Secularists, we have no right to the proud title of Freethinkers. If you want to be paid for your good lives by living for ever in a lazy and useless fashion in an idle heaven; if you want to be bribed into nobility of life; if, like silly children, you learn your lesson not to gain knowledge but to win sugar-plums, then you had better go back to your creeds and your churches; they are all you are fit for; you are not worthy to be free. But we—who, having caught a glimpse of the beauty of Truth, deem the possession of her worth more than all the world beside; who have made up our minds to do our work ungrudgingly, asking for no reward beyond the results which spring up from our labour—we will spread the Gospel of Freethought among men, until the sad minor melodies of Christianity have sobbed out their last mournful notes on the dying evening breeze, and on the fresh morning winds shall ring out the chorus of hope and joyfulness, from the glad lips of men whom the Truth has at last set free."[20]

The intellectual comprehension of the sources of evil and the method of its extinction was the second great plank in my ethical platform. The study of Darwin and Herbert Spencer, of Huxley, Büchner and Haeckel, had not only convinced me of the truth of evolution, but, with help from W.H. Clifford, Lubbock, Buckle, Lecky, and many another, had led me to see in the evolution of the social instinct the explanation of the growth of conscience and of the strengthening of man's mental and moral nature. If man by study of the conditions surrounding him and by the application of intelligence to the subdual of external nature, had already accomplished so much, why should not further persistence along the same road lead to his complete emancipation? All the evil, anti-social side of his nature was an inheritance from his brute ancestry, and could be gradually eradicated; he could not only "let the ape and tiger die," but he could kill them out." It may be frankly acknowledged that man inherits from his brute progenitors various bestial tendencies which are in course of elimination. The wild-beast desire to fight is one of these, and this has been encouraged, not checked, by religion. Another bestial tendency is the lust of the male for the female apart from love, duty, and loyalty; this again has been encouraged by religion, as witness the polygamy and concubinage of the Hebrews—as in Abraham, David, and Solomon, not to mention the precepts of the Mosaic laws—the bands of male and female prostitutes in connection with Pagan temples, and the curious outbursts of sexual passion in connection with religious revivals and missions. Another bestial tendency is greed, the strongest grabbing all he can and trampling down the weak, in the mad struggle for wealth; how and when has religion modified this tendency, sanctified as it is in our present civilisation? All these bestial tendencies will be eradicated only by the recognition of human duty, of the social bond. Religion has not eradicated them, but science, by tracing

---

[20] "The Gospels of Christianity and Freethought." 1874.

them to their source in our brute ancestry, has explained them and has shown them in their true light. As each recognises that the anti-social tendencies are the bestial tendencies in man, and that man in evolving further must evolve out of these, each also feels it part of his personal duty to curb these in himself, and so to rise further from the brute. This rational 'co-operation with Nature' distinguishes the scientific from the religious person, and this constraining sense of obligation is becoming stronger and stronger in all those who, in losing faith in God, have gained hope for man."[21]

For this rational setting of oneself on the side of the forces working for evolution implied active co-operation by personal purity and nobility." To the Atheist it seems that the knowledge that the perfecting of the race is only possible by the improvement of the individual, supplies the most constraining motive which can be imagined for efforts after personal perfection. The Theist may desire personal perfection, but his desire is self-centred; each righteous individual is righteous, as it were, alone, and his righteousness does not benefit his fellows save as it may make him helpful and loving in his dealings with them. The Atheist desires personal perfection not only for his joy in it as beautiful in itself, but because science has taught him the unity of the race, and he knows that each fresh conquest of his over the baser parts of his nature, and each strengthening of the higher, is a gain for all, and not for himself alone."[22]

Besides all this, the struggle against evil, regarded as transitory and as a necessary concomitant of evolution, loses its bitterness. "In dealing with evil, Atheism is full of hope instead of despair. To the Christian, evil is as everlasting as good; it exists by the permission of God, and, therefore, by the will of God. Our nature is corrupt, inclined to evil; the devil is ever near us, working all sin and all misery. What hope has the Christian face to face with a world's wickedness? what answer to the question, Whence comes sin? To the Atheist the terrible problem has in it no figure of despair. Evil comes from ignorance, we say; ignorance of physical and of moral facts. Primarily, from ignorance of physical order; parents who dwell in filthy, unventilated, unweathertight houses, who live on insufficient, innutritious, unwholesome food, will necessarily be unhealthy, will lack vitality, will probably have disease lurking in their veins; such parents will bring into

---

[21] "A World without God." 1885.
[22] "A World without God." 1885.

the world ill-nurtured children, in whom the brain will generally be the least developed part of the body; such children, by their very formation, will incline to the animal rather than to the human, and by leading an animal, or natural, life will be deficient in those qualities which are necessary in social life. Their surroundings as they grow up, the home, the food, the associates, all are bad. They are trained into vice, educated into criminality; so surely as from the sown corn rises the wheat-ear, so from the sowing of misery, filth, and starvation shall arise crime. And the root of all is poverty and ignorance. Educate the children, and give them fair wage for fair work in their maturity, and crime will gradually diminish and ultimately disappear. Man is God-made, says Theism; man is circumstance-made, says Atheism. Man is the resultant of what his parents were, of what his surroundings have been and are, and of what they have made him; himself the result of the past he modifies the actual, and so the action and reaction go on, he himself the effect of what is past, and one of the causes of what is to come. Make the circumstances good and the results will be good, for healthy bodies and healthy brains may be built up, and from a State composed of such the disease of crime will have disappeared. Thus is our work full of hope; no terrible will of God have we to struggle against; no despairful future to look forward to, of a world growing more and more evil, until it is, at last, to burned up; but a glad, fair future of an ever-rising race, where more equal laws, more general education, more just division, shall eradicate pauperism, destroy Ignorance, nourish Independence, a future to be made the grander by our struggles, a future to be made the nearer by our toil."[23]

This joyous, self-reliant facing of the world with the resolute determination to improve it is characteristic of the noblest Atheism of our day. And it is thus a distintly elevating factor in the midst of the selfishness, luxury, and greed of modern civilisation. It is a virile virtue in the midst of the calculating and slothful spirit which too ofter veils itself under the pretence or religion. It will have no putting off of justice to a far-off day of reckoning, and it is ever spurred on by the feeling, "The night cometh, when no man can work." Bereft of all hope of a personal future, it binds up its hopes with that of the race; unbelieving in any aid from Deity, it struggles the more strenuously to work out man's salvation by his own strength. "To us there is but small comfort in Miss Cobbe's assurance that 'earth's wrongs and

---

[23] "The Gospel of Atheism." 1876.

agonies' 'will be righted hereafter.' Granting for a moment that man survives death what certainty have we that 'the next world' will be any improvement on this? Miss Cobbe assures us that this is 'God's world'; whose world will the next be, if not also His? Will He be stronger there or better, that He should set right in that world the wrongs He has permitted here? Will He have changed His mind, or have become weary of the contemplation of suffering? To me the thought that the world was in the hands of a God who permitted all the present wrongs and pains to exist would be intolerable, maddening in its hopelessness. There is every hope of righting earth's wrongs and of curing earth's pains if the reason and skill of man which have already done so much are free to do the rest; but if they are to strive against omnipotence, hopeless indeed is the future of the world. It is in this sense that the Atheist looks on good as 'the final goal of ill,' and believing that that goal will be reached the sooner the more strenuous the efforts of each individual, he works in the glad certainty that he is aiding the world's progress thitherward. Not dreaming of a personal reward hereafter, not craving a personal payment from heavenly treasury, he works and loves, content that he is building a future fairer than his present, joyous that he is creating a new earth for a happier race."[24]

Such was the creed and such the morality which governed my life and thoughts from 1874 to 1886, and with some misgivings to 1889, and from which I drew strength and happiness amid all outer struggles and distress. And I shall ever remain grateful for the intellectual and moral training it gave me, for the self-reliance it nurtured, for the altruism it inculcated, for the deep feeling of the unity of man that it fostered, for the inspiration to work that it lent. And perhaps the chief debt of gratitude I owe to Freethought is that it left the mind ever open to new truth, encouraged the most unshrinking questioning of Nature, and shrank from no new conclusions, however adverse to the old, that were based on solid evidence. I admit sorrowfully that all Freethinkers do not learn this lesson, but I worked side by side with Charles Bradlaugh, and the Freethought we strove to spread was strong-headed and broad-hearted.

The antagonism which, as we shall see in a few moments, blazed out against me from the commencement of my platform work, was based partly on ignorance, was partly aroused by my direct attacks on Christianity, and by the combative spirit I myself

[24] "A World without God." 1885.

showed in those attacks, and very largely by my extreme Radicalism in politics. I had against me all the conventional beliefs and traditions of society in general, and I attacked them, not with bated breath and abundant apologies, but joyously and defiantly, with sheer delight in the intellectual strife. I was fired, too, with passionate sympathy for the sufferings of the poor, for the overburdened, overdriven masses of the people, not only here but in every land, and wherever a blow was struck at Liberty or Justice my pen or tongue brake silence. It was a perpetual carrying of the fiery cross, and the comfortable did not thank me for shaking them out of their soft repose.

The antagonism that grew out of ignorance regarded Atheism as implying degraded morality and bestial life, and they assailed my conduct not on evidence that it was evil, but on the presumption that an Atheist must be immoral. Thus a Christian opponent at Leicester assailed me as a teacher of free love, fathering on me views which were maintained in a book that I had not read, but which, before I had ever seen the *National Reformer*, had been reviewed in its columns—as it was reviewed in other London papers—and had been commended for its clear statement of the Malthusian position, but not for its contention as to free love, a theory to which Mr. Bradlaugh was very strongly opposed. Nor were the attacks confined to the ascription to me of theories which I did not hold, but agents of the Christian Evidence Society, in their street preaching, made the foulest accusations against me of personal immorality. Remonstrances addressed to the Rev. Mr. Engström, the secretary of the society, brought voluble protestations of disavowal and disapproval; but as the peccant agents were continued in their employment, the apologies were of small value. No accusation was too coarse, no slander too baseless, for circulation by these men; and for a long time these indignities caused me bitter suffering, outraging my pride, and soiling my good name. The time was to come when I should throw that good name to the winds for the sake of the miserable, but in those early days I had done nothing to merit, even ostensibly, such attacks. Even by educated writers, who should have known better, the most wanton accusations of violence and would-be destructiveness were brought against Atheists; thus Miss Frances Power Cobbe wrote in the *Contemporary Review* that loss of faith in God would bring about the secularisation *or destruction* of all cathedrals, churches, and chapels. "Why," I wrote in answer, "should cathedrals, churches, and chapels be destroyed? Atheism will utilise, not destroy, the beautiful edifices which, once wasted on God, shall hereafter be consecrated for man. Destroy Westminster Abbey, with its exquisite arches, its glorious tones of soft, rich colour, its stonework light as if of cloud, its dreamy, subdued twilight, soothing as the 'shadow of a great rock in a weary land'? Nay, but reconsecrate it to humanity. The fat cherubs who tumble over guns and banners on soldiers' graves will fitly be removed to some spot where their clumsy forms will no longer mar the upward-springing grace of lines of pillar and of arch; but the glorious building wherein now barbaric psalms are chanted and droning canons preach of Eastern follies, shall hereafter echo the majestic music of Wagner and Beethoven, and the teachers of the future shall there unveil to thronging multitudes the beauties and the wonders of the world. The 'towers and spires' will not be effaced, but they will no longer be symbols of a religion which sacrifices earth to heaven and Man to God."[25] Between the cultured and the uncultured burlesques of Atheism we came off pretty badly, being for the most part regarded, as the late Cardinal Manning termed us, as mere "cattle."

The moral purity and elevation of Atheistic teaching were overlooked by many who heard only of my bitter attacks on Christian theology. Against the teachings of eternal torture, of the vicarious atonement, of the infallibility of the Bible, I levelled all the strength of my brain and tongue, and I exposed the history of the Christian Church with unsparing hand, its persecutions, its religious wars, its cruelties, its oppressions. Smarting under the suffering inflicted on myself, and wroth with the cruel pressure continually put on Freethinkers by Christian employers, speaking under constant threats of prosecution, identifying Christianity with the political and social tyrannies of Christendom, I used every weapon that history, science, criticism, scholarship could give me against the Churches; eloquence, sarcasm, mockery, all were called on to make breaches in the wall of traditional belief and crass superstition.

To argument and reason I was ever ready to listen, but I turned a front of stubborn defiance to all attempts to compel assent to Christianity by appeals to force. "The threat and the enforcement of legal and social penalties against unbelief can never compel belief. Belief must be gained by demonstration; it can never be forced by punishment. Persecution makes the stronger among us

---

[25] "A World without God." 1885.

bitter; the weaker among us hypocrites; it never has made and never can make an honest convert."[26]

That men and women are now able to speak and think as openly as they do, that a broader spirit is visible in the Churches, that heresy is no longer regarded as morally disgraceful—these things are very largely due to the active and militant propaganda carried on under the leadership of Charles Bradlaugh, whose nearest and most trusted friend I was. That my tongue was in the early days bitterer than it should have been, I frankly acknowledge; that I ignored the services done by Christianity and threw light only on its crimes, thus committing injustice, I am ready to admit. But these faults were conquered long ere I left the Atheistic camp, and they were the faults of my personality, not of the Atheistic philosophy. And my main contentions were true, and needed to be made; from many a Christian pulpit to-day may be heard the echo of the Freethought teachings; men's minds have been awakened, their knowledge enlarged; and while I condemn the unnecessary harshness of some of my language, I rejoice that I played my part in that educating of England which has made impossible for evermore the crude superstitions of the past, and the repetition of the cruelties and injustices under which preceding heretics suffered.

But my extreme political views had also much to do with the general feeling of hatred with which I was regarded. Politics, as such, I cared not for at all, for the necessary compromises of political life were intolerable to me; but wherever they touched on the life of the people they became to me of burning interest. The land question, the incidence of taxation, the cost of Royalty, the obstructive power of the House of Lords—these were the matters to which I put my hand; I was a Home Ruler, too, of course, and a passionate opponent of all injustice to nations weaker than ourselves, so that I found myself always in opposition to the Government of the day. Against our aggressive and oppressive policy in Ireland, in the Transvaal, in India, in Afghanistan, in Burmah, in Egypt, I lifted up my voice in all our great towns, trying to touch the consciences of the people, and to make them feel the immorality of a land-stealing, piratical policy. Against war, against capital punishment, against flogging, demanding

---

[26] "The Christian Creed." 1884.

national education instead of big guns, public libraries instead of warships—no wonder I was denounced as an agitator, a firebrand, and that all orthodox society turned up at me its most respectable nose.

CHAPTER VIII

At Work

From this sketch of the inner sources of action let me turn to the actions themselves, and see how the outer life was led which fed itself at these springs.

I have said that the friendship between Mr. Bradlaugh and myself dated from our first meeting, and a few days after our talk in Turner Street he came down to see me at Norwood. It was characteristic of the man that he refused my first invitation, and bade me to think well ere I asked him to my house. He told me that he was so hated by English society that any friend of his would be certain to suffer, and that I should pay heavily for any friendship extended to him. When, however, I wrote to him, repeating my invitation, and telling him that I had counted the cost, he came to see me. His words came true; my friendship for him alienated from me even many professed Freethinkers, but the strength and the happiness of it outweighed a thousand times the loss it brought, and never has a shadow of regret touched me that I clasped hands with him in 1874, and won the noblest friend that woman ever had. He never spoke to me a harsh word; where we differed, he never tried to override my judgment, nor force on me his views; we discussed all points of difference as equal friends; he guarded me from all suffering as far as friend might, and shared with me all the pain he could not turn aside; all the brightness of my stormy life came to me through him, from his tender thoughtfulness, his ever-ready sympathy, his generous love. He was the most unselfish man I ever knew, and as patient as he was strong. My quick, impulsive nature found in him the restful strength it needed, and learned from him the self-control it lacked.

He was the merriest of companions in our rare hours of relaxation; for many years he was wont to come to my house in the morning, after the hours always set aside by him for receiving poor men who wanted advice on legal and other matters—for he was a veritable poor man's lawyer, always ready to help and counsel—and, bringing his books and papers, he would sit writing, hour after hour, I equally busy with my own work, now and then, perhaps, exchanging a word, breaking off just for lunch and dinner, and working on again in the evening till about ten o'clock—he always went early to bed when at home—

he would take himself off again to his lodgings, about three-quarters of a mile away. Sometimes he would play cards for an hour, euchre being our favourite game. But while we were mostly busy and grave, we would make holiday sometimes, and then he was like a boy, brimming over with mirth, full of quaint turns of thought and speech; all the country round London has for me bright memories of our wanderings—Richmond, where we tramped across the park, and sat under its mighty trees; Windsor, with its groves of bracken; Kew, where we had tea in a funny little room, with watercress *ad libitum*; Hampton Court, with its dishevelled beauties; Maidenhead and Taplow, where the river was the attraction; and, above all, Broxbourne, where he delighted to spend the day with his fishing-rod, wandering along the river, of which he knew every eddy. For he was a great fisherman, and he taught me all the mysteries of the craft, mirthfully disdainful of my dislike of the fish when I had caught them. And in those days he would talk of all his hopes of the future, of his work, of his duty to the thousands who looked to him for guidance, of the time when he would sit in Parliament as member for Northampton, and help to pass into laws the projects of reform for which he was battling with pen and tongue. How often he would voice his love of England, his admiration of her Parliament, his pride in her history. Keenly alive to the blots upon it in her sinful wars of conquest, in the cruel wrongs inflicted upon subject peoples, he was yet an Englishman to the heart's core, but feeling above all the Englishman's duty, as one of a race that had gripped power and held it, to understand the needs of those he ruled, and to do justice willingly, since compulsion to justice there was none. His service to India in the latest years of his life was no suddenly accepted task. He had spoken for her, pleaded for her, for many a long year, through press and on platform, and his spurs as member for India were won long ere he was member of Parliament.

A place on the staff of the *National Reformer* was offered me by Mr. Bradlaugh a few days after our first meeting, and the small weekly salary thus earned—it was only a guinea, for national reformers are always poor—was a very welcome addition to my resources. My first contribution appeared in the number for August 30, 1874, over the signature of "Ajax," and I wrote in it regularly until Mr. Bradlaugh died; from 1877 until his death I sub-edited it, so as to free him from all the technical trouble and the weary reading of copy, and for part of this period was also co-editor. I wrote at first under a *nom de guerre*, because the work I was doing for Mr. Scott would have been prejudiced had my name appeared in the columns of the terrible *National Reformer*, and until this work—commenced and paid for—was concluded I did not feel at liberty to use my own name. Afterwards, I signed my *National Reformer* articles, and the tracts written for Mr. Scott appeared anonymously.

> The name was suggested by the famous statue of "Ajax Crying for Light," a cast of which may be seen in the centre walk by any visitor to the Crystal Palace, Sydenham. The cry through the darkness for light, even though light should bring destruction, was one that awoke the keenest sympathy of response from my heart:
>
> "If our fate be death
>
> Give light, and let us die!"

To see, to know, to understand, even though the seeing blind, though the knowledge sadden, though the understanding shatter the dearest hopes—such has ever been the craving of the upward-striving mind in man. Some regard it as a weakness, as a folly, but I am sure that it exists most strongly in some of the noblest of our race; that from the lips of those who have done most in lifting the burden of ignorance from the overstrained and bowed shoulders of a stumbling world has gone out most often into the empty darkness the pleading, impassioned cry:

"Give light!"

The light may come with a blinding flash, but it is light none the less, and we can see.

And now the time had come when I was to use that gift of speech which I had discovered in Sibsey Church that I possessed, and to use it to move hearts and brains all over the English land. In 1874, tentatively, and in 1875 definitely, I took up this keen weapon, and have used it ever since. My first attempt was at a garden party, in a brief informal debate, and I found that words came readily and smoothly: the second in a discussion at the Liberal Social Union on the opening of museums and art galleries on Sunday. My first lecture was given at the Co-operative Institute, 55, Castle Street, Oxford Street, on August 25, 1874. Mr. Greening—then, I think, the secretary—had invited me to read a paper before the society, and had left me the choice of the subject. I resolved that my first public lecture should be on behalf of my own sex, so I selected for my theme, "The Political Status of Women," and wrote thereon a paper. But it was a very nervous person who presented herself at the Co-operative Institute on that August evening. When a visit to the dentist is made, and one stands on the steps outside, desiring to run away ere the neat little boy in buttons opens the door and beams on one with a smile of compassionate superiority and implike triumph, then the world seems dark and life is as a huge blunder. But all such feelings are poor and weak as compared with the sinking of the heart and the trembling of the knees which seize upon the unhappy lecturer as he advances towards his first audience, and as before his eyes rises a ghastly vision of a tongue-tied would-be lecturer, facing rows of listening faces, listening to—silence. But to my surprise all this miserable feeling vanished the moment I was on my feet and was looking at the faces before me. I felt no tremor of nervousness from the first word to the last, and as I heard my own voice ring out over the attentive listeners I was conscious of power and of pleasure, not of fear. And from that day to this my experience has been the same; before a lecture I am horribly nervous, wishing myself at the ends of the earth, heart beating violently, and sometimes overcome by deadly sickness. Once on my feet, I feel perfectly at my ease, ruler of the crowd, master of myself. I often jeer at myself mentally as I feel myself throbbing and fearful, knowing that when I stand up I shall be all right, and yet I cannot conquer the physical terror and trembling, illusory as I know them to be. People often say to me, "You look too ill to go on the platform." And I smile feebly and say I am all right, and I often fancy that the more miserably nervous I am in the ante-room, the better I speak when once on the platform. My second lecture was delivered on September 27th, at Mr. Moncure D. Conway's Chapel, in St. Paul's Road, Camden Town, and redelivered a few weeks later at a Unitarian Chapel, where the Rev. Peter Dean was minister. This was on the "True Basis of Morality," and was later printed as a pamphlet, which attained a wide circulation. This was all I did in the way of speaking in 1874, but I took silent part in an electioneering struggle at Northampton, where a seat for the House of Commons had fallen vacant by the death of Mr. Charles Gilpin. Mr. Bradlaugh had contested the borough as a Radical in 1868, obtaining 1,086 votes, and again in February, 1874, when he received 1,653; of these no less than 1,060 were plumpers, while his four opponents had only 113, 64, 21 and 12 plumpers respectively; this band formed the compact and personally loyal following which was to win the seat for its chief in 1880, after twelve years of steady struggle, and to return him over and over again to Parliament during the long contest which followed his election, and which ended in his final triumph. They never wavered in their allegiance to "our Charlie," but stood by him through evil report and good report, when he was outcast as when he was triumphant, loving him with a deep, passionate devotion, as honourable to them as it was precious to him. I have seen him cry like a child at evidences of their love for him, he whose courage no danger could daunt, and who was never seen to blench before hatred nor change his stern immobility in the face of his foes. Iron to enmity, he was soft as a woman to kindness; unbending as steel to pressure, he was ductile as wax to love. John Stuart Mill had the insight in 1868 to see his value, and the courage to recognise it. He strongly supported his candidature, and sent a donation to his election expenses. In his "Autobiography" he wrote (pp. 311, 312):—

"He had the support of the working classes; having heard him speak I knew him to be a man of ability, and he had proved that he was the reverse of a demagogue by placing himself in strong opposition to the prevailing opinion of the Democratic party on two such important subjects as Malthusianism and Proportional Representation. Men of this sort, who, while sharing the democratic feeling of the working classes, judge political questions for themselves, and have the courage to assert their individual convictions against popular opposition, were needed, as it seemed to me, in Parliament; and I did not think that Mr. Bradlaugh's anti-religious opinions (even though he had been intemperate in the expression of them) ought to exclude him."

It has been said that Mr. Mill's support of Mr. Bradlaugh's candidature at Northampton cost him his own seat at Westminster, and so bitter was bigotry at that time that the statement is very likely to be true. On this, Mr. Mill himself said: "It was the right thing to do, and if the election were yet to take place, I would do it again."

At this election of September, 1874—the second in the year, for the general election had taken place in the February, and Mr. Bradlaugh had been put up and defeated during his absence in America—I went down to Northampton to report electioneering incidents for the *National Reformer*, and spent some days there

in the whirl of the struggle. The Whig party was more bitter against Mr. Bradlaugh than was the Tory. Strenuous efforts were made to procure a Liberal candidate, who would be able at least to prevent Mr. Bradlaugh's return, and, by dividing the Liberal and Radical party, should let in a Tory rather than the detested Radical. Messrs. Bell and James and Dr. Pearce came on the scene only to disappear. Mr. Jacob Bright and Mr. Arnold Morley were vainly suggested. Mr. Ayrton's name was whispered. Major Lumley was recommended by Mr. Bernal Osborne. Dr. Kenealy proclaimed himself ready to come to the rescue of the Whigs. Mr. Tillett, of Norwich, Mr. Cox, of Belper, were invited, but neither would consent to oppose a good Radical who had fought two elections at Northampton and had been the chosen of the Radical workers for six years. At last Mr. William Fowler, a banker, accepted the task of handing over the representation of a Liberal and Radical borough to a Tory, and duly succeeded in giving the seat to Mr. Mereweather, a very reputable Tory lawyer. Mr. Bradlaugh polled 1,766, thus adding another 133 voters to those who had polled for him in the previous February.

That election gave me my first experience of anything in the nature of rioting. The violent abuse levelled against Mr. Bradlaugh by the Whigs, and the foul and wicked slanders circulated against him, assailing his private life and family relations, had angered almost to madness those who knew and loved him; and when it was found that the unscrupulous Whig devices had triumphed, had turned the election against him, and given over the borough to a Tory, the fury broke out into open violence. One illustration may be given as a type of these cruel slanders. It was known that Mr. Bradlaugh was separated from his wife, and it was alleged that being an Atheist, and, (therefore!) an opponent of marriage, he had deserted his wife and children, and left them to the workhouse. The cause of the separation was known to very few, for Mr. Bradlaugh was chivalrously honourable to women, and he would not shield his own good name at the cost of that of the wife of his youth and the mother of his children. But since his death his only remaining child has, in devotion to her father's memory, stated the melancholy truth: that Mrs. Bradlaugh gave way to drink; that for long years he bore with her and did all that man could do to save her; that finally, hopeless of cure, he broke up his home, and placed his wife in the care of her parents in the country, leaving her daughters with her, while he worked for their support. No man could have acted more generously and wisely under these cruel circumstances than he did, but it was, perhaps, going to an extreme of Quixotism, that he concealed the real state of the case, and let the public blame him as it would. His Northampton followers did not know the facts, but they knew him as an upright, noble man, and these brutal attacks on his personal character drove them wild. Stray fights had taken place during the election over these slanders, and, defeated by such foul weapons, the people lost control of their passions. As Mr. Bradlaugh was sitting well-nigh exhausted in the hotel, after the declaration of the poll, the landlord rushed in, crying to him to go out and try to stop the people, or there would be murder done at the "Palmerston," Mr. Fowler's headquarters; the crowd was charging the door, and the windows were being broken with showers of stones. Weary as he was, Mr. Bradlaugh sprang to his feet, and swiftly made his way to the rescue of those who had maligned and defeated him. Flinging himself before the doorway, from which the door had just been battered down, he knocked down one or two of the most violent, drove the crowd back, argued and scolded them into quietness, and finally dispersed them. But at nine o'clock he had to leave Northampton to catch the mail steamer for America at Queenstown, and after he had left, word went round that he had gone, and the riot he had quelled broke out afresh. The Riot Act was at last read, the soldiers were called out, stones flew freely, heads and windows were broken, but no very serious harm was done. The "Palmerston" and the printing-office of the *Mercury*, the Whig organ, were the principal sufferers; doors and windows disappearing somewhat completely. The day after the election I returned home, and soon after fell ill with a severe attack of congestion of the lungs. Soon after my recovery I left Norwood and settled in a house in Westbourne Terrace, Bayswater, where I remained till 1876.

In the following January (1875), after much thought and self-analysis, I resolved to give myself wholly to propagandist work, as a Freethinker and a Social Reformer, and to use my tongue as well as my pen in the struggle. I counted the cost ere I determined on this step, for I knew that it would not only outrage the feelings of such new friends as I had already made, but would be likely to imperil my custody of my little girl. I knew that an Atheist was outside the law, obnoxious to its penalties, but deprived of its protection, and that the step I contemplated might carry me into conflicts in which everything might be lost and nothing could be gained. But the desire to spread liberty and truer thought among men, to war against bigotry and superstition, to make the world freer and better than I found it—all this impelled me with a force that would not be denied. I seemed to hear the voice of Truth ringing over the battlefield: "Who will go? Who will speak for me?" And I sprang forward with passionate enthusiasm, with resolute cry: "Here am I, send me!" Nor have I ever regretted for one hour that resolution, come to in solitude, carried out amid the surging life of men, to devote to that sacred cause every power of brain and tongue that I possessed. Very solemn to me is the responsibility of the public teacher, standing forth in Press and on platform to partly mould the thought of his time, swaying thousands of readers and hearers year after year. No weightier responsibility can any take, no more sacred charge. The written and the spoken word start forces none may measure, set working brain after brain, influence numbers unknown to the forthgiver of the word, work for good or for evil all down the stream of time. Feeling the greatness of the career, the solemnity of the duty, I pledged my word then to the cause I loved that no effort on my part should be wanted to render myself worthy of the privilege of service that I took; that I would read and study, and would train every faculty that I had; that I would polish my language, discipline my thought, widen my knowledge; and this, at least, I may say, that if I have written and spoken much, I have studied and thought more, and that I have not given to my mistress Truth that "which hath cost me nothing."

This same year (1875) that saw me launched on the world as a public advocate of Freethought, saw also the founding of the Theosophical Society to which my Freethought was to lead me. I have often since thought with pleasure that at the very time I began lecturing in England, H.P. Blavatsky was at work in the United States, preparing the foundation on which in November, 1875, the Theosophical Society was to be raised. And with deeper pleasure yet have I found her writing of what she called the noble work against superstition done by Charles Bradlaugh and myself, rendering the propaganda of Theosophy far more practicable and safer than it would otherwise have been. The fight soon began, and with some queer little skirmishes. I was a member of the "Liberal Social Union," and one night a discussion arose as to the admissibility of Atheists to the Society. Dr. Zerffi declared that he would not remain a member if avowed Atheists were admitted. I promptly declared that I was an Atheist, and that the basis of the union was liberty of opinion. The result was that I found myself cold-shouldered, and those that had been warmly cordial to me merely as a non-Christian looked askance at me when I had avowed that my scepticism had advanced beyond their "limits of religious thought." The Liberal Social Union soon knew me no more, but in the wider field of work open before me, the narrow-mindedness of this petty clique troubled me not at all.

I started my definite lecturing work at South Place Chapel in January, 1875, Mr. Moncure D. Conway presiding for me, and I find in the *National Reformer* for January 17th, the announcement that "Mrs. Annie Besant ('Ajax') will lecture at South Place Chapel, Finsbury, on 'Civil and Religious Liberty.'" Thus I threw off my pseudonym, and rode into the field of battle with uplifted visor. The identification led to an odd little exhibition of bigotry. I had been invited by the Dialectical Society to read a paper, and had selected for subject, "The Existence of God." (It may be noted, in passing, that young students and speakers always select the most tremendous subjects for their discourses. One advances in modesty as one advances in knowledge, and after eighteen years of platform work, I am far more dubious than I was at their beginning as to my power of dealing in any sense adequately with the problems of life.) The Dialectical Society had for some years held their meetings in a room in Adam Street, rented from the Social Science Association. When the members gathered as usual on February 17th, the door was found to be locked, and they had to gather on the stairs; they found that "Ajax's" as yet undelivered paper was too much for Social Science nerves, and that entrance to their ordinary meeting-room was then and thenceforth denied them. So they, with "Ajax," found refuge at the Charing Cross Hotel, and speculated merrily on the eccentricities of religious bigotry.

On February 12th I started on my first provincial lecturing tour, and after speaking at Birkenhead that evening went on by the night mail to Glasgow. Some races—dog races—I think, had been going on, and very unpleasant were many of the passengers waiting on the platform. Some Birkenhead friends had secured me a compartment, and watched over me till the train began to move. Then, after we had fairly started, the door was flung open by a porter, and a man was thrust in who half tumbled on to the seat. As he slowly recovered he stood up, and as his money rolled out of his hand on to the floor, and he gazed vaguely at it, I saw to my horror that he was drunk. The position was not pleasant, for the train was an express, and was not timed to stop for a considerable time. My odious fellow-passenger spent some time on the floor, hunting after his scattered coins; then he slowly gathered himself up and presently became conscious of my presence. He studied me for some time, and then proposed to shut the window. I assented quietly, not wanting to discuss a trifle and feeling in deadly terror—alone at night in an express with a man not drunk enough to be helpless, but too drunk to be controlled. Never before nor since have I felt so thoroughly frightened. I can see him still, swaying as he stood, with eyes bleared and pendulous lips—but I sat there quiet and outwardly unmoved, as is always my impulse in danger till I see some way of escape, only grasping a penknife in my pocket, with a desperate resolve to use my feeble weapon as soon as the need arose. The man came towards me with a fatuous leer, when a jarring noise was heard and the train began to slacken.

"What is that?" stammered my drunken companion.

"They are putting on the brakes to stop the train," I answered very slowly and distinctly, though a very passion of relief made it hard to say quietly the measured words.

The man sat down stupidly, staring at me, and in a minute or two the train pulled up at a station—it had been stopped by signal. My immobility was gone. In a moment I was at the window, called the guard, and explained rapidly that I was a woman travelling alone, and that a half-drunken man was in the carriage. With the usual kindness of a railway official, he at once moved me and my baggage into another compartment, into which he locked me, and he kept a friendly watch over me at every station at which we stopped until he landed me safely at Glasgow.

At Glasgow a room had been taken for me at a temperance hotel, and it seemed to me so new and lonely a thing to be "all on my own account" in a strange hotel in a strange city, that I wanted to sit down and cry. This feeling, to which I was too proud to yield, was probably partly due to the extreme greyness and grubbiness of my surroundings. Things are better now, but in those days temperance hotels were for the most part lacking in cleanliness. Abstinence from alcohol and a superfluity of "matter in the wrong place" do not seem necessary correlatives, yet I rarely went to a temperance hotel in which water was liberally used for other purposes than that of drinking. From Glasgow I went north to Aberdeen, where I found a very stern and critical audience. Not a sound broke the stillness as I walked up the hall; not a sound as I ascended the platform and faced the people; the canny Scot was not going to applaud a stranger at sight; he was going to see what she was like first. In grim silence they listened; I could not move them; they were granite like their own granite city, and I felt I would like to take off my head and throw it at them, if only to break that hard wall. After about twenty minutes, a fortunate phrase drew a hiss from some child of the Covenanters. I made a quick retort, there was a burst of cheering, and the granite vanished. Never after that did I have to complain of the coldness of an Aberdeen audience. Back to London from Aberdeen, and a long, weary journey it was, in a third-class carrlage In the cold month of February; but the labour had in it a joy that outpaid all physical discomfort, and the feeling that I had found my work in the world gave a new happiness to life.

On February 28th I stood for the first time on the platform of the Hall of Science, Old Street, St. Luke's, London, and was received with that warmth of greeting which Secularists are always so ready to extend to any who sacrifice aught to join their ranks. That hall is identified in my mind with many a bitter struggle, with both victory and defeat, but whether in victory or in defeat I found there always welcome; and the love and the courage wherewith Secularists stood by me have overpaid a thousandfold any poor services I was fortunate enough to render, while in their ranks, to the cause of Liberty, and wholly prevent any bitterness arising in my mind for any unfriendliness shown me by some, who have perhaps overstepped kindness and justice in their sorrowful wrath at my renunciation of Materialism and Atheism. So far as health was concerned, the lecturing acted as a tonic. My chest had always been a little delicate, and when I consulted a doctor on the possibility of my standing platform work, he answered, "It will either kill you or cure you." It entirely cured the lung weakness, and I grew strong and vigorous instead of being frail and delicate, as of old.

It would be wearisome to go step by step over eighteen years of platform work, so I will only select here and there incidents illustrative of the whole. And here let me say that the frequent attacks made on myself and others, that we were attracted to Free-thought propaganda by the gains it offered, formed a somewhat grotesque contrast to the facts. On one occasion I spent eight days in Northumberland and Durham, gave twelve lectures, and made a deficit of eleven shillings on the whole. Of course such a thing could not happen in later years, when I had made my name by sheer hard work, but I fancy that every Secularist lecturer could tell of similar experiences in the early days of "winning his way." The fact is that from Mr. Bradlaugh downwards every one of us could have earned a competence with comparative ease in any other line of work, and could have earned it with public approval instead of amid popular reproach. Much of my early lecturing was done in Northumberland and Durham; the miners there are, as a rule, shrewd and hard-headed men, and very cordial is the greeting given by them to those they have reason to trust. At Seghill and at Bedlington I have slept in their cottages and have been welcomed to their tables, and I have a vivid memory of one evening at Seghill, after a lecture, when my host, himself a miner, invited about a dozen of his comrades to supper to meet me; the talk ran on politics, and I soon found that my companions knew more of English politics, had a far shrewder notion of political methods, and were, therefore, much better worth talking to, than most of the ordinary men met at dinner parties "in society." They were of the "uneducated" class despised by "gentlemen," and had not then the franchise, but politically they were far better educated than their social superiors, and were far better fitted to discharge the duties of citizenship. How well, too, do I remember a ten-mile drive in a butcher's cart, to give a lecture in an out-of-the-way spot, unapproached by railway. Such was the jolting as we rattled over rough roads and stony places, that I felt as though all my bones were broken, and as though I should collapse on the platform like a bag half-filled with stones. How kind they were to me, those genial, cordial miners, how careful for my comfort, and how motherly were the women! Ah! if opponents of my views who did not know me were often cruel and malignant, there was compensation in the love and honour in which good men and women all the country over held me, and their devotion outweighed the hatred, and many a time and often soothed a weary and aching heart.

Lecturing in June, 1875, at Leicester, I came for the first time across a falsehood that brought sore trouble and cost me more pain than I care to tell. An irate Christian opponent, in the discussion that followed the lecture, declared that I was responsible for a book entitled, "The Elements of Social Science," which was, he averred, "The Bible of Secularists." I had never heard of the book, but as he stated that it was in favour of the abolition of marriage, and that Mr. Bradlaugh agreed with it, I promptly contradicted him; for while I knew nothing about the book, I knew a great deal about Mr. Bradlaugh, and I knew that on the marriage question he was conservative rather than revolutionary. He detested "Free Love" doctrines, and had thrown himself strongly on the side of the agitation led so heroically for many years by Mrs. Josephine Butler. On my return to London after the lecture I naturally made inquiry as to the volume and its contents, and I found that it had been written by a Doctor of Medicine some years before, and sent to the *National Reformer* for review, as to other journals, in ordinary course of business. It consisted of three parts—the first advocated, from the standpoint of medical science, what is roughly known as "Free Love"; the second was entirely medical; the third consisted of a clear and able exposition of the law of population as laid down by the Rev. Mr. Malthus, and—following the lines of John Stuart Mill—insisted that it was the duty of married persons to voluntarily limit their families within their means of subsistence. Mr. Bradlaugh, in reviewing the book, said that it was written "with honest and pure intent and purpose," and recommended to working men the exposition of the law of population. His enemies took hold of this recommendation, declared that he shared the author's views on the impermanence of the marriage tie, and, despite his reiterated contradictions, they used extracts against marriage from the book as containing his views. Anything more meanly vile it would be difficult to conceive, but such were the weapons used against him all his life, and used often by men whose own lives contrasted most unfavourably with his own. Unable to find anything in his own writings to serve their purpose, they used this book to damage him with those who knew nothing at first-hand of his views. What his enemies feared were not his views on marriage—which, as I have said, was conservative—but his Radicalism and his Atheism. To discredit him as politician they maligned him socially, and the idea that a man desires "to abolish marriage and the home," is a most convenient poniard, and the one most certain to wound. This was the origin of his worst difficulties, to be intensified, ere long, by his defence of Malthusianism. On me also fell the same lash, and I found myself held up to hatred as upholder of views that I abhorred.

I may add that far warmer praise than that bestowed on this book by Mr. Bradlaugh was given by other writers, who were never attacked in the same way.

In the *Reasoner*, edited by Mr. George Jacob Holyoake, I find warmer praise of it than in the *National Reformer*, in the review the following passage appears:—

"In some respects all books of this class are evils: but it would be weakness and criminal prudery—a prudery as criminal as vice itself—not to say that such a book as the one in question is not only a far lesser evil than the one that it combats, but in one sense a book which it is a mercy to issue and courage to publish."

The *Examiner*, reviewing the same book, declared it to be—

"A very valuable, though rather heterogeneous book. This is, we believe, the only book that has fully, honestly, and in a scientific spirit recognised all the elements in the problem—How are mankind to triumph over poverty, with its train of attendant evils?—and fearlessly endeavoured to find a practical solution."

The *British Journal of Homoeopathy* wrote:—

"Though quite out of the province of our journal, we cannot refrain from stating that this work is unquestionably the most remarkable one, in many respects, we have ever met with. Though we differ *toto coelo* from the author in his views of religion and morality, and hold some of his remedies to tend rather to a dissolution than a reconstruction of society, yet we are bound to admit the benevolence and philanthropy of his motives. The scope of the work is nothing less than the whole field of political economy."

Ernest Jones and others wrote yet more strongly, but out of all these Charles Bradlaugh alone has been selected for reproach, and has had the peculiar views of the anonymous author fathered on himself.

Some of the lecture work in those days was pretty rough. In Darwen, Lancashire, in June, 1875, stone-throwing was regarded as a fair argument addressed to the Atheist lecturer. At Swansea, in March, 1876, the fear of violence was so great that a guarantee against damage to the hall was exacted by the proprietor, and no local friend had the courage to take the chair for me. In September, 1876, at Hoyland, thanks to the exertions of Mr. Hebblethwaite, a Primitive Methodist, and two

Protestant missionaries, I found the hall packed with a crowd that yelled at me with great vigour, stood on forms, shook fists at me, and otherwise showed feelings more warm than friendly. Taking advantage of a lull in the noise, I began to speak, and the tumult sank into quietness; but as I was leaving the hall it broke out afresh, and I walked slowly through a crowd that yelled and swore and struck at me, but somehow those nearest always shrank back and let me pass. In the dark, outside the hall, they took to kicking, but only one kick reached me, and the attempts to overturn the cab were foiled by the driver, who put his horse at a gallop. Later in the same month Mr. Bradlaugh and I visited Congleton together, having been invited there by Mr. and Mrs. Wolstenholme Elmy. Mr. Bradlaugh lectured on the first evening to an accompaniment of broken windows, and I, sitting with Mrs. Elmy facing the platform, received a rather heavy blow on the back of the head from a stone thrown by some one in the room. We had a mile and a half to walk from the hall to the house, and were accompanied all the way by a stone-throwing crowd, who sang hymns at the tops of their voices, with interludes of curses and foul words. On the following evening I lectured, and our stone-throwing admirers escorted us to the hall; in the middle of the lecture a man shouted, "Put her out!" and a well-known wrestler of the neighbourhood, named Burbery, who had come to the hall with some friends to break up the meeting, stood up as at a signal in front of the platform and loudly interrupted. Mr. Bradlaugh, who was in the chair, told him to sit down, and, as he persisted in interrupting, informed him that he must either be quiet or go out. "Put me out!" shouted Mr. Burbery, striking an attitude. Mr. Bradlaugh left the platform and walked up to the noisy swashbuckler, who at once grappled with him and tried to throw him. But Mr. Burbery had not reckoned on the massive strength of his opponent, and when the "throw" was complete Mr. Burbery was underneath. Amid much excitement Mr. Burbery was propelled towards the door, being gently used on the way as a battering-ram against his friends who rushed to the rescue, and at the door was handed over to the police. The chairman then resumed his normal duties, with a brief "Go on" to me, and I promptly went on, finishing the lecture in peace. But outside the hall there was plenty of stone-throwing, and Mrs. Elmy received a cut on the temple from a flint. This stormy work gradually lessened, and my experience of it was a mere trifle compared to that which my predecessors had faced. Mr. Bradlaugh's early experiences involved much serious rioting, and Mrs. Harriet Law, a woman of much courage and of strong natural ability, had many a rough meeting in her lecturing days.

In September, 1875, Mr. Bradlaugh again sailed for America, still to earn money there to pay his debts. Unhappily he was struck down by typhoid fever, and all his hopes of freeing himself thus were destroyed. His life was well-nigh despaired of, but the admirable skill of physician and nurse pulled him through. Said the *Baltimore Advertiser:*—

"This long and severe illness has disappointed the hopes and retarded the object for which he came to this country; but he is gentleness and patience itself in his sickness in this strange land, and has endeared himself greatly to his physicians and attendants by his gratitude and appreciation of the slightest attention."

His fortitude in face of death was also much commented on, lying there as he did far from home and from all he loved best. Never a quiver of fear touched him as he walked down into the valley of the shadow of death; the Rev. Mr. Frothingham bore public and admiring testimony in his own church to Mr. Bradlaugh's noble serenity, at once fearless and unpretending, and, himself a Theist, gave willing witness to the Atheist's calm strength. He came back to us at the end of September, worn to a shadow, weak as a child, and for many a long month he bore the traces of his wrestle with death.

One part of my autumn's work during his absence was the delivery and subsequent publication of six lectures on the French Revolution. That stormy time had for me an intense fascination. I brooded over it, dreamed over it, and longed to tell the story from the people's point of view. I consequently read a large amount of the current literature of the time, as well as Louis Blanc's monumental work and the histories of Michelet, Lamartine, and others. Fortunately for me, Mr. Bradlaugh had a splendid collection of books on the subject, and ere we left England he brought me two cabs-full of volumes, aristocratic, ecclesiastical, democratic, and I studied all these diligently, and lived in them, till the French Revolution became to me as a drama in which I had myself taken part, and the actors were to me as personal friends and foes. In this, again, as in so much of my public work, I have to thank Mr. Bradlaugh for the influence which led me to read fully all sides of a question, and to read most carefully those from which I differed most, ere I considered myself competent to write or to speak thereon. From 1875 onwards I held office as one of the vice-presidents of the National Secular Society—a society founded on a broad basis of liberty, with the inspiring motto, "We Search for Truth." Mr. Bradlaugh was president, and I held office under him till he resigned his post in February, 1890, nine months after I had joined the Theosophical Society. The N.S.S., under his judicious and far-sighted leadership, became a real force in the country, theologically and politically, embracing large numbers of men and women who were Freethinkers as well as Radicals, and forming a nucleus of earnest workers, able to gather round them still larger numbers of others, and thus to powerfully affect public opinion. Once a year the society met in conference, and many a strong and lasting friendship between men living far apart dated from these yearly gatherings, so that all over the country spread a net-work of comradeship between the staunch followers of "our Charlie." These were the men and women who paid his election expenses over and over again, supported him in his Parliamentary struggle, came up to London to swell the demonstrations in his favour. And round them grew up a huge party—"the largest personal following of any public man since Mr. Gladstone," it was once said by an eminent man—who differed from him in theology, but passionately supported him in politics; miners, cutlers, weavers, spinners, shoemakers, operatives of every trade, strong, sturdy, self-reliant men who loved him to the last.

CHAPTER IX

The Knowlton Pamphlet

The year 1877 dawned, and in its early days began a struggle which, ending in victory all along the line, brought with it pain and anguish that I scarcely care to recall. An American physician, Dr. Charles Knowlton, convinced of the truth of the teaching of the Rev. Mr. Malthus, and seeing that that teaching had either no practical value or tended to the great increase of prostitution, unless married people were taught to limit their families within their means of livelihood—wrote a pamphlet on the voluntary limitation of the family. It was published somewhere in the Thirties—about 1835, I think—and was sold unchallenged in England as well as in America for some forty years. Philosophers of the Bentham school, like John Stuart Mill, endorsed its teachings, and the bearing of population on poverty was an axiom in economic literature. Dr. Knowlton's work was a physiological treatise, advocating conjugal prudence and parental responsibility; it argued in favour of early marriage, with a view to the purity of social life; but as early marriage between persons of small means generally implies a large family, leading either to pauperism or to lack of necessary food, clothing, education, and fair start in life for the children, Dr. Knowlton advocated the restriction of the number of the family within the means of subsistence, and stated the methods by which this restriction could be carried out. The book was never challenged till a disreputable Bristol bookseller put some copies on sale to which he added some improper pictures, and he was prosecuted and convicted. The publisher of the *National Reformer* and of Mr. Bradlaugh's and my books and pamphlets had taken over a stock of Knowlton's pamphlets among other literature he bought, and he was prosecuted and, to our great dismay, pleaded guilty. We at once removed our publishing from his hands, and after careful deliberation we decided to publish the incriminated pamphlet in order to test the right of discussion on the population question, when, with the advice to limit the family, information was given as to how that advice could be followed. We took a little shop, printed the pamphlet, and sent notice to the police that we would commence the sale at a certain day and hour, and ourselves sell the pamphlet, so that no one else might be endangered by our action. We resigned our offices in the National Secular Society that we might not injure the society, but the executive first, and then the Annual Conference, refused to accept the resignations.

Our position as regarded the pamphlet was simple and definite; had it been brought to us for publication, we stated, we should not have published it, for it was not a treatise of high merit; but, prosecuted as immoral because it advised the limitation of the family, it at once embodied the right of publication. In a preface to the republished edition, we wrote:—

"We republish this pamphlet, honestly believing that on all questions affecting the happiness of the people, whether they be theological, political, or social, fullest right of free discussion ought to be maintained at all hazards. We do not personally endorse all that Dr. Knowlton says: his 'Philosophical Proem' seems to us full of philosophical mistakes, and—as we are neither of us doctors—we are not prepared to endorse his medical views; but since progress can only be made through discussion, and no discussion is possible where differing opinions are suppressed, we claim the right to publish all opinions, so that the public, enabled to see all sides of a question, may have the materials for forming a sound judgment."

We were not blind to the danger to which this defiance of the authorities exposed us, but it was not the danger of failure, with the prison as penalty, that gave us pause. It was the horrible misconceptions that we saw might arise; the odious imputations on honour and purity that would follow. Could we, the teachers of a lofty morality, venture to face a prosecution for publishing what would be technically described as an obscene book, and risk the ruin of our future, dependent as that was on our fair fame? To Mr. Bradlaugh it meant, as he felt, the almost certain destruction of his Parliamentary position, the forging by his own hands of a weapon that in the hands of his foes would be well-nigh fatal. To me it meant the loss of the pure reputation I prized, the good name I had guarded—scandal the most terrible a woman could face. But I had seen the misery of the poor, of my sister-women with children crying for bread; the wages of the workmen were often sufficient for four, but eight or ten they could not maintain. Should I set my own safety, my own good name, against the helping of these? Did it matter that my reputation should be ruined, if its ruin helped to bring remedy to this otherwise hopeless wretchedness of thousands? What was worth all my talk about self-sacrifice and self-surrender, if, brought to the test, I failed? So, with heart aching but steady, I came to my resolution; and though I know now that I was wrong intellectually, and blundered in the remedy, I was right morally in the will to sacrifice all to help the poor, and I can rejoice that I faced a storm of obloquy fiercer and harder to bear than any other which can ever touch me again. I learned a lesson of stern indifference to all judgments from without that were not endorsed by condemnation from within. The long suffering that followed was a splendid school for the teaching of endurance.

The day before the pamphlet was put on sale we ourselves delivered copies to the Chief Clerk of the Magistrates at Guildhall, to the officer in charge at the City Police Office in Old Jewry, and to the Solicitor for the City of London. With each pamphlet was a notice that we would attend and sell the book from 4 to 5 p.m. on the following day, Saturday, March 24th. This we accordingly did, and in order to save trouble we offered to attend daily at the shop from 10 to 11 a.m. to facilitate our arrest, should the authorities determine to prosecute. The offer was readily accepted, and after some little delay—during which a deputation from the Christian Evidence Society waited upon Mr. Cross to urge the Tory Government to prosecute us—warrants were issued against us and we were arrested on April 6th. Letters of approval and encouragement came from the most diverse quarters, including among their writers General Garibaldi, the well-known economist, Yves Guyot, the great French constitutional lawyer, Emile Acollas, together with letters literally by the hundred from poor men and women thanking and blessing us for the stand taken. Noticeable were the numbers of letters from clergymen's wives, and wives of ministers of all denominations.

After our arrest we were taken to the police-station in Bridewell Place, and thence to the Guildhall, where Alderman Figgins was sitting, before whom we duly appeared, while in the back of the court waited what an official described as "a regular waggon-load of bail." We were quickly released, the preliminary investigation being fixed for ten days later—April 17th. At the close of the day the magistrate released us on our own recognisances, without bail; and it was so fully seen on all sides that we were fighting for a principle that no bail was asked for during the various stages of the trial. Two days later we were committed for trial at the Central Criminal Court, but Mr. Bradlaugh moved for a writ of *certiorari* to remove the trial to the Court of Queen's Bench; Lord Chief Justice Cockburn said he would grant the writ if "upon looking at it (the book), we think its object is the legitimate one of promoting knowledge on a matter of human interest," but not if the science were only a cover for impurity, and he directed that copies of the book should be handed in for perusal by himself and Mr. Justice Mellor. Having read the book they granted the writ.

The trial commenced on June 18th before the Lord Chief Justice of England and a special jury, Sir Hardinge Giffard, the Solicitor-General of the Tory Government, leading against us, and we defending ourselves. The Lord Chief Justice "summed up strongly for an acquittal," as a morning paper said; he declared that "a more ill-advised and more injudicious proceeding in the way of a prosecution was probably never brought into a court of justice," and described us as "two enthusiasts who have been actuated by a desire to do good in a particular department of society." He then went on to a splendid statement of the law of population, and ended by praising our straightforwardness and asserting Knowlton's honesty of intention. Every one in court thought that we had won our case, but they had not taken into account the religious and political hatred against us and the presence on the jury of such men as Mr. Walter, of the *Times*. After an hour and thirty-five minutes of delay the verdict was a compromise: "We are unanimously of opinion that the book in question is calculated to deprave public morals, but at the same time we entirely exonerate the defendants from any corrupt motive in publishing it." The Lord Chief Justice looked troubled, and said that he should have to translate the verdict into one of guilty, and on that some of the jury turned to leave the box, it having been agreed—we heard later from one of them—that if the verdict were not accepted in that form they should retire again, as six of the jury were against convicting us; but the foreman, who was bitterly hostile, jumped at the chance of snatching a conviction, and none of those in our favour had the courage to contradict him on the spur of the moment, so the foreman's "Guilty" passed, and the judge set us free, on Mr. Bradlaugh's recognisances to come up for judgment that day week.

On that day we moved to quash the indictment and for a new trial, partly on a technical ground and partly on the ground that the verdict, having acquitted us of wrong motive, was in our favour, not against us. On this the Court did not agree with us, holding that the part of the indictment alleging corrupt motive was superfluous. Then came the question of sentence, and on this the Lord Chief Justice did his best to save us; we were acquitted of any intent to violate the law; would we submit to the verdict of the jury and promise not to sell the book? No, we would not; we claimed the right to sell, and meant to vindicate it. The Judge pleaded, argued, finally got angry with us, and, at last, compelled to pass sentence, he stated that if we would have yielded he would have let us go free without penalty, but that as we would set ourselves against the law, break it and defy it—a sore offence from the judge's point of view—he could only pass a heavy sentence on each of six months' imprisonment, a fine of £200, and recognisances of £500 for two years, and this, as he again repeated, upon the assumption "that they do intend to set the law at defiance." Even despite this he made us first-class misdemeanants. Then, as Mr. Bradlaugh stated that we should move for a writ of error, he liberated us on Mr. Bradlaugh's recognisance for £100, the queerest comment on his view of the case and of our characters, since we were liable jointly to £1,400 under the sentence, to say nothing of the imprisonment. But prison and money penalties vanished into thin air, for the writ of error was granted, proved successful, and the verdict was quashed.

Then ensued a somewhat anxious time. We were resolute to continue selling; were our opponents equally resolved to prosecute us? We could not tell. I wrote a pamphlet entitled "The Law of Population," giving the arguments which had convinced me of its truth, the terrible distress and degradation entailed on families by overcrowding and the lack of the necessaries of life, pleading for early marriages that prostitution might be destroyed, and limitation of the family that pauperism might be avoided; finally, giving the information which rendered early marriage without these evils possible. This pamphlet was put in circulation as representing our view of the subject, and we again took up the sale of Knowlton's. Mr. Bradlaugh carried the war into the enemy's country, and commenced an action against the police for the recovery of some pamphlets they had seized; he carried the action to a successful issue, recovered the pamphlets, bore them off in triumph, and we sold them all with an inscription across them, "Recovered from the police." We continued the sale of Knowlton's tract for some time, until we received an intimation that no further prosecution would be attempted, and on this we at once dropped its publication, substituting for it my "Law of Population."

But the worst part of the fight, for me, was to come. Prosecution of the "Law of Population" was threatened, but never commenced; a worse weapon against me was in store. An attempt had been made in August, 1875, to deprive me of the custody of my little girl by hiding her away when she went on her annual visit of one month to her father, but I had promptly recovered her by threatening to issue a writ of *habeas corpus.* Now it was felt that the Knowlton trial might be added to the charges of blasphemy that could be urged against me, and that this double-barrelled gun might be discharged with effect. I received notice in January, 1878, that an application was to be made to the High Court of Chancery to deprive me of the child, but the petition was not filed till the following April. Mabel was dangerously ill with scarlet fever at the time, and though this fact was communicated to her father I received a copy of the petition while sitting at her bedside. The petition alleged that, "The said Annie Besant is, by addresses, lectures, and writings, endeavouring to propagate the principles of Atheism, and has published a book entitled 'The Gospel of Atheism.' She has also associated herself with an infidel lecturer and author named Charles Bradlaugh in giving lectures and in publishing books and pamphlets, whereby the truth of the Christian religion is impeached, and disbelief in all religion inculcated."

It further alleged against me the publication of the Knowlton pamphlet, and the writing of the "Law of Population." Unhappily, the petition came for hearing before the then Master of the Rolls, Sir George Jessel, a man animated by the old spirit of Hebrew bigotry, to which he had added the time-serving morality of a "man of the world," sceptical as to all sincerity, and contemptuous of all devotion to an unpopular cause. The treatment I received at his hands on my first appearance in court told me what I had to expect. I had already had some experience of English judges, the stately kindness and gentleness of the Lord Chief Justice, the perfect impartiality and dignified courtesy of the Lords Justices of Appeal. My astonishment, then, can be imagined when, in answer to a statement by Mr. Ince, Q.C., that I appeared in person, I heard a harsh, loud voice exclaim:

"Appear in person? A lady appear in person? Never heard of such a thing! Does the lady really appear in person?"

As the London papers had been full of my appearing in person in the other courts and had contained the high compliments of the Lord Chief Justice on my conduct of my own case, Sir George Jessel's pretended astonishment seemed a little overdone. After a variety of similar remarks delivered in the most grating tones and in the roughest manner, Sir George Jessel tried to obtain his object by browbeating me directly. "Is this the lady?"

"I am the respondent, my lord, Mrs. Besant."

"Then I advise you, Mrs. Besant, to employ counsel to represent you, if you can afford it; and I suppose you can."

"With all submission to your lordship, I am afraid I must claim my right of arguing my case in person."

"You will do so if you please, of course, but I think you had much better appear by counsel. I give you notice that, if you do not, you must not expect to be shown any consideration. You will not be heard by me at any greater length than the case requires, nor allowed to go into irrelevant matter, as persons who argue their own cases usually do."

"I trust I shall not do so, my lord; but in any case I shall be arguing under your lordship's complete control."

This encouraging beginning may be taken as a sample of the case—it was one long fight against clever counsel, aided by a counsel instead of a judge on the bench. Only once did judge and counsel fall out. Mr. Ince and Mr. Bardswell had been arguing that my Atheism and Malthusianism made me an unfit guardian for my child; Mr. Ince declared that Mabel, educated by me, would "be helpless for good in this world," and "hopeless for good hereafter, outcast in this life and damned in the next." Mr. Bardswell implored the judge to consider that my custody of her "would be detrimental to the future prospects of the child in society, to say nothing of her eternal prospects." Had not the matter been to me of such heart-breaking importance, I could have laughed at the mixture of Mrs. Grundy, marriage establishment, and hell, presented as an argument for robbing a mother of her child. But Mr. Bardswell carelessly forgot that Sir George Jessel was a Jew, and lifting eyes to heaven in horrified appeal, he gasped out:

"Your lordship, I think, will scarcely credit it, but Mrs. Besant says, in a later affidavit, that she took away the Testament from the child because it contained coarse passages unfit for a child to read."

The opportunity was too tempting for a Jew to refrain from striking at a book written by apostate Jews, and Sir George Jessel answered sharply:

126

"It is not true to say there are no passages unfit for a child's reading, because I think there are a great many."

"I do not know of any passages that could fairly be called coarse."

"I cannot quite assent to that."

Barring this little episode judge and counsel showed a charming unanimity. I distinctly said I was an Atheist, that I had withdrawn the child from religious instruction at the day-school she attended, that I had written various anti-Christian books, and so on; but I claimed the child's custody on the ground that the deed of separation distinctly gave it to me, and had been executed by her father after I had left the Christian Church, and that my opinions were not sufficient to invalidate it. It was admitted on the other side that the child was admirably cared for, and there was no attempt at attacking my personal character. The judge stated that I had taken the greatest possible care of the child, but decided that the mere fact of my refusing to give the child religious instruction was sufficient ground for depriving me of her custody. Secular education he regarded as "not only reprehensible, but detestable, and likely to work utter ruin to the child, and I certainly should upon this ground alone decide that this child ought not to remain another day under the care of her mother."

Sir George Jessel denounced also my Malthusian views in a fashion at once so brutal and so untruthful as to facts, that some years later another judge, the senior puisne judge of the Supreme Court of New South Wales, declared in a judgment delivered in his own court that there was "no language used by Lord Cockburn which justified the Master of the Rolls in assuming that Lord Cockburn regarded the book as obscene," and that "little weight is to be attached to his opinion on a point not submitted for his decision"; he went on to administer a sharp rebuke for the way in which Sir George Jessel travelled outside the case, and remarked that "abuse, however, of an unpopular opinion, whether indulged in by judges or other people, is not argument, nor can the vituperation of opponents in opinion prove them to be immoral." However, Sir George Jessel was all-powerful in his own court, and he deprived me of my child, refusing to stay the order even until the hearing of my appeal against his decision. A messenger from the father came to my house, and the little child was carried away by main force, shrieking and struggling, still weak from the fever, and nearly frantic with fear and passionate resistance. No access to her was given me, and I gave notice that if access were denied me, I would sue for a restitution of conjugal rights, merely that I might see my children. But the strain had been too great, and I nearly went mad, spending hours pacing up and down the empty rooms, striving to weary myself to exhaustion that I might forget. The loneliness and silence of the house, of which my darling had always been the sunshine and the music, weighed on me like an evil dream; I listened for the patter of the dancing feet, and merry, thrilling laughter that rang through the garden, the sweet music of the childish voice; during my sleepless nights I missed in the darkness the soft breathing of the little child; each morning I longed in vain for the clinging arms and soft, sweet kisses. At last health broke down, and fever struck me, and mercifully gave me the rest of pain and delirium instead of the agony of conscious loss. Through that terrible illness, day after day, Mr. Bradlaugh came to me, and sat writing beside me, feeding me with ice and milk, refused from all others, and behaving more like a tender mother than a man friend; he saved my life, though it seemed to me for awhile of little value, till the first months of lonely pain were over. When recovered, I took steps to set aside an order obtained by Mr. Besant during my illness, forbidding me to bring any suit against him, and even the Master of the Rolls, on hearing that all access had been denied to me, and the money due to me stopped, uttered words of strong condemnation of the way in which I had been treated. Finally the deed of separation executed in 1873 was held to be good as protecting Mr. Besant from any suit brought by me, whether for divorce or for restitution of conjugal rights, while the clauses giving me the custody of the child were set aside. The Court of Appeal in April, 1879, upheld the decision, the absolute right of the father as against a married mother being upheld. This ignoring of all right to her children on the part of the married mother is a scandal and a wrong that has since been redressed by Parliament, and the husband has no longer in his grasp this instrument of torture, whose power to agonise depends on the tenderness and strength of the motherliness of the wife. In the days when the law took my child from me, it virtually said to all women: "Choose which of these two positions, as wife and mother, you will occupy. If you are legally your husband's wife, you can have no legal claim to your children; if legally you are

your husband's mistress, your rights as mother are secure."
That stigma on marriage is now removed.

One thing I gained in the Court of Appeal. The Court expressed a
strong view as to my right of access, and directed me to apply to
Sir George Jessel for it, adding that it could not doubt he would
grant it. Under cover of this I applied to the Master of the Rolls,
and obtained liberal access to the children; but I found that my
visits kept Mabel in a continual state of longing and fretting for
me, while the ingenious forms of petty insult that were devised
against me and used in the children's presence would soon
become palpable to them and cause continual pain. So, after a
painful struggle with myself, I resolved to give up the right of
seeing them, feeling that thus only could I save them from
constantly recurring conflict, destructive of all happiness and of
all respect for one or the other parent. Resolutely I turned my
back on them that I might spare them trouble, and determined
that, robbed of my own, I would be a mother to all helpless
children I could aid, and cure the pain at my own heart by
soothing the pain of others.

As far as regards this whole struggle over the Knowlton
pamphlet, victory was finally won all along the line. Not only did
we, as related, recover all our seized pamphlets, and continue
the sale till all prosecution and threat of prosecution were
definitely surrendered; but my own tract had an enormous sale,
so that when I withdrew it from sale in June, 1891, I was offered a
large sum for the copyright, an offer which I, of course, refused.
Since that time not a copy has been sold with my knowledge or
permission, but long ere that the pamphlet had received a very
complete legal vindication. For while it circulated untouched in
England, a prosecution was attempted against it in New South
Wales, but was put an end to by an eloquent and luminous
judgment by the senior puisne judge of the Supreme Court, Mr.
Justice Windmeyer, in December, 1888. This judge, the most
respected in the great Australian colony, spoke out plainly and
strongly on the morality of such teaching. "Take the case," he
said, "of a woman married to a drunken husband, steadily ruining
his constitution and hastening to the drunkard's doom, loss of
employment for himself, semi-starvation for his family, and
finally death, without a shilling to leave those whom he has
brought into the world, but armed with the authority of the law
to treat his wife as his slave, ever brutally insisting on the
indulgence of his marital rights. Where is the immorality, if,
already broken in health from unresting maternity, having

already a larger family than she can support when the miserable breadwinner has drunk himself to death, the woman avails herself of the information given in this book, and so averts the consequences of yielding to her husband's brutal insistence on his marital rights? Already weighted with a family that she is unable to decently bring up, the immorality, it seems to me, would be in the reckless and criminal disregard of precautions which would prevent her bringing into the world daughters whose future outlook as a career would be prostitution, or sons whose inherited taint of alcoholism would soon drag them down with their sisters to herd with the seething mass of degenerate and criminal humanity that constitutes the dangerous classes of great cities. In all these cases the appeal is from thoughtless, unreasoning prejudice to conscience, and, if listened to, its voice will be heard unmistakably indicating where the path of duty lies."

The judge forcibly refused to be any party to the prohibition of such a pamphlet, regarding it as of high service to the community. He said: "So strong is the dread of the world's censure upon this topic that few have the courage openly to express their views upon it; and its nature is such that it is only amongst thinkers who discuss all subjects, or amongst intimate acquaintances, that community of thought upon the question is discovered. But let any one inquire amongst those who have sufficient education and ability to think for themselves, and who do not idly float, slaves to the current of conventional opinion, and he will discover that numbers of men and women of purest lives, of noblest aspirations, pious, cultivated, and refined, see no wrong in teaching the ignorant that it is wrong to bring into the world children to whom they cannot do justice, and who think it folly to stop short in telling them simply and plainly how to prevent it. A more robust view of morals teaches that it is puerile to ignore human passions and human physiology. A clearer perception of truth and the safety of trusting to it teaches that in law, as in religion, it is useless trying to limit the knowledge of mankind by any inquisitorial attempts to place upon a judicial Index Expurgatorius works written with an earnest purpose, and commending themselves to thinkers of well-balanced minds. I will be no party to any such attempt. I do not believe that it was ever meant that the Obscene Publication Act should apply to cases of this kind, but only to the publication of such matter as all good men would regard as lewd and filthy, to lewd and bawdy novels, pictures and exhibitions, evidently published and given for lucre's sake. It could never have been intended to stifle the expression of thought by the earnest-minded on a subject of transcendent national importance like the present, and I will not strain it for that purpose. As pointed out by Lord Cockburn in the case of the Queen v. Bradlaugh and Besant, all prosecutions of this kind should be regarded as mischievous, even by those who disapprove the opinions sought to be stifled, inasmuch as they only tend more widely to diffuse the teaching objected to. To those, on the other hand, who desire its promulgation, it must be a matter of congratulation that this, like all attempted persecutions of thinkers, will defeat its own object, and that truth, like a torch, 'the more it's shook it shines.'"

The argument of Mr. Justice Windmeyer for the Neo-Malthusian position was (as any one may see who reads the full text of the judgment) one of the most luminous and cogent I have ever read. The judgment was spoken of at the time in the English press as a "brilliant triumph for Mrs. Besant," and so I suppose it was; but no legal judgment could undo the harm wrought on the public mind in England by malignant and persistent misrepresentation. What that trial and its results cost me in pain no one but myself will ever know; on the other hand, there was the passionate gratitude evidenced by letters from thousands of poor married women—many from the wives of country clergymen and curates—thanking and blessing me for showing them how to escape from the veritable hell in which they lived. The "upper classes" of society know nothing about the way in which the poor live; how their overcrowding destroys all sense of personal dignity, of modesty, of outward decency, till human life, as Bishop Fraser justly said, is "degraded below the level of the swine." To such, and among such I went, and I could not grudge the price that then seemed to me as the ransom for their redemption. To me, indeed, it meant the losing of all that made life dear, but for them it seemed to be the gaining of all that gave hope of a better future. So how could I hesitate—I whose heart had been fired by devotion to an ideal Humanity, inspired by that Materialism that is of love and not of hate?

And now, in August, 1893, we find the *Christian World,* the representative organ of orthodox Christian Protestantism, proclaiming the right and the duty of voluntary limitation of the family. In a leading article, after a number of letters had been inserted, it said:—

131

"The conditions are assuredly wrong which bring one member of the married partnership into a bondage so cruel. It is no less evident that the cause of the bondage in such cases lies in the too rapid multiplication of the family. There was a time when any idea of voluntary limitation was regarded by pious people as interfering with Providence. We are beyond that now, and have become capable of recognising that Providence works through the common sense of individual brains. We limit population just as much by deferring marriage from prudential motives as by any action that may be taken after it. Apart from certain methods of limitation, the morality of which is gravely questioned by many, there are certain easily-understood physiological laws of the subject, the failure to know and to observe which is inexcusable on the part either of men or women in these circumstances. It is worth noting in this connection that Dr. Billings, in his article in this month's *Forum*, on the diminishing birth-rate of the United States, gives as one of the reasons the greater diffusion of intelligence, by means of popular and school treatises on physiology, than formerly prevailed."

Thus has opinion changed in sixteen years, and all the obloquy poured on us is seen to have been the outcome of ignorance and bigotry.

As for the children, what was gained by their separation from me? The moment they were old enough to free themselves, they came back to me, my little girl's too brief stay with me being ended by her happy marriage, and I fancy the fears expressed for her eternal future will prove as groundless as the fears for her temporal ruin have proved to be! Not only so, but both are treading in my steps as regards their views of the nature and destiny of man, and have joined in their bright youth the Theosophical Society to which, after so many struggles, I won my way.

The struggle on the right to discuss the prudential restraint of population did not, however, conclude without a martyr. Mr. Edward Truelove, alluded to above, was prosecuted for selling a treatise by Robert Dale Owen on "Moral Physiology," and a pamphlet entitled, "Individual, Family, and National Poverty." He was tried on February 1, 1878, before the Lord Chief Justice in the Court of Queen's Bench, and was most ably defended by Professor W.A. Hunter. The jury spent two hours in considering their verdict, and returned into court and stated that they were unable to agree. The majority of the jury were ready to convict, if they felt sure that Mr. Truelove would not be punished, but one of them boldly declared in court: "As to the book, it is written in plain language for plain people, and I think that many more persons ought to know what the contents of the book are." The jury was discharged, in consequence of this one man's courage, but Mr. Truelove's persecutors—the Vice Society—were determined not to let their victim free. They proceeded to trial a second time, and wisely endeavoured to secure a special jury, feeling that as prudential restraint would raise wages by limiting the supply of labour, they would be more likely to obtain a verdict from a jury of "gentlemen" than from one composed of workers. This attempt was circumvented by Mr. Truelove's legal advisers, who let a *procedendo* go which sent back the trial to the Old Bailey. The second trial was held on May 16th at the Central Criminal Court before Baron Pollock and a common jury, Professor Hunter and Mr. J.M. Davidson appearing for the defence. The jury convicted, and the brave old man, sixty-eight years of age, was condemned to four months' imprisonment and £50 fine for selling a pamphlet which had been sold unchallenged, during a period of forty-five years, by James Watson, George Jacob Holyoake, Austin Holyoake, and Charles Watts. Mr. Grain, the counsel employed by the Vice Society, most unfairly used against Mr. Truelove my "Law of Population," a pamphlet which contained, Baron Pollock said, "the head and front of the offence in the other [the Knowlton] case." I find an indignant protest against this odious unfairness in the *National Reformer* for May 19th: "My 'Law of Population' was used against Mr. Truelove as an aggravation of his offence, passing over the utter meanness—worthy only of Collette—of using against a prisoner a book whose author has never been attacked for writing it—does Mr. Collette, or do the authorities, imagine that the severity shown to Mr. Truelove will in any fashion deter me from continuing the Malthusian propaganda? Let me here assure them, one and all, that it will do nothing of the kind; I shall continue to sell the 'Law of Population' and to advocate scientific checks to population, just as though Mr. Collette and his Vice Society were all dead and buried. In commonest justice they are bound to prosecute me, and if they get, and keep, a verdict against me, and succeed in sending me to prison, they will only make people more anxious to read my book, and make me more personally powerful as a teacher of the views which they attack."

A persistent attempt was made to obtain a writ of error in Mr. Truelove's case, but the Tory Attorney-General, Sir John Holker, refused it, although the ground on which it was asked was one of the grounds on which a similar writ had been granted to Mr. Bradlaugh and myself. Mr. Truelove was therefore compelled to suffer his sentence, but memorials, signed by 11,000 persons, asking for his release, were sent to the Home Secretary from every part of the country, and a crowded meeting in St. James's Hall, London, demanded his liberation with only six dissentients. The whole agitation did not shorten Mr. Truelove's sentence by a single day, and he was not released from Coldbath Fields Prison until September 5th. On the 12th of the same month the Hall of Science was crowded with enthusiastic friends, who assembled to do him honour, and he was presented with a beautifully-illuminated address and a purse containing £177 (subsequent subscriptions raised the amount to £197 16s. 6d.).

It is scarcely necessary to say that one of the results of the prosecution was a great agitation throughout the country, and a wide popularisation of Malthusian views. Some huge demonstrations were held in favour of free discussion; on one occasion the Free Trade Hall, Manchester, was crowded to the doors; on another the Star Music Hall, Bradford, was crammed in every corner; on another the Town Hall, Birmingham, had not a seat or a bit of standing-room unoccupied. Wherever we went, separately or together, it was the same story, and not only were Malthusian lectures eagerly attended, and Malthusian literature eagerly bought, but curiosity brought many to listen to our Radical and Freethought lectures, and thousands heard for the first time what Secularism really meant. The Press, both London and provincial, agreed in branding the prosecution as foolish, and it was generally remarked that it resulted only in the wider circulation of the indicted book, and the increased popularity of those who had stood for the right of publication. The furious attacks since made upon us have been made chiefly by those who differ from us in theological creed, and who have found a misrepresentation of our prosecution served them as a convenient weapon of attack. During the last few years public opinion has been gradually coming round to our side, in consequence of the pressure of poverty resulting from widespread depression of trade, and during the sensation caused in 1884 by "The Bitter Cry of Outcast London," many writers in the *Daily News*—notably Mr. G.R. Sims—boldly alleged that the distress was to a great extent due to the large families of the poor, and mentioned that we had been prosecuted for giving the very knowledge which would bring salvation to the sufferers in our great cities.

Among the useful results of the prosecution was the establishment of the Malthusian League, "to agitate for the abolition of all penalties on the public discussion of the population question," and "to spread among the people, by all practicable means, a knowledge of the law of population, of its consequences, and of its bearing upon human conduct and morals." The first general meeting of the League was held at the Hall of Science on July 26, 1877, and a council of twenty persons was elected, and this council on August 2nd elected Dr. C.R. Drysdale, M.D., President; Mr. Swaagman, Treasurer; Mrs. Besant, Secretary; Mr. Shearer, Assistant-Secretary; and Mr. Hember, Financial Secretary. Since 1877 the League, under the same indefatigable president, has worked hard to carry out its objects; it has issued a large number of leaflets and tracts; it supports a monthly journal, the *Malthusian;* numerous lectures have been delivered under its auspices in all parts of the country; and it has now a medical branch, into which none but duly qualified medical men and women are admitted, with members in all European countries.

Another result of the prosecution was the accession of "D." to the staff of the *National Reformer.* This able and thoughtful writer came forward and joined our ranks as soon as he heard of the attack on us, and he further volunteered to conduct the journal during our expected imprisonment. From that time to this—a period of fifteen years—articles from his pen appeared in its columns week by week, and during all that time not one solitary difficulty arose between editors and contributor. In public a trustworthy colleague, in private a warm and sincere friend, "D." proved an unmixed benefit bestowed upon us by the prosecution.

Nor was "D." the only friend brought to us by our foes. I cannot ever think of that time without remembering that the prosecution brought me first into close intimacy with Mrs. Annie Parris—the wife of Mr. Touzeau Parris, the Secretary of the Defence Committee throughout all the fight—a lady who, during that long struggle, and during the, for me, far worse struggle that succeeded it, over the custody of my daughter, proved to me the most loving and sisterly of friends. One or two other friendships which will, I hope, last my life, date from that same time of strife and anxiety.

The amount of money subscribed by the public during the Knowlton and succeeding prosecutions gives some idea of the interest felt in the struggle. The Defence Fund Committee in March, 1878, presented a balance-sheet, showing subscriptions amounting to £1,292 5s. 4d., and total expenditure in the Queen v. Bradlaugh and Besant, the Queen v. Truelove, and the appeal against Mr. Vaughan's order (the last two up to date) of £1,274 10s. This account was then closed and the balance of £17 15s. 4d. passed on to a new fund for the defence of Mr. Truelove, the carrying on of the appeal against the destruction of the Knowlton pamphlet, and the bearing of the costs incident on the petition lodged against myself. In July this new fund had reached £196 16s. 7d., and after paying the remainder of the costs in Mr. Truelove's case, a balance of £26 15s. 2d. was carried on. This again rose to £247 15s. 2-1/2d., and the fund bore the expenses of Mr. Bradlaugh's successful appeal on the Knowlton pamphlet, the petition and subsequent proceedings in which I was concerned in the Court of Chancery, and an appeal on Mr. Truelove's behalf, unfortunately unsuccessful, against an order for the destruction of the Dale Owen pamphlet. This last decision was given on February 21, 1880, and on this the Defence Fund was closed. On Mr. Truelove's release, as mentioned above, a testimonial to the amount of £197 16s. 6d. was presented to him, and after the close of the struggle some anonymous friend sent to me personally £200 as "thanks for the courage and ability shown." In addition to all this, the Malthusian League received no less than £455 11s. 9d. during the first year of its life, and started on its second year with a balance in hand of £77 5s. 8d.

A somewhat similar prosecution in America, in which the bookseller, Mr. D.M. Bennett, sold a book with which he did not agree, and was imprisoned, led to our giving him a warm welcome when, after his release, he visited England. We entertained him at the Hall of Science at a crowded gathering, and I was deputed as spokesman to present him with a testimonial. This I did in the following speech, quoted here in order to show the spirit then animating me:—

"Friends, Mr. Bradlaugh has spoken of the duty that calls us here to-night. It is pleasant to think that in our work that duty is one to which we are not unaccustomed. In our army there are more true soldiers than traitors, more that are faithful to the trust of keeping the truth than those who shrink when the hour of danger comes. And I would ask Mr. Bennett to-night not to measure English feeling towards him by the mere number of those present. They that are here are representatives of many thousands of our fellow-countrymen. Glance down this middle table, and you will see that it is not without some right that we claim to welcome you in the name of multitudes of the citizens of England. There are those who taunt us with want of loyalty, and with the name of infidels. In what church will they find men and women more loyal to truth and conscience? The name infidel is not for us so long as we are faithful to the truth we know. If I speak, as I have done, of national representation in this hall this evening, tell me, you who know those who sit here, who have watched some of them for years, others of them but for a brief time, do I not speak truth? Take them one by one. Your President but a little while ago in circumstances similar to those wherein our guest himself was placed, with the true lover's keenness that recognises the mistress under all disguise, beholding his mistress Liberty in danger, under circumstances that would have blinded less sure eyes, leapt to her rescue. He risked the ambition of his life rather than be disloyal to liberty. And next is seated a woman, who, student of a noble profession, thought that liberty had greater claim upon her than even her work. When we stood in worse peril than even loss of liberty, she risked her own good name for the truth's sake. One also is here who, eminent in his own profession, came with the weight of his position and his right to speak, and gave a kindred testimony. One step further, and you see one who, soldier to liberty, throughout a long and spotless life, when the task was far harder than it is to-day, when there were no greetings, no welcomes, when to serve was to peril name as well as liberty, never flinched from the first until now. He is crowned with the glory of the jail, that was his for no crime but for claiming the right to publish that wherein the noblest thought is uttered in the bravest words. And next to him is another who speaks for liberty, who has brought culture, university degree, position in men's sight, and many friends, and cast them all at her beloved feet. Sir, not alone the past and the present greet you to-night. The future also greets you with us. We have here also those who are training themselves to walk in the footsteps of the one most dear to them, who shall carry on, when we have passed away, the work which we shall have dropped from our hands. But he whom we delight to honour at this hour in truth honours us, in that he allows us to offer him the welcome that it is our glory and our pleasure to give. He has fought bravely. The Christian creed had in its beginning more traitors and less true hearts than the creed of to-day. We are happy to-day not only in the thought of what manner of men we have for leaders, but in the thought of what manner of men we have as soldiers in our army. Jesus had twelve apostles. One betrayed Him for thirty pieces of silver; a second denied Him. They all forsook Him and fled. We can scarcely point to one who has thus deserted our sacred cause. The traditions of our party tell us of many who went to jail because they claimed for all that right of free speech which is the heritage of all. One of the most famous members of our body in England, Richard Carlile, turned bookseller to sell books that were prosecuted. This man became Free-thinker, driven thereto by the bigotry and wickedness of the Churches. He sold the books of Hone not because he agreed with them, but because Hone was prosecuted. He saw that the book in whose prosecution freedom was attacked was the book for the freeman to sell; and the story of our guest shows that in all this England and America are one. Those who gave Milton to the world can yet bring forth men of the same stamp in continents leagues asunder. Because our friend was loyal and true, prison had to him no dread. It was far, far less of dishonour to wear the garb of the convict than to wear that of the hypocrite. The society we represent, like his society in America, pleads for free thought, speaks for free speech, claims for every one, however antagonistic, the right to speak the thought he feels. It is better that this should be, even though the thought be wrong, for thus the sooner will its error be discovered—better if the thought be right, for then the sooner does the gladness of a new truth find place in the heart of man. As the mouthpiece, Sir, of our National Secular Society, and of its thousands of members, I speak to you now:—

"'ADDRESS.

"'*We seek for Truth.*'

"'To D.M. Bennett.

"'In asking you to accept at the hands of the National Secular Society of England this symbol of cordial sympathy and brotherly welcome, we are but putting into act the motto of our Society. "We seek for Truth" is our badge, and it is as Truthseeker that we do you homage to-night. Without free speech no search for Truth is possible; without free speech no discovery of Truth is useful; without free speech progress is checked, and the nations no longer march forward towards the nobler life which the future holds for man. Better a thousandfold abuse of free speech than denial of free speech. The abuse dies in a day; the denial slays the life of the people and entombs the hope of the race.

"'In your own country you have pleaded for free speech, and when, under a wicked and an odious law, one of your fellow-citizens was imprisoned for the publication of his opinions, you, not sharing the opinions but faithful to liberty, sprang forward to defend in him the principle of free speech which you claimed for yourself, and sold his book while he lay in prison. For this act you were in turn arrested and sent to jail, and the country which won its freedom by the aid of Paine in the eighteenth century disgraced itself in the nineteenth by the imprisonment of a heretic. The Republic of the United States dishonoured herself, and not you, in Albany penitentiary. Two hundred thousand of your countrymen pleaded for your release, but bigotry was too strong. We sent you greeting in your captivity; we rejoiced when the time came for your release. We offer you to-night our thanks and our hope—thanks for the heroism which never flinched in the hour of battle, hope for a more peaceful future, in which the memory of a past pain may be a sacred heritage and not a regret.

"'Charles Bradlaugh, *President.*'

"Soldier of liberty, we give you this. Do in the future the same good service that you have done in the past, and your reward shall be in the love that true men shall bear to you."

That, however, which no force could compel me to do, which I refused to threats of fine and prison, to separation from my children, to social ostracism, and to insults and ignominy worse to bear than death, I surrendered freely when all the struggle was over, and a great part of society and of public opinion had adopted the view that cost Mr. Bradlaugh and myself so dear. I may as well complete the story here, so as not to have to refer to it again. I gave up Neo-Malthusianism in April, 1891, its renunciation being part of the outcome of two years' instruction from Mdme. H.P. Blavatsky, who showed me that however justifiable Neo-Malthusianism might be while man was regarded only as the most perfect outcome of physical evolution, it was wholly incompatible with the view of man as a spiritual being, whose material form and environment were the results of his own mental activity. Why and how I embraced Theosophy, and accepted H.P. Blavatsky as teacher, will soon be told in its proper place. Here I am concerned only with the why and how of my renunciation of the Neo-Malthusian teaching, for which I had fought so hard and suffered so much.

When I built my life on the basis of Materialism I judged all actions by their effect on human happiness in this world now and in future generations, regarding man as an organism that lived on earth and there perished, with activities confined to earth and limited by physical laws. The object of life was the ultimate building-up of a physically, mentally, morally perfect man by the cumulative effects of heredity—mental and moral tendencies being regarded as the outcome of material conditions, to be slowly but surely evolved by rational selection and the transmission to offspring of qualities carefully acquired by, and developed in, parents. The most characteristic note of this serious and lofty Materialism had been struck by Professor W. K. Clifford in his noble article on the "Ethics of Belief."

Taking this view of human duty in regard to the rational co-operation with nature in the evolution of the human race, it became of the first importance to rescue the control of the generation of offspring from mere blind brute passion, and to transfer it to the reason and to the intelligence; to impress on parents the sacredness of the parental office, the tremendous responsibility of the exercise of the creative function. And since, further, one of the most pressing problems for solution in the older countries is that of poverty, the horrible slums and dens into which are crowded and in which are festering families of eight and ten children, whose parents are earning an uncertain 10s., 12s., 15s., and 20s. a week; since an immediate palliative is wanted, if popular risings impelled by starvation are to be avoided; since the lives of men and women of the poorer classes, and of the worst paid professional classes, are one long, heart-breaking struggle "to make both ends meet and keep respectable"; since in the middle class marriage is often avoided, or delayed till late in life, from the dread of the large family, and late marriage is followed by its shadow, the prevalence of vice and the moral and social ruin of thousands of women; for these, and many other reasons, the teaching of the duty of limiting the family within the means of subsistence is the logical outcome of Materialism linked with the scientific view of evolution, and with a knowledge of the physical law, by which evolution is accelerated or retarded. Seeking to improve the physical type, scientific Materialism, it seemed to me, must forbid parentage to any but healthy married couples; it must restrict childbearing within the limits consistent with the thorough health and physical well-being of the mother; it must impose it as a duty never to bring children into the world unless the conditions for their fair nurture and development are present. Regarding it as hopeless, as well as mischievous, to preach asceticism, and looking on the conjunction of nominal celibacy with widespread prostitution as inevitable, from the constitution of human nature, scientific Materialism—quite rationally and logically—advises deliberate restriction of the production of offspring, while sanctioning the exercise of the sexual instinct within the limits imposed by temperance, the highest physical and mental efficiency, the good order and dignity of society, and the self-respect of the individual.

In all this there is nothing which for one moment implies approval of licentiousness, profligacy, unbridled self-indulgence. On the contrary, it is a well-considered and intellectually-defensible scheme of human evolution, regarding all natural instincts as matters for regulation, not for destruction, and seeking to develop the perfectly healthy and well-balanced physical body as the necessary basis for the healthy and well-balanced mind. If the premises of Materialism be true, there is no answer to the Neo-Malthusian conclusions; for even those Socialists who have bitterly opposed the promulgation of Neo-Malthusianism—regarding it as a "red herring intended to draw the attention of the proletariat away from the real cause of poverty, the monopoly of land and capital by a class"—admit that when society is built on the foundation of common property in all that is necessary for the production of wealth, the time will come for the consideration of the population question. Nor do I now see, any more than I saw then, how any Materialist can rationally avoid the Neo-Malthusian position. For if man be the outcome of purely physical causes, it is with these that we must deal in guiding his future evolution. If he be related but to terrestrial existence, he is but the loftiest organism of earth; and, failing to see his past and his future, how should my eyes not have been then blinded to the deep-lying causes of his present woe? I brought a material cure to a disease which appeared to me to be of material origin; but how when the evil came from a subtler source, and its causes lay not on the material plane? How if the remedy only set up new causes for a future evil, and, while immediately a palliative, strengthened the disease itself, and ensured its reappearance in the future? This was the view of the problem set before me by H.P. Blavatsky when she unrolled the story of man, told of his origin and his destiny, showed me the forces that went to the making of man, and the true relation between his past, his present, and his future.

For what is man in the light of Theosophy? He is a spiritual intelligence, eternal and uncreate, treading a vast cycle of human experience, born and reborn on earth millennium after millennium, evolving slowly into the ideal man. He is not the product of matter, but is encased in matter, and the forms of matter with which he clothes himself are of his own making. For the intelligence and will of man are creative forces—not creative *ex nihilo*, but creative as is the brain of the painter—and these forces are exercised by man in every act of thought. Thus he is ever creating round him thought-forms, moulding subtlest matter into shape by these energies, forms which persist as tangible realities when the body of the thinker has long gone back to earth and air and water. When the time for rebirth into this earth-life comes for the soul these thought-forms, its own progeny, help to form the tenuous model into which the molecules of physical matter are builded for the making of the body, and matter is thus moulded for the new body in which the soul is to dwell, on the lines laid down by the intelligent and volitional life of the previous, or of many previous, incarnations. So does each man create for himself in verity the form wherein he functions, and what he is in his present is the inevitable outcome of his own creative energies in his past. Applying this to the Neo-Malthusian theory, we see in sexual love not only a passion which man has in common with the brute, and which forms, at the present stage of evolution, a necessary part of human nature, but an animal passion that may be trained and purified into a human emotion, which may be used as one of the levers in human progress, one of the factors in human growth. But, instead of this, man in the past has made his intellect the servant of his passions; the abnormal development of the sexual instinct in man—in whom it is far greater and more continuous than in any brute—is due to the mingling with it of the intellectual element, all sexual thoughts, desires, and imaginations having created thought-forms, which have been wrought into the human race, giving rise to a continual demand, far beyond nature, and in marked contrast with the temperance of normal animal life. Hence it has become one of the most fruitful sources of human misery and human degradation, and the satisfaction of its imperious cravings in civilised countries lies at the root of our worst social evils. This excessive development has to be fought against, and the instinct reduced within natural limits, and this will certainly never be done by easy-going self-indulgence within the marital relation any more than by self-indulgence outside it. By none other road than that of self-control and self-denial can men and women now set going the causes which will build for them brains and bodies of a higher type for their future return to earth-life. They have to hold this instinct in complete control, to transmute it from passion into tender and self-denying affection, to develop the intellectual at the expense of the animal, and thus to raise the whole man to the human stage, in which every intellectual and physical capacity shall subserve the purposes of the soul. From all this it follows that Theosophists should sound the note of self-restraint within marriage, and the gradual—for with the mass it cannot be sudden—restriction of the sexual relation to the perpetuation of the race.

Such was the bearing of Theosophical teaching on Neo-Malthusianism, as laid before me by H.P. Blavatsky, and when I urged, out of my bitter knowledge of the miseries endured by the poor, that it surely might, for a time at least, be recommended as a palliative, as a defence in the hands of a woman against intolerable oppression and enforced suffering, she bade me look beyond the moment, and see how the suffering must come back and back with every generation, unless we sought to remove the roots of wrong. "I do not judge a woman," she said, "who has resort to such means of defence in the midst of circumstances so evil, and whose ignorance of the real causes of all this misery is her excuse for snatching at any relief. But it is not for you, an Occultist, to continue to teach a method which you now know must tend to the perpetuation of the sorrow." I felt that she was right, and though I shrank from the decision—for my heart somewhat failed me at withdrawing from the knowledge of the poor, so far as I could, a temporary palliative of evils which too often wreck their lives and bring many to an early grave, worn old before even middle age has touched them—yet the decision was made. I refused to reprint the "Law of Population," or to sell the copyright, giving pain, as I sadly knew, to all the brave and loyal friends who had so generously stood by me in that long and bitter struggle, and who saw the results of victory thrown away on grounds to them inadequate and mistaken! Will it always be, I wonder, in man's climbing upward, that every step must be set on his own heart and on the hearts of those he loves?

CHAPTER X

At War All Round

Coming back to my work after my long and dangerous illness, I took up again its thread, heartsick, but with courage unshaken, and I find myself in the *National Reformer* for September 15, 1878, saying in a brief note of thanks that "neither the illness nor the trouble which produced it has in any fashion lessened my determination to work for the cause." In truth, I plunged into work with added vigour, for only in that did I find any solace, but the pamphlets written at this time against Christianity were marked with considerable bitterness, for it was Christianity that had robbed me of my child, and I struck mercilessly at it in return. In the political struggles of that time, when the Beaconsfield Government was in full swing, with its policy of annexation and aggression, I played my part with tongue and pen, and my articles in defence of an honest and liberty-loving policy in India, against the invasion of Afghanistan and other outrages, laid in many an Indian heart a foundation of affection for me, and seem to me now as a preparation for the work among Indians to which much of my time and thought to-day are given. In November of this same year (1878) I wrote a little book on "England, India, and Afghanistan" that has brought me many a warm letter of thanks, and with this, the carrying on of the suit against Mr. Besant before alluded to, two and often three lectures every Sunday, to say nothing of the editorial work on the *National Reformer*, the secretarial work on the Malthusian League, and stray lectures during the week, my time was fairly well filled. But I found that in my reading I developed a tendency to let my thoughts wander from the subject in hand, and that they would drift after my lost little one, so I resolved to fill up the gaps in my scientific education, and to amuse myself by reading up for some examinations; I thought it would serve as an absorbing form of recreation from my other work, and would at the same time, by making my knowledge exact, render me more useful as a speaker on behalf of the causes to which my life was given.

At the opening of the new year (1879) I met for the first time a man to whom I subsequently owed much in this department of work—Edward B. Aveling, a D.Sc. of London University, and a marvellously able teacher of scientific subjects, the very ablest, in fact, that I have ever met. Clear and accurate in his knowledge, with a singular gift for lucid exposition, enthusiastic in his love of science, and taking vivid pleasure in imparting his knowledge to others, he was an ideal teacher. This young man, in January, 1879, began writing under initials for the *National Reformer*, and in February I became his pupil, with the view of matriculating in June at the London University, an object which was duly accomplished. And here let me say to any one in mental trouble, that they might find an immense relief in taking up some intellectual recreation of this kind; during that spring, in addition to my ordinary work of writing, lecturing, and editing—and the lecturing meant travelling from one end of England to the other—I translated a fair-sized French volume, and had the wear-and-tear of pleading my case for the custody of my daughter in the Court of Appeal, as well as the case before the Master of the Rolls; and I found it the very greatest relief to turn to algebra, geometry, and physics, and forget the harassing legal struggles in wrestling with formulae and problems. The full access I gained to my children marked a step in the long battle of Freethinkers against disabilities, for, as noted in the *National Reformer* by Mr. Bradlaugh, it was "won with a pleading unequalled in any case on record for the boldness of its affirmation of Freethought," a pleading of which he generously said that it deserved well of the party as "the most powerful pleading for freedom of opinion to which it has ever been our good fortune to listen."

In the London *Daily News* some powerful letters of protest appeared, one from Lord Harberton, in which he declared that "the Inquisition acted on no other principle" than that applied to me; and a second from Mr. Band, in which he sarcastically observed that "this Christian community has for some time had the pleasure of seeing her Majesty's courts repeatedly springing engines of torture upon a young mother—a clergyman's wife who dared to disagree with his creed—and her evident anguish, her long and expensive struggles to save her child, have proved that so far as heretical mothers are concerned modern defenders of the faith need not envy the past those persuasive instruments which so long secured the unity of the Church. In making Mrs. Besant an example, the Master of the Rolls and Lord Justice James have been careful not to allow any of the effect to be lost by confusion of the main point—the intellectual heresy—with side questions. There was a Malthusian matter in the case, but the judges were very clear in stating that without any reference whatever to that, they would simply, on the ground of Mrs. Besant's 'religious, or anti-religious, opinions,' take her child from her." The great provincial papers took a similar tone, the *Manchester Examiner* going so far as to say of the ruling of the judges: "We do not say they have done so wrongly. We only say that the effect of their judgment is cruel, and it shows that the holding of unpopular opinions is, in the eye of the law, an offence which, despite all we had thought to the contrary, may be visited with the severest punishment a woman and a mother can be possibly called on to bear." The outcome of all this long struggle and of another case of sore injustice—in which Mrs. Agar-Ellis, a Roman Catholic, was separated from her children by a judicial decision obtained against her by her husband, a Protestant—was a change in the law which had vested all power over the children in the hands of the father, and from thenceforth the rights of the married mother were recognised to a limited extent. A small side-fight was with the National Sunday League, the president of which, Lord Thurlow, strongly objected to me as one of the vice-presidents. Mr. P.A. Taylor and others at once resigned their offices, and, on the calling of a general meeting, Lord Thurlow was rejected as president. Mr. P.A. Taylor was requested to assume the presidency, and the vice-presidents who had resigned were, with myself, re-elected. Little battles of this sort were a running accompaniment of graver struggles during all these battling years.

And through all the struggles the organised strength of the Freethought party grew, 650 new members being enrolled in the National Secular Society in the year 1878-79, and in July, 1879, the public adhesion of Dr. Edward B. Aveling brought into the ranks a pen of rare force and power, and gave a strong impulse to the educational side of our movement. I presided for him at his first lecture at the Hall of Science on August 10, 1879, and he soon paid the penalty of his boldness, finding himself, a few months later, dismissed from the Chair of Comparative Anatomy at the London Hospital, though the Board admitted that all his duties were discharged with punctuality and ability. One of the first results of his adhesion was the establishment of two classes under the Science and Art Department at South Kensington, and these grew year after year, attended by numbers of young men and women, till in 1883 we had thirteen classes in full swing, as well as Latin, and London University Matriculation classes; all these were taught by Dr. Aveling and pupils that he had trained. I took advanced certificates, one in honours, and so became qualified as a science teacher in eight different sciences, and Alice and Hypatia Bradlaugh followed a similar course, so that winter after winter we kept these classes going from September to the following May, from 1879 until the year 1888. In addition to these Miss Bradlaugh carried on a choral union.

Personally I found that this study and teaching together with attendance at classes held for teachers at South Kensington, the study for passing the First B.Sc. and Prel. Sc. Examinations at London University, and the study for the B.Sc. degree at London, at which I failed in practical chemistry three times—a thing that puzzled me not a little at the time, as I had passed a far more difficult practical chemical examination for teachers at South Kensington—all this gave me a knowledge of science that has stood me in good stead in my public work. But even here theological and social hatred pursued me.

When Miss Bradlaugh and myself applied for permission to attend the botany class at University College, we were refused, I for my sins, and she only for being her father's daughter; when I had qualified as teacher, I stood back from claiming recognition from the Department for a year in order not to prejudice the claims of Mr. Bradlaugh's daughters, and later, when I had been recognised, Sir Henry Tyler in the House of Commons attacked the Education Department for accepting me, and actually tried to prevent the Government grant being paid to the Hall of Science Schools because Dr. Aveling, the Misses Bradlaugh, and myself were unbelievers in Christianity. When I asked permission to go to the Botanical Gardens in Regent's Park the curator refused it, on the ground that his daughters studied there. On every side repulse and insult, hard to struggle against, bitter to bear. It was against difficulties of this kind on every side that we had to make our way, handicapped in every effort by our heresy. Let our work be as good as it might—and our Science School was exceptionally successful—the subtle fragrance of heresy was everywhere distinguishable, and when Mr. Bradlaugh and myself are blamed for bitterness in our anti-Christian advocacy, this constant gnawing annoyance and petty persecution should be taken into account. For him it was especially trying, for he saw his daughters—girls of ability and of high character, whose only crime was that they were his—insulted, sneered at, slandered, continually put at a disadvantage, because they were his children and loved and honoured him beyond all others.

It was in October, 1879, that I first met Herbert Burrows, though I did not become intimately acquainted with him till the Socialist troubles of the autumn of 1887 drew us into a common stream of work. He came as a delegate from the Tower Hamlets Radical Association to a preliminary conference, called by Mr. Bradlaugh, at the Hall of Science, on October 11th, to consider the advisability of holding a great London Convention on Land Law Reform, to be attended by delegates from all parts of the kingdom. He was appointed on the Executive Committee with Mr. Bradlaugh, Mr. Mottershead, Mr. Nieass, and others. The Convention was successfully held, and an advanced platform of Land Law Reform adopted, used later by Mr. Bradlaugh as a basis for some of the proposals he laid before Parliament.

CHAPTER XI

Mr. Bradlaugh's Struggle

And now dawned the year 1880, the memorable year in which commenced Mr. Bradlaugh's long Parliamentary battle. After a long and bitter struggle he was elected, with Mr. Labouchere, as member for Northampton, at the general election, and so the prize so long fought for was won. Shall I ever forget that election day, April 2, 1880? How at four o'clock Mr. Bradlaugh came into the room at the "George", where his daughters and I were sitting, flung himself into a chair with, "There's nothing more to do; our last man is polled." Then the waiting for the declaration through the long, weary hours of suspense, till as the time drew near we knelt by the window listening—listening to the hoarse murmur of the crowd, knowing that presently there would be a roar of triumph or a howl of anger when the numbers were read out from the steps of the Town Hall. And now silence sank, and we knew the moment had come, and we held our breath, and then—a roar, a wild roar of joy and exultation, cheer after cheer, ringing, throbbing, pealing, and then the mighty surge of the crowd bringing him back, their member at last, waving hats, handkerchiefs, a very madness of tumultuous delight, and the shrill strains of "Bradlaugh for Northampton!" with a ring of triumph in them they had never had before. And he, very grave, somewhat shaken by the outpour of love and exultation, very silent, feeling the weight of new responsibility more than the gladness of victory. And then the next morning, as he left the town, the mass of men and women, one sea of heads from hotel to station, every window crowded, his colours waving everywhere, men fighting to get near him, to touch him, women sobbing, the cries, "Our Charlie, our Charlie; we've got you and we'll keep you." How they loved him, how they joyed in the triumph won after twelve years of strife. Ah me! we thought the struggle over, and it was only beginning; we thought our hero victorious, and a fiercer, crueller fight lay in front. True, he was to win that fight, but his life was to be the price of the winning; victory for him was to be final, complete, but the laurel-wreath was to fall upon a grave.

From a photograph by T. Westley, 57, Vernon Street, Northampton.
CHARLES BRADLAUGH AND HENRY LABOUCHERE.

The outburst of anger from the more bigoted of the Christian community was as savage as the outburst of delight had been exultant, but we recked little of it. Was he not member, duly elected, without possibility of assailment in his legal right? Parliament was to meet on April 29th, the swearing-in beginning on the following day, and Mr. Bradlaugh had taken counsel with some other Freethinking members as to the right of Freethinkers to affirm. He held that under the Act 29 and 30 Vict. c. 19, and the Evidence Amendment Acts 1869 and 1870, the right to substitute affirmation for oath was clear; he was willing to take the oath as a necessary form if obligatory, but, believing it to be optional, he preferred affirmation. On May 3rd he presented himself and, according to the evidence of Sir Erskine May, the Clerk of the House, given before the second Select Committee on his case, he "came to the table and delivered the following statement in writing to the Clerk: 'To the Right Honourable the Speaker of the House of Commons. I, the undersigned, Charles Bradlaugh, beg respectfully to claim to be allowed to affirm, as a person for the time being by law permitted to make a solemn affirmation or declaration, instead of taking an oath. (Signed) Charles Bradlaugh.' And being asked by the Clerk upon what grounds he claimed to make an affirmation, he answered: 'By virtue of the Evidence Amendment Acts, 1869 and 1870.' Whereupon the Clerk reported to Mr. Speaker" the claim, and Mr. Speaker told Mr. Bradlaugh that he might address the House on the matter. "Mr. Bradlaugh's observations were very short. He repeated that he relied upon the Evidence Further Amendment Act, 1869, and the Evidence Amendment Act, 1870, adding: 'I have repeatedly, for nine years past, made an affirmation in the highest courts of jurisdiction in this realm. I am ready to make such a declaration or affirmation.' Substantially those were the words which he addressed to the Speaker." This was the simple, quiet, and dignified scene which took place in the House. Mr. Bradlaugh was directed to withdraw, and he withdrew, and, after debate, a Select Committee was appointed to consider whether he could make affirmation; that Committee decided against the claim, and gave in its report on May 20th. On the following day Mr. Bradlaugh presented himself at the table of the House to take the oath in the form prescribed by the law, and on the objection of Sir Henry Drummond Wolff, who submitted a motion that he should not be allowed to take the oath, another Committee was appointed.

Before this Committee Mr. Bradlaugh stated his case, and pointed out that the legal obligation lay on him to take the oath, adding: "Any form that I went through, any oath that I took, I should regard as binding upon my conscience in the fullest degree. I would go through no form, I would take no oath, unless I meant it to be so binding." He wrote in the same sense to the *Times*, saying that he should regard himself "as bound, not by the letter of its words, but by the spirit which the affirmation would have conveyed, had I been permitted to use it." The Committee reported against him, and on June 23rd he was heard at the Bar of the House, and made a speech so self-restrained, so noble, so dignified, that the House, in defiance of all its own rules, broke out over and over again into applause. In the debate that preceded his speech, members had lost sight of the ordinary rules of decency, and had used expressions against myself wholly gratuitous in such a quarrel; the grave rebuke to him who "was wanting in chivalry, because, while I can answer for myself and am able to answer for myself, nothing justified the introduction of any other name beside my own to make prejudice against me," brought irrepressible cheers. His appeal was wholly to the law. "I have not yet used—I trust no passion may tempt me into using—any words that would seem to savour of even a desire to enter into conflict with this House. I have always taught, preached, and believed the supremacy of Parliament, and it is not because for a moment the judgment of one Chamber of Parliament should be hostile to me that I am going to deny the ideas I have always held; but I submit that one Chamber of Parliament—even its grandest Chamber, as I have always held this to be—had no right to override the law. The law gives me the right to sign that roll, to take and subscribe the oath, and to take my seat there [with a gesture towards the benches]. I admit that the moment I am in the House, without any reason but your own good will, you can send me away. That is your right. You have full control over your members. But you cannot send me away until I have been heard in my place, not a suppliant as I am now, but with the rightful audience that each member has always had. I am ready to admit, if you please, for the sake of argument, that every opinion I hold is wrong and deserves punishment. Let the law punish it. If you say the law cannot, then you admit that you have no right, and I appeal to public opinion against the iniquity of a decision which overrides the law and denies me justice. I beg your pardon, sir, and that of the House too, if in this warmth there seems to lack respect for its dignity. And as I shall have, if your decision be against me, to come to that table when your decision is given, I beg you, before the step is taken in which we may both lose our dignity—mine is not much, but yours is that of the Commons of England—I beg you, before the gauntlet is fatally thrown, I beg you, not in any sort of menace, not in any sort of boast, but as one man against six hundred, to give me that justice which on the other side of this hall the judges would give me, were I pleading there before them."

But no eloquence, no plea for justice, could stay the tide of Tory and religious bigotry, and the House voted that he should not be allowed to take the oath. Summoned to the table to hear the decision communicated by the Speaker, he answered that decision with the words firmly spoken: "I respectfully refuse to obey the order of the House, because that order was against the law." The Speaker appealed to the House for direction, and on a division—during which the Speaker and Charles Bradlaugh were left together in the chamber—the House ordered the enforcement of Mr. Bradlaugh's withdrawal. Once more the order is given, once more the refusal made, and then the Serjeant-at-

Arms was bidden to remove him. Strange was the scene as little Captain Cosset walked up to the member of Herculean proportions, and men wondered how the order would be enforced; but Charles Bradlaugh was not the man to make a vulgar brawl, and the light touch on his shoulder was to him the touch of an authority he admitted and to which he bowed. So he gravely accompanied his small captor, and was lodged in the Clock Tower of the House as prisoner until the House should further consider what to do with him—the most awkward prisoner it had ever had, in that in his person it was imprisoning the law.

In a special issue of the *National Reformer*, giving an account of the Committee's work and of Mr. Bradlaugh's committal to the Clock Tower, I find the following from my own pen: "The Tory party, beaten at the polls by the nation, has thus, for the moment, triumphed in the House of Commons. The man chosen by the Radicals of Northampton has been committed to prison on the motion of the Tory ex-Chancellor of the Exchequer, simply because he desires to discharge the duty laid upon him by his constituency and by the law of the land. As this paper goes to press, I go to Westminster to receive from him his directions as to the conduct of the struggle with the nation into which the House of Commons has so recklessly plunged." I found him busily writing, prepared for all events, ready for a long imprisonment. On the following day a leaflet from my pen, "Law Makers and Law Breakers," appealed to the people; after reciting what had happened, it concluded: "Let the people speak. Gladstone and Bright are for Liberty, and the help denied them within the House must come to them from without. No time must be lost. While we remain idle, a representative of the people is illegally held in prison. Northampton is insulted, and in this great constituency every constituency is threatened. On freedom of election depends our liberty; on freedom of conscience depends our progress. Tory squires and lordlings have defied the people and measured their strength against the masses. Let the masses speak." But there was no need to make appeals, for the outrage itself caused so swiftly a growl of anger that on the very next day the prisoner was set free, and there came protest upon protest against the high-handed action of the House. In Westminster Hall 4,000 people gathered to cheer Mr. Bradlaugh when he came to the House on the day after his liberation. In less than a week 200 meetings had thundered out their protest. Liberal associations, clubs, societies, sent up messages of anger and of demand for justice. In Trafalgar Square there gathered—

so said the papers—the largest crowd ever seen there, and on the Thursday following—the meeting was held on Monday—the House of Commons rescinded its resolution, refusing to allow Mr. Bradlaugh to affirm, and admitted him on Friday, July 2nd, to take his seat after affirmation. "At last the bitter struggle is over," I wrote, "and law and right have triumphed. The House of Commons has, by rescinding the resolution passed by Tories and Ultramontanes, re-established its good name in the eyes of the world. The triumph is not one of Freethought over Christianity, nor is it over the House of Commons; it is the triumph of law, brought about by good men—of all shades of opinion, but of one faith in justice—over Tory contempt of law and Ultramontane bigotry. It is the reassertion of civil and religious liberty under the most difficult circumstances, the declaration that the House of Commons is the creation of the people, and not a club of the aristocracy with the right of blackballing in its own hands."

The battle between Charles Bradlaugh and his persecutors was now transferred to the law courts. As soon as he had taken his seat he was served with a writ for having voted without having taken the oath, and this began the wearisome proceedings by which his defeated enemies boasted that they would make him bankrupt, and so vacate the seat he had so hardly gained. Rich men like Mr. Newdegate sued him, putting forward a man of straw as nominal plaintiff; for many a weary month Mr. Bradlaugh kept all his enemies at bay, fighting each case himself; defeated time after time, he fought on, finally carrying the cases to the House of Lords, and there winning them triumphantly. But they were won at such heavy cost of physical strength and of money, that they undermined his strength and burdened him heavily with debt. For all this time he had not only to fight in the law courts and to attend scrupulously to his Parliamentary duties, but he had to earn his living by lecturing and writing, so that his nights away from the House were spent in travelling and his days in incessant labour. Many of his defeated foes turned their weapons against me, hoping thus to give him pain; thus Admiral Sir John Hay, at Wigton, used language of me so coarse that the *Scotsman* and *Glasgow Herald* refused to print it, and the editor of the *Scotsman* described it as "language so coarse that it could have hardly dropped from a yahoo." August 25th found me at Brussels, whither I went, with Miss Hypatia Bradlaugh, to represent the English Freethinkers at the International Freethought Conference. It was an interesting gathering, attended by men of world-wide reputation, including

Dr. Ludwig Büchner, a man of noble and kindly nature. An International Federation of Freethinkers was there founded, which did something towards bringing together the Freethinkers of different countries, and held interesting congresses in the following years in London and Amsterdam; but beyond these meetings it did little, and lacked energy and vitality. In truth, the Freethought party in each country had so much to do in holding its own that little time and thought could be given to international organisation. For myself, my introduction to Dr. Büchner, led to much interesting correspondence, and I translated, with his approval, his "Mind in Animals," and the enlarged fourteenth edition of "Force and Matter," as well as one or two pamphlets. This autumn of 1880 found the so-called Liberal Government in full tilt against the Irish leaders, and I worked hard to raise English feeling in defence of Irish freedom even against attack by one so much honoured as was Mr. Gladstone. It was uphill work, for harsh language had been used against England and all things English, but I showed by definite figures—all up and down England—that life and property were far safer in Ireland than in England, that Ireland was singularly free from crime save in agrarian disputes, and I argued that these would disappear if the law should step in between landlord and tenant, and by stopping the crimes of rack-renting and most brutal eviction, put an end to the horrible retaliations that were born of despair and revenge. A striking point on these evictions I quoted from Mr. T.P. O'Connor, who, using Mr. Gladstone's words that a sentence of eviction was a sentence of starvation, told of 15,000 processes of eviction issued in that one year. The autumn's work was varied by the teaching of science classes, a debate with a clergyman of the Church of England, and an operation which kept me in bed for three weeks, but which, on the other hand, was useful, for I learned to write while lying on my back, and accomplished in this fashion a good part of the translation of "Mind in Animals."

And here let me point a moral about hard work. Hard work kills no one. I find a note in the *National Reformer* in 1880 from the pen of Mr. Bradlaugh: "It is, we fear, useless to add that, in the judgment of her best friends, Mrs. Besant has worked far too hard during the last two years." This is 1893, and the thirteen years' interval has been full of incessant work, and I am working harder than ever now, and in splendid health. Looking over the *National Reformer* for all these years, it seems to me that it did really fine educational work; Mr. Bradlaugh's strenuous utterances on political and theological matters; Dr. Aveling's luminous and beautiful scientific teachings; and to my share fell much of the educative work on questions of political and national morality in our dealings with weaker nations. We put all our hearts into our work, and the influence exercised was distinctly in favour of pure living and high thinking.

In the spring of 1881 the Court of Appeal decided against Mr. Bradlaugh's right to affirm as Member of Parliament, and his seat was declared vacant, but he was at once returned again by the borough of Northampton, despite the virulence of slander directed against him, so that he rightly described the election as "the most bitter I have ever fought." His work in the House had won him golden opinions in the country, and he was already recognised as a power there; so Tory fear was added to bigoted hatred, and the efforts to keep him out of the House were increased.

He was introduced to the House as a new member to take his seat by Mr. Labouchere and Mr. Burt, but Sir Stafford Northcote intervened, and after a lengthy debate, which included a speech from Mr. Bradlaugh at the Bar, a majority of thirty-three refused to allow him to take the oath. After a prolonged scene, during which Mr. Bradlaugh declined to withdraw and the House hesitated to use force, the House adjourned, and finally the Government promised to bring in an Affirmation Bill, and Mr. Bradlaugh promised, with the consent of his constituents, to await the decision of the House on this Bill. Meantime, a League for the Defence of Constitutional Rights was formed, and the agitation in the country grew: wherever Mr. Bradlaugh went to speak vast crowds awaited him, and he travelled from one end of the country to the other, the people answering his appeal for justice with no uncertain voice. On July 2nd, in consequence of Tory obstruction, Mr. Gladstone wrote to Mr. Bradlaugh that the Government were going to drop the Affirmation Bill, and Mr. Bradlaugh thereupon determined to present himself once more in the House, and fixed on August 3rd as the date of such action, so that the Irish Land Bill might get through the House ere any delay in business was caused by him. The House was then closely guarded with police; the great gates were closed, reserves of police were packed in the law courts, and all through July this state of siege continued. On August 2nd there was a large meeting in Trafalgar Square, at which delegates were present from all parts of England, and from as far north as Edinburgh, and on Wednesday, August 3rd, Mr. Bradlaugh went down to the House. His last words to me were: "The people know you better than they know any one, save myself; whatever happens, mind, whatever happens, let them do no violence; I trust to you to keep them quiet." He went to the House entrance with Dr. Aveling, and into the House alone. His daughters and I went together, and with some hundreds of others carrying petitions—ten only with each petition, and the ten rigidly counted and allowed to pass through the gate, sufficiently opened to let one through at a time—reached Westminster Hall, where we waited on the steps leading to the passage of the lobby.

An inspector ordered us off. I gently intimated that we were within our rights. Dramatic order: "Four officers this way." Up they marched and looked at us, and we looked at them. "I think you had better consult Inspector Denning before you use violence," I remarked placidly. They thought they had, and in a few moments up came the inspector, and seeing that we were standing in a place where we had a right to be, and were doing no harm, he rebuked his over-zealous subordinates, and they retired and left us in peace. A man of much tact and discretion was Inspector Denning. Indeed, all through this, the House of Commons police behaved admirably well. Even in the attack they were ordered to make on Mr. Bradlaugh, the police used as little violence as they could. It was Mr. Erskine, the Deputy Serjeant-at-Arms, and his ushers, who showed the brutality; as Dr. Aveling wrote at the time: "The police disliked their work, and, as brave men, had a sympathy for a brave man. Their orders they obeyed rigidly. This done, they were kindness itself." Gradually the crowd of petitioners grew and grew; angry murmurs were heard, for no news came from the House, and they loved "Charlie," and were mostly north country men, sturdy and independent. They thought they had a right to go into the lobby, and suddenly, with the impulse that will sway a crowd to a single action there was a roar, "Petition, petition, justice, justice," and they surged up the steps, charging at the policemen who held the door. Flashed into my mind my chief's charge, his words, "I trust to you to keep them quiet," and as the police sprang forward to meet the crowd I threw myself between them, with all the advantage of the position of the top of the steps that I had chosen, so that every man in the charging crowd saw me, and as they checked themselves in surprise I bade them stop for his sake, and keep for him the peace which he had bade us should not be broken. I heard afterwards that as I sprang forward the police laughed—

they must have thought me a fool to face the rush of the charging men; but I knew his friends would never trample me down, and as the crowd stopped the laugh died out, and they drew back and left me my own way.

Sullenly the men drew back, mastering themselves with effort, reining in their wrath, still for his sake. Ah! had I known what was going on inside, would I have kept his trust unbroken! and, as many a man said to me afterwards in northern towns, "Oh! if you had let us go we would have carried him into the House up to the Speaker's chair." We heard a crash inside, and listened, and there was sound of breaking glass and splintering wood, and in a few minutes a messenger came to me: "He is in Palace Yard." And we went thither and saw him standing, still and white, face set like marble, coat torn, motionless, as though carved in stone, facing the members' door. Now we know the whole shameful story: how as that one man stood alone, on his way to claim his right, alone so that he could do no violence, fourteen men, said the Central News, police and ushers, flung themselves upon him, pushed and pulled him down the stairs, smashing in their violence the glass and wood of the passage door; how he struck no blow, but used only his great strength in passive resistance— " Of all I have ever seen, I never saw one man struggle with ten like that," said one of the chiefs, angrily disdainful of the wrong he was forced to do—till they flung him out into Palace Yard. An eye-witness thus reported the scene in the Press: "The strong, broad, heavy, powerful frame of Mr. Bradlaugh was hard to move, with its every nerve and muscle strained to resist the coercion. Bending and straining against the overpowering numbers, he held every inch with surprising tenacity, and only surrendered it after almost superhuman exertions to retain it. The sight—little of it as was seen from the outside—soon became sickening. The overborne man appeared almost at his last gasp. The face, in spite of the warmth of the struggle, had an ominous pallor. The limbs barely sustained him. The Trafalgar Square phrase that this man might be broken but not bent occurred to minds apprehensive at the present appearance of him."

They flung him out, and swift, short words were there interchanged. "I nearly did wrong at the door," he said afterwards, "I was very angry. I said to Inspector Denning, 'I shall come again with force enough to overcome it,' He said, 'When?' I said, 'Within a minute if I raise my hand.'" He stood in Palace Yard, and there outside the gate was a vast sea of heads, the men who had journeyed from all parts of England for love of him, and in defence of the great right he represented of a constituency to send to Parliament the man of its choice. Ah! he was never greater than in that moment of outrage and of triumphant wrong; with all the passion of a proud man surging within him, insulted by physical violence, injured by the cruel wrenching of all his muscles—so that for weeks his arms had to be swathed in bandages—he was never greater than when he conquered his own wrath, crushed down his own longing for battle, stirred to flame by the bodily struggle, and the bodily injury, and with thousands waiting within sound of his voice, longing to leap to his side, he gave the word to tell them to meet him that evening away from the scene of conflict, and meanwhile to disperse quietly, "no riot, no disorder." But how he suffered mentally no words of mine may tell, and none can understand how it wrung his heart who does not know how he reverenced the great Parliament of England, how he honoured law, how he believed in justice being done; it was the breaking down of his national ideals, of his pride in his country, of his belief that faith would be kept with a foe by English gentlemen, who with all their faults, he thought, held honour and chivalry dear. "No man will sleep in gaol for me to-night," he said to me that day; "no woman can blame me for her husband killed or wounded, but—" A wave of agony swept over his face, and from that fatal day Charles Bradlaugh was never the same man. Some hold their ideals lightly, but his heart-strings were twined round his; some care little for their country—he was an Englishman, law-abiding, liberty-loving, to his heart's core, of the type of the seventeenth-century patriot, holding England's honour dear. It was the treachery that broke his heart; he had gone alone, believing in the honour of his foes, ready to submit to expulsion, to imprisonment, and it was the latter that he expected; but he never dreamed that, going alone amongst his foes, they would use brutal and cowardly violence, and shame every Parliamentary tradition by personal outrage on a duly-elected member, outrage more worthy of a slum pot-house than of the great Commons House, the House of Hampden and of Vane, the House that had guarded its own from Royal violence, and had maintained its privileges in the teeth of kings.

These stormy scenes brought about a promise of Government aid; Mr. Bradlaugh failed to get any legal redress, as, indeed, he expected to fail, on the ground that the officials of the House were covered by the House's order, but the Government promised to support his claim to his seat during the next session, and thus prevented the campaign against them on which we had resolved. I had solely on my own responsibility organised a great band of people pledged to refrain from the use of all excisable articles after a certain date, and to withdraw all their moneys in the Savings Bank, thus seriously crippling the financial resources of the Government. The response from the workers to my appeal to "Stop the supplies" was great and touching. One man wrote that as he never drank nor smoked he would leave off tea; others that though tobacco was their one luxury, they would forego it; and so on. Somewhat reluctantly, I asked the people to lay aside this formidable weapon, as "we have no right to embarrass the Government financially save when they refuse to do the first duty of a Government to maintain law. They have now promised to do justice, and we must wait." Meanwhile the injuries inflicted on Mr. Bradlaugh, rupturing the sheaths of some of the muscles of the arm, laid him prostrate, and various small fights went on during the temporary truce in the great struggle. I turned up in the House two or three times, haled thither, though not in person, by the people who kept Mr. Bradlaugh out, and a speech of mine became the subject of a question by Mr. Ritchie, while Sir Henry Tyler waged war on the science classes. Another joy was added to life by the use of my name—which by all these struggles had gained a marketable value—as author of pamphlets I had never seen, and this forgery of my name by unscrupulous people in the colonies caused me a good deal of annoyance. In the strengthening of the constitutional agitation in the country, the holding of an International Congress of Freethinkers in London, the studying and teaching of science, the delivering of courses of scientific lectures in the Hall of Science, a sharp correspondence with the Bishop of Manchester, who had libelled Secularists, and which led to a fiery pamphlet, "God's Views on Marriage," as retort—in all these matters the autumn months sped rapidly away. One incident of that autumn I record with regret. I was misled by very partial knowledge of the nature of the experiments performed, and by my fear that if scientific men were forbidden to experiment on animals with drugs they would perforce experiment with them on the poor in hospitals, to write two articles, republished as a pamphlet, against Sir Eardley Wilmot's Bill for the "Total Suppression of Vivisection." I limited my approval to highly skilled men engaged in original investigations, and took the representations made of the character of the experiments without sufficient care to verify them. Hence the publication of the one thing I ever wrote for which I feel deep regret and shame, as against the whole trend and efforts of my life. I am thankful to say that Dr. Anna Kingsford answered my articles, and I readily inserted her replies in the paper in which mine had appeared—our *National Reformer*—and she touched that question of the moral sense to which my nature at once responded. Ultimately, I looked carefully into the subject, found that vivisection abroad was very different from vivisection in England, saw that it was in very truth the fiendishly cruel thing that its opponents alleged, and destroyed my partial defence of even its less brutal form.

1882 saw no cessation of the struggles in which Mr. Bradlaugh and those who stood by him were involved. On February 7th he was heard for the third time at the Bar of the House of Commons, and closed his speech with an offer that, accepted, would have closed the contest. "I am ready to stand aside, say for four or five weeks, without coming to that table, if the House within that time, or within such time as its great needs might demand, would discuss whether an Affirmation Bill should pass or not. I want to obey the law, and I tell you how I might meet the House still further, if the House will pardon me for seeming to advise it. Hon. members have said that would be a Bradlaugh Relief Bill. Bradlaugh is more proud than you are. Let the Bill pass without applying to elections that have taken place previously, and I will undertake not to claim my seat, and when the Bill has passed I will apply for the Chiltern Hundreds. I have no fear. If I am not fit for my constituents, they shall dismiss me, but you never shall. The grave alone shall make me yield." But the House would do nothing. He had asked for 100,000 signatures in favour of his constitutional right, and on February 8th, 9th, and 10th 1,008 petitions, bearing 241,970 signatures, were presented; the House treated them with contemptuous indifference. The House refused to declare his seat vacant, and also refused to allow him to fill it, thus half-disfranchising Northampton, while closing every avenue to legal redress. Mr. Labouchere—who did all a loyal colleague could do to assist his brother member—brought in an Affirmation Bill; it was blocked. Mr. Gladstone, appealed to support the law declared by his own Attorney-General, refused to do anything. An *impasse* was created, and all the enemies of freedom rejoiced. Out of this position of what the *Globe* called "quiet omnipotence" the House was shaken by an audacious defiance, for on February 21st the member it was trying to hold at arm's length took the oath in its startled face, went to his seat, and—waited events. The House then expelled him—and, indeed, it could scarcely do anything else after such defiance—

and Mr. Labouchere moved for a new writ, declaring that Northampton was ready, its "candidate was Charles Bradlaugh, expelled this House." Northampton, ever steadfast, returned him for the third time—the vote in his favour showing an increase of 359 over the second bye-election—and the triumph was received in all the great towns of England with wild enthusiasm. By the small majority of fifteen in a House of 599 members—and this due to the vacillation of the Government—he was again refused the right to take his seat. But now the whole Liberal Press took up his quarrel; the oath question became a test question for every candidate for Parliament, and the Government was warned that it was alienating its best friends. The *Pall Mall Gazette* voiced the general feeling. "What is the evidence that an Oaths Bill would injure the Government in the country? Of one thing we may be sure, that if they shirk the Bill they will do no good to themselves at the elections. Nobody doubts that it will be made a test question, and any Liberal who declines to vote for such a Bill will certainly lose the support of the Northampton sort of Radicalism in every constituency. The Liberal Press throughout the country is absolutely unanimous. The political Non-conformists are for it. The local clubs are for it. All that is wanted is that the Government should pick up a little more moral courage, and recognise that even in practice honesty is the best policy." The Government did not think so, and they paid the penalty, for one of the causes that led to their defeat at the polls was the disgust felt at their vacillation and cowardice in regard to the rights of constituencies. Not untruly did I write, in May, 1882, that Charles Bradlaugh was a man "who by the infliction of a great wrong had become the incarnation of a great principle"; for the agitation in the country grew and grew, until, returned again to Parliament at the General Election, he took the oath and his seat, brought in and carried an Oaths Bill, not only giving Members of Parliament the right to affirm, but making Freethinkers competent as jurymen, and relieving witnesses from the insult hitherto put upon those who objected to swearing; he thus ended an unprecedented struggle by a complete victory, weaving his name for ever into the constitutional history of his country.

In the House of Lords, Lord Redesdale brought in a Bill disqualifying Atheists from sitting in Parliament, but in face of the feeling aroused in the country, the Lords, with many pathetic expressions of regret, declined to pass it. But, meanwhile, Sir Henry Tyler in the Commons was calling out for prosecutions for blasphemy to be brought against Mr. Bradlaugh and his friends, while he carried on his crusade against Mr. Bradlaugh's daughters, Dr. Aveling, and myself, as science teachers. I summed up the position in the spring of 1882 in the following somewhat strong language: "This short-lived 'Parliamentary Declaration Bill' is but one of the many clouds which presage a storm of prosecution. The reiterated attempts in the House of Commons to force the Government into prosecuting heretics for blasphemy; the petty and vicious attacks on the science classes at the Hall; the odious and wicked efforts of Mr. Newdegate to drive Mr. Bradlaugh into the Bankruptcy Court; all these are but signs that the heterogeneous army of pious and bigoted Christians are gathering together their forces for a furious attack on those who have silenced them in argument, but whom they hope to conquer by main force, by sheer brutality. Let them come. Free-thinkers were never so strong, never so united, never so well organised as they are to-day. Strong in the goodness of our cause, in our faith in the ultimate triumph of Truth, in our willingness to give up all save fidelity to the sacred cause of liberty of human thought and human speech, we await gravely and fearlessly the successors of the men who burned Bruno, who imprisoned Galileo, who tortured Vanini—the men who have in their hands the blood-red cross of Jesus of Nazareth, and in their hearts the love of God and the hate of man."

CHAPTER XII

Still Fighting

All this hot fighting on the religious field did not render me blind to the misery of the Irish land so dear to my heart, writhing in the cruel grip of Mr. Forster's Coercion Act. An article "Coercion in Ireland and its Results," exposing the wrongs done under the Act, was reprinted as a pamphlet and had a wide circulation.

I pleaded against eviction—7,020 persons had been evicted during the quarter ending in March—for the trial of those imprisoned on suspicion, for indemnity for those who before the Land Act had striven against wrongs the Land Act had been carried to prevent, and I urged that "no chance is given for the healing measures to cure the sore of Irish disaffection until not only are the prisoners in Ireland set at liberty, but until the brave, unfortunate Michael Davitt stands once more a free man on Irish soil." At last the Government reconsidered its policy and resolved on juster dealings; it sent Lord Frederick Cavendish over to Ireland, carrying with him the release of the "suspects," and scarcely had he landed ere the knife of assassination struck him—a foul and cowardly murder of an innocent messenger of peace. I was at Blackburn, to lecture on "The Irish Question," and as I was walking towards the platform, my heart full of joy for the dawning hope of peace, a telegram announcing the assassination was placed in my hands. Never shall I forget the shock, the incredulous horror, the wave of despair. "It is not only two men they have killed," I wrote, a day or two later; "they have stabbed the new-born hope of friendship between two countries, and have reopened the gulf of hatred that was just beginning to close." Alas! the crime succeeded in its object, and hurried the Government into new wrong. Hastily a new Coercion Bill was brought in, and rushed through its stages in Parliament, and, facing the storm of public excitement, I pleaded still, "Force no remedy," despite the hardship of the task. "There is excessive difficulty in dealing with the Irish difficulty at the present moment. Tories are howling for revenge on a whole nation as answer to the crime committed by a few; Whigs are swelling the outcry; many Radicals are swept away by the current, and feeling that 'something must be done,' they endorse the Government action, forgetting to ask whether the 'something' proposed is the wisest thing. A few stand firm, but they are very few—too few to prevent the new Coercion Bill from passing into law. But few though we be who lift up the voice of protest against the wrong which we are powerless to prevent, we may yet do much to make the new Act of brief duration, by so rousing public opinion as to bring about its early repeal. When the measure is understood by the public half the battle will be won; it is accepted at the moment from faith in the Government; it will be rejected when its true character is grasped. The murders which have given birth to this repressive measure came with a shock upon the country, which was the more terrible from the sudden change from gladness and hope to darkness and despair. The new policy was welcomed so joyfully; the messenger of the new policy was slain ere yet the pen was dry which had signed the orders of mercy and of liberty. Small wonder that cry of horror should be followed by measures of vengeance; but the murders were the work of a few criminals, while the measure of vengeance strikes the whole of the Irish people. I plead against the panic which confounds political agitation and political redressal of wrong with crime and its punishment; the Government measure gags every mouth in Ireland, and puts, as we shall see, all political effort at the mercy of the Lord-Lieutenant, the magistracy, and the police." I then sketched the misery of the peasants in the grip of absentee landlords, the turning out on the roadside to die of the mother with new-born babe at her breast, the loss of "all thought of the sanctity of human life when the lives of the dearest are reckoned as less worth than the shillings of overdue rack-rental." I analysed the new Act: "When this Act passes, trial by jury, right of public meeting, liberty of press, sanctity of house, will one and all be held at the will of the Lord-Lieutenant, the irresponsible autocrat of Ireland, while liberty of person will lie at the mercy of every constable. Such is England's way of governing Ireland in the year 1882. And this is supposed to be a Bill for the 'repression of crime.'" Bluntly, I put the bald truth: "The plain fact is that the murderers have succeeded. They saw in the new policy the reconciliation of England and Ireland; they knew that friendship would follow justice, and that the two countries, for the first time in history, would clasp hands. To prevent this they dug a new gulf, which they hoped the English nation would not span; they sent a river of blood across the road of friendship, and they flung two corpses to bar the newly-opened gate of reconciliation and peace. They have succeeded."

Into this whirl of political and social strife came the first whisper to me of the Theosophical Society, in the shape of a statement of its principles, which conveyed, I remarked, "no very definite idea of the requirements for membership, beyond a dreamy, emotional, scholarly interest in the religio-philosophic fancies of the past." Also a report of an address by Colonel Olcott, which led me to suppose that the society held to "some strange theory of 'apparitions' of the dead, and to some existence outside the physical and apart from it." These came to me from some Hindû Freethinkers, who asked my opinion as to Secularists joining the Theosophical Society, and Theosophists being admitted to the National Secular Society. I replied, judging from these reports, that "while Secularists would have no right to refuse to enrol Theosophists, if they desired it, among their members, there is a radical difference between the mysticism of Theosophy and the scientific materialism of Secularism. The exclusive devotion to this world implied in the profession of Secularism leaves no room for other-worldism; and consistent members of our body cannot join a society which professes belief therein."[27]

H.P. Blavatsky penned a brief article in the *Theosophist* for August, 1882, in which she commented on my paragraph, remarking, in her generous way, that it must have been written "while labouring under entirely misconceived notions about the real nature of our society. For one so highly intellectual and keen as that renowned writer to dogmatise and issue autocratic ukases, after she has herself suffered so cruelly and undeservedly at the hands of blind bigotry and social prejudice in her lifelong struggle for *freedom of thought* seems, to say the least, absurdly inconsistent." After quoting my paragraph she went on: "Until proofs to the contrary, we prefer to believe that the above lines were dictated to Mrs. Besant by some crafty misrepresentations from Madras, inspired by a mean personal revenge rather than a desire to remain consistent with the principles of 'the scientific materialism of Secularism.' We beg to assure the Radical editors of the *National Reformer* that they were both very strangely misled by false reports about the Radical editors of the *Theosophist.* The term 'supernaturalists' can no more apply to the latter than to Mrs. A. Besant and Mr. C. Bradlaugh."

H.P. Blavatsky, when she commented, as she occasionally did, on the struggles going on in England, took of them a singularly large-hearted and generous view. She referred with much admiration to Mr. Bradlaugh's work and to his Parliamentary struggle, and spoke warmly of the services he had rendered to

---

[27] *National Reformer*, June 18, 1882]

liberty. Again, in pointing out that spiritualistic trance orations by no means transcended speeches that made no such claim, I find her first mention of myself: "Another lady orator, of deservedly great fame, both for eloquence and learning—the good Mrs. Annie Besant—without believing in controlling spirits, or for that matter in her own spirit, yet speaks and writes such sensible and wise things, that we might almost say that one of her speeches or chapters contains more matter to benefit humanity than would equip a modern trance-speaker for an entire oratorical career."[28] I have sometimes wondered of late years whether, had I met her then or seen any of her writings, I should have become her pupil. I fear not; I was still too much dazzled by the triumphs of Western Science, too self-assertive, too fond of combat, too much at the mercy of my own emotions, too sensitive to praise and blame. I needed to sound yet more deeply the depths of human misery, to hear yet more loudly the moaning of "the great Orphan," Humanity, to feel yet more keenly the lack of wider knowledge and of clearer light if I were to give effective help to man, ere I could bow my pride to crave admittance as pupil to the School of Occultism, ere I could put aside my prejudices and study the Science of the Soul.

The long-continued attempts of Sir Henry Tyler and his friends to stimulate persecutions for blasphemy at length took practical shape, and in July, 1882, Mr. Foote, the editor, Mr. Ramsey, the publisher, and Mr. Whittle, the printer of the *Freethinker*, were summoned for blasphemy by Sir Henry Tyler himself. An attempt was made to involve Mr. Bradlaugh in the proceedings, and the solicitors promised to drop the case against the editor and printer if Mr. Bradlaugh would himself sell them some copies of the paper. But however ready Mr. Bradlaugh had always shown himself to shield his subordinates by taking his sins on his own shoulders, he saw no reason why he should assume responsibility for a paper over which he had no control, and which was, he thought, by its caricatures, lowering the tone of Freethought advocacy and giving an unnecessary handle to its foes. He therefore answered that he would sell the solicitors any works published by himself or with his authority, and sent them a catalogue of the whole of such works. The object of this effort of Sir Henry Tyler's was obvious enough, and Mr. Bradlaugh commented: "The above letters make it pretty clear that Sir Henry W. Tyler having failed in his endeavour to get the science classes stopped at the Hall of Science, having also failed in his

[28] *Theosophist*, June, 1882.

attempt to induce Sir W. Vernon Harcourt to prosecute myself and Mrs. Besant as editors and publishers of this journal, desires to make me personally and criminally responsible for the contents of a journal I neither edit nor publish, over which I have not a shadow of control, and in which I have not the smallest interest. Why does Sir H.W. Tyler so ardently desire to prosecute, me for blasphemy? Is it because two convictions will under the 9th and 10th Will. III. cap. 32, render me 'for ever' incapable of sitting in Parliament?" The *Whitehall Review* frankly put this forward as an object to be gained, and Mr. Bradlaugh was summoned to the Mansion House on a charge of publishing blasphemous libels in the *Freethinker*, meanwhile Sir Henry Tyler put a notice on the Order Book to deprive "the daughters of Mr. Charles Bradlaugh" of the grant they had earned as science teachers, and got an order which proved to be invalid, but which was acted on, to inspect Mr. Bradlaugh's and my own private banking accounts, I being no party to the case. Looking back, I marvel at the incredible meannesses to which Sir Henry Tyler and others stooped in defence of "religion"—Heaven save the mark! Let me add that his motion in the House of Commons was a complete failure, and it was emphasised by the publication at the same time of the successful work, both as teachers and as students, of the "daughters of Mr. Charles Bradlaugh," and of my being the only student in all England who had succeeded in taking honours in botany.

I must pause a moment to chronicle, in September, 1882, the death of Dr. Pusey, whom I had sought in the whirl of my early religious struggles. I wrote an article on him in the *National Reformer*, and ended by laying a tribute on his grave: "A strong man and a good man. Utterly out of harmony with the spirit of his own time, looking with sternly-rebuking eyes on all the eager research, the joyous love of nature, the earnest inquiry into a world doomed to be burnt up at the coming of its Judge. An ascetic, pure in life, stern in faith, harsh to unbelievers because sincere in his own cruel creed, generous and tender to all who accepted his doctrines and submitted to his Church. He never stooped to slander those with whom he disagreed. His hatred of heresy led him not to blacken the character of heretics, nor to descend to the vulgar abuse used by pettier priests. And therefore I, who honour courage and sincerity wherever I find them; I, who do homage to steadfastness wherever I find it; I, Atheist, lay my small tribute of respect on the bier of this noblest of the Anglo-Catholics, Edward Bouverie Pusey."

As a practical answer to the numberless attacks made on us, and as a result of the enormous increase of circulation given to our theological and political writings by these harassing persecutions, we moved our publishing business to 63, Fleet Street, at the end of September, 1882, a shop facing that at which Richard Carlile had carried on his publishing business for a great time, and so seemed still redolent with memories of his gallant struggles. Two of the first things sold here were a pamphlet of mine, a strong protest against our shameful Egyptian policy, and a critical volume on "Genesis" which Mr. Bradlaugh found time to write in the intervals of his busy life. Here I worked daily, save when out of London, until Mr. Bradlaugh's death in 1891, assisted in the conduct of the business by Mr. Bradlaugh's elder daughter—a woman of strong character with many noble qualities, who died rather suddenly in December, 1888, and in the work on the *National Reformer*, first by Dr. Aveling, and then by Mr. John Robertson, its present editor. Here, too, from 1884 onwards, worked with me Thornton Smith, one of Mr. Bradlaugh's most devoted disciples, who became one of the leading speakers of the National Secular Society; like her well-loved chief, she was ever a good friend and a good fighter, and to me the most loyal and loving of colleagues, one of the few—the very few—Freethinkers who were large-hearted and generous enough not to turn against me when I became a Theosophist. A second of these—alas! I could count them on my fingers—was the John Robertson above mentioned, a man of rare ability and wide culture, somewhat too scholarly for popular propagandism of the most generally effective order, but a man who is a strength to any movement, always on the side of noble living and high thinking, loyal-natured as the true Scot should be, incapable of meanness or treachery, and the most genial and generous of friends.

Among the new literary ventures that followed on our taking the large publishing premises in Fleet Street was a sixpenny magazine, edited by myself, and entitled *Our Corner*; its first number was dated January, 1883, and for six years it appeared regularly, and served me as a useful mouthpiece in my Socialist and Labour propagandist work. Among its contributors were Moncure D. Conway, Professor Ludwig Büchner, Yves Guyot, Professor Ernst Haeckel, G. Bernard Shaw, Constance Naden, Dr. Aveling, J.H. Levy, J.L. Joynes, Mrs. Edgren, John Robertson, and many another, Charles Bradlaugh and I writing regularly each month.

1883 broke stormily, fights on every hand, and a huge constitutional agitation going on in the country, which forced the Government into bringing in an Affirmation Bill; resolutions from Liberal Associations all over the land; preparations to oppose the re-election of disloyal members; no less than a thousand delegates sent up to London by clubs, Trade Unions, associations of every sort; a meeting that packed Trafalgar Square; an uneasy crowd in Westminster Hall; a request from Inspector Denning that Mr. Bradlaugh would go out to them—they feared for his safety inside; a word from him, "The Government have pledged themselves to bring in an Affirmation Bill at once;" roar after roar of cheering; a veritable people's victory on that 15th of February, 1883. It was the answer of the country to the appeal for justice, the rebuke of the electors to the House that had defied them.

Scarcely was this over when a second prosecution for blasphemy against Messrs. Foote, Ramsey, and Kemp began, and was hurried on in the Central Criminal Court, before Mr. Justice North, a bigot of the sternest type. The trial ended in a disagreement of the jury, Mr. Foote defending himself in a splendid speech. The judge acted very harshly throughout, interrupted Mr. Foote continuously, and even refused bail to the defendants during the interval between the first and second trial; they were, therefore, confined in Newgate from Thursday to Monday, and we were only allowed to see them through iron bars and lattice, as they exercised in the prison yard between 8:30 and 9:30 a.m. Brought up to trial again on Monday, they were convicted, and Mr. Foote was sentenced to a year's imprisonment, Mr. Ramsey to nine months, and Mr. Kemp to three months. Mr. Foote especially behaved with great dignity and courage in a most difficult position, and heard his cruel sentence without wincing, and with the calm words, "My Lord, I thank you; it is worthy your creed." A few of us at once stepped in, to preserve to Mr. Ramsey his shop, and to Mr. Foote his literary property; Dr. Aveling undertook the editing of the *Freethinker* and of Mr. Foote's magazine *Progress*; the immediate necessities of their families were seen to; Mr. and Mrs. Forder took charge of the shop, and within a few days all was in working order. Disapproving as many of us did of the policy of the paper, there was no time to think of that when a blasphemy prosecution had proved successful, and we all closed up in the support of men imprisoned for conscience' sake. I commenced a series of articles on "The Christian Creed; what it is blasphemy to deny," showing what Christians must believe under peril of prosecution. Everywhere a tremendous impulse was given to the Freethought movement, as men awakened to the knowledge that blasphemy laws were not obsolete.

From over the sea came a word of sympathy from the pen of H.P. Blavatsky in the *Theosophist*. "We prefer Mr. Foote's actual position to that of his severe judge. Aye, and were we in his guilty skin, we would feel more proud, even in the poor editor's present position, than we would under the wig of Mr. Justice North."

In April, 1883, the long legal struggles of Mr. Bradlaugh against Mr. Newdegate and his common informer, that had lasted from July 2, 1880, till April 9, 1883, ended in his complete victory by the judgment of the House of Lords in his favour. "Court after Court decided against me," he wrote; "and Whig and Tory journals alike mocked at me for my persistent resistance. Even some good friends thought that my fight was hopeless, and that the bigots held me fast in their toils. I have, however, at last shaken myself free of Mr. Newdegate and his common informer. The judgment of the House of Lords in my favour is final and conclusive, and the boasts of the Tories that I should be made bankrupt for the penalties, have now, for ever, come to naught. Yet but for the many poor folk who have stood by me with their help and sympathy, I should have long since been ruined. The days and weeks spent in the Law Courts, the harassing work connected with each stage of litigation, the watching daily when each hearing was imminent, the absolute hindrance of all provincial lecturing—it is hardly possible for any one to judge the terrible mental and pecuniary strain of all this long-drawn-out struggle." Aye! it killed him at last, twenty years before his time, sapping his splendid vitality, undermining his iron constitution.

The blasphemy trial of Mr. Bradlaugh, Mr. Foote, and Mr. Ramsey now came on, but this time in the Queen's Bench, before the Lord Chief Justice Coleridge. I had the honour of sitting between Mr. Bradlaugh and Mr. Foote, charged with the duty of having ready for the former all his references, and with a duplicate brief to mark off point after point as he dealt with it. Messrs. Foote and Ramsey were brought up in custody, but were brave and bright with courage unbroken. Mr. Bradlaugh applied to have his case taken separately, as he denied responsibility for the paper, and the judge granted the application; it was clearly proved that he and I—the "Freethought Publishing Company"—had never had anything to do with the production of the paper; that until November, 1881, we published it, and then refused to publish it any longer; that the reason for the refusal was the addition of comic Bible illustrations as a feature of the paper. I was called as witness and began with a difficulty; claiming to affirm, I was asked by the judge if the oath would not be binding on my conscience; I answered that any promise was binding on me whatever the form, and after some little argument the judge found a way out of the insulting form by asking whether the "invocation of the Deity added anything to it of a binding nature—added any sanction?" "None, my Lord," was the prompt reply, and I was allowed to affirm. Sir Hardinge Giffard subjected me to a very stringent cross-examination, doing his best to entangle me, but the perfect frankness of my answers broke all his weapons of finesse and inuendo.

Some of the incidents of the trial were curious; Sir Hardinge Giffard's opening speech was very able and very unscrupulous. All facts in Mr. Bradlaugh's favour were distorted or hidden; anything that could be used against him was tricked out in most seductive fashion. Among the many monstrous perversions of the truth made by this most pious counsel, was the statement that changes of publisher, and of registration of the *Freethinker* were made in consequence of a question as to prosecuting it put in the House of Commons. The change of publisher was admittedly made in November; the registration was made for the first time in November, and could not be changed, as there was no previous one. The House of Commons was not sitting in November; the question alluded to was asked in the following February. This one deliberate lie of the "defender of the faith" will do as well as quoting a score of others to show how wickedly and maliciously he endeavoured to secure an unjust verdict.

The speech over, a number of witnesses were called. Sir Hardinge did not call witnesses who knew the facts, such as Mr. Norrish, the shopman, or Mr. Whittle, the printer. These he carefully avoided, although he subpoenaed both, because he did not want the real facts to come out. But he put in two solicitor's clerks, who had been hanging about the premises, and buying endless *National Reformers* and *Freethinkers*, sheaves of them which were never used, but by which Sir Hardinge hoped to convey the impression of a mass of criminality. He put in a gentleman from the British Museum, who produced two large books, presumed to be *National Reformers* and *Freethinkers*; what they were brought for nobody understood, the counsel for the Crown as little as any one, and the judge, surveying them over his spectacles, treated them with supreme contempt, as utterly irrelevant. Then a man came to prove that Mr. Bradlaugh was rated for Stonecutter Street, a fact no one disputed. Two policemen came to say they had seen him go in. "You saw many people go in, I suppose?" queried the Lord Chief Justice. On the whole the most miserably weak and obviously malicious case that could be brought into a court of law.

One witness, however, must not be forgotten—Mr. Woodhams, bank manager. When he stated that Mr. Maloney, the junior counsel for the Crown, had inspected Mr. Bradlaugh's banking account, a murmur of surprise and indignation ran round the court. "Oh! Oh!" was heard from the crowd of barristers behind. The judge looked down incredulously, and for a moment the examination was stopped by the general movement. Unless Sir Hardinge Giffard is a splendid actor, he was not aware of the infamous proceeding, for he looked as startled as the rest of his legal brethren.

Another queer incident occurred, showing, perhaps more than aught else, Mr. Bradlaugh's swift perception of the situation and adaptation to the environment. He wanted to read the Mansion House deposition of Norrish, to show why he was not called; the judge objected, and declined to allow it to be read. A pause while you might count five; then; "Well, I think I may say the learned counsel did not call Norrish because " and then the whole substance of the deposition was given in supposititious form. The judge looked down a minute, and then went off into silent laughter impossible to control at the adroit change of means and persistent gaining of end; barristers all round broke into ripples of laughter unrestrained; a broad smile pervaded the jury box; the only unmoved person was the defendant who proceeded in his grave statement as to what Norrish "might" have been asked. The nature of the defence was very clearly stated by Mr. Bradlaugh: "I shall ask you to find that this prosecution is one of the steps in a vindictive attempt to oppress and to crush a political opponent—that it was a struggle that commenced on my return to Parliament in 1880. If the prosecutor had gone into the box I should have shown you that he was one of the first then in the House to use the suggestion of blasphemy against me there. Since then I have never had any peace until the Monday of this week. Writs for penalties have been served, and suits of all kinds have been taken against me. On Monday last the House of Lords cleared me from the whole of one set, and, gentlemen, I ask you to-day to clear me from another. Three times I have been re-elected by my constituents, and what Sir Henry Tyler asks you to do is to send me to them branded with the dishonour of a conviction, branded not with the conviction for publishing heresy, but branded with the conviction, dishonourable to me, of having lied in this matter. I have no desire to have a prison's walls closed on me, but I would sooner ten times that, than that my constituents should think that for one moment I lied to escape the penalties. I am not indicted for anything I have ever written or caused to be written. As my Lord at the very first stage this morning pointed out, it is no question with me, Are the matters indicted blasphemous, or are they not blasphemous? Are they defensible, or are they not defensible? That is not my duty here. On this I make no comment. I have no duty here of even discussing the policy of the blasphemy laws, although I cannot help thinking that, if I were here making my defence against them, I might say that they were bad laws unfairly revived, doing more mischief to those who revive them than to those whom they are revived against. But it is not for anything I have said myself; it is not for anything I have written myself; it is not for anything I have published myself. It is an endeavour to make me technically liable for a publication with which I have nothing whatever to do, and I will ask you to defeat that here. Every time I have succeeded I have been met with some new thing. When I first fought it was hoped to defeat my election. When I was re-elected it was sought to make me bankrupt by enormous penalties, and when I escaped the suit for enormous penalties they hope now to destroy me by this. I have no question here about defending my heresy, not because I am not ready to defend it when it is challenged in the right way, and it there be anything in it that the law can challenge. I have never gone back from anything I have ever said; I have never gone back from anything I have ever written; I have never gone back from anything I have ever done; and I ask you not to allow this Sir Henry Whatley Tyler, who dares not come here to-day, to use you as the assassin uses the dagger, to stab a man from behind whom he never dares to face."

The summing up by Lord Coleridge was perfect in eloquence, in thought, in feeling. Nothing more touching could be imagined than the conflict between the real religious feeling, abhorrent of heresy, and the determination to be just, despite all prejudice. The earnest effort lest the prejudice he felt as a Christian should weigh also in the minds of the jury, and should cause them to pervert justice. The absolute pleading to them to do what was right and not to admit against the unbeliever what they would not admit in ordinary cases. Then the protest against prosecution of opinions; the admission of the difficulties in the Hebrew Scriptures, and the pathetic fear lest by persecution "the sacred truths might be struck through the sides of those who are their enemies." For intellectual clearness and moral elevation this exquisite piece of eloquence, delivered in a voice of silvery beauty, would be hard to excel, and Lord Coleridge did this piece of service to the religion so dear to his heart, that he showed that a Christian judge could be just and righteous in dealing with a foe of his creed.

There was a time of terrible strain waiting for the verdict, and when at last it came, "Not Guilty," a sharp clap of applause hailed it, sternly and rightly reproved by the judge. It was echoed by the country, which almost unanimously condemned the prosecution as an iniquitous attempt on the part of Mr. Bradlaugh's political enemies to put a stop to his political career. Thus the *Pall Mall Gazette* wrote:—

"Whatever may be the personal or political or religious aversion which is excited by Mr. Bradlaugh, it is impossible for even his bitterest opponents to deny the brilliance of the series of victories which he has won in the law courts. His acquittal in the blasphemy prosecution of Saturday was but the latest of a number of encounters in which he has succeeded in turning the tables upon his opponents in the most decisive fashion. The policy of baiting Mr. Bradlaugh which has been persisted in so long, savours so strongly of a petty and malignant species of persecution that it is well that those who indulge in it should be made to smart for their pains. The wise and weighty words used by the Lord Chief Justice in summing up should be taken seriously to heart: 'Those persons are to be deprecated who would pervert the law, even with the best intentions, and "do evil that good may come, whose damnation" (says the apostle) "is just."' Without emulating the severity of the apostle, we may say that it is satisfactory that the promoters of all these prosecutions should be condemned in costs."

In the separate trial of Messrs. Foote and Ramsey, Mr. Foote again defended himself in a speech of marked ability, and spoken of by the judge as "very striking." Lord Coleridge made a noble charge to the jury, in which he strongly condemned prosecutions of unpopular opinions, pointing out that no prosecution short of extermination could be effective, and caustically remarking on the very easy form of virtue indulged in by persecutors. "As a general rule," he said, "persecution, unless far more extreme than in England in the nineteenth century is possible, is certain to be in vain. It is also true, and I cannot help assenting to it, that it is a very easy form of virtue. It is a more difficult form of virtue, quietly and unostentatiously to obey what we believe to be God's will in our own lives. It is not very easy to do it; and it makes much less noise in the world. It is very easy to turn upon somebody else who differs from us, and in the guise of zeal of God's honour to attack somebody of a difference of opinion, whose life may be more pleasing to God and more conducive to His honour than our own. And when it is done by persons whose own lives are not free from reproach and who take that particular form of zeal for God which consists in putting the criminal law in force against others, that, no doubt, does more to create a sympathy with the defendant than with the prosecutor. And if it should be done by those who enjoy the wit of Voltaire, and who do not turn away from the sneers of Gibbon, and rather relish the irony of Hume, our feelings do not go with the prosecutors, and we are rather disposed to sympathise with the defendant. It is still worse if the person who takes such a course takes it, not from a kind of notion that God wants his assistance, and that he can give it less on his own account than by prosecuting others— but it is mixed up with anything of partisan or political feeling, then nothing can be more foreign to what is high-minded, or religious, or noble, in men's conduct; and indeed, it seems to me that any one who will do that, not for the honour of God but for the purpose of the ban, deserves the most disdainful disapprobation."

The jury disagreed, and a *nolle prosequi* was entered. The net results of the trials were a large addition to the membership of the National Secular Society, an increase of circulation of Freethought literature, the raising of Mr. Foote for a time to a position of great influence and popularity, and the placing of his name in history as a brave martyr for liberty of speech. The offence against good taste will be forgotten; the loyalty to conviction and to courage will remain. History does not ask if men who suffered for heresy ever published a rough word; it asks, Were they brave in their steadfastness; were they faithful to the truth they saw? It may be well to place on record Mr. Foote's punishment for blasphemy: he spent twenty-two hours out of the twenty-four alone in his cell; his only seat was a stool without a back; his employment was picking matting; his bed was a plank with a thin mattress. During the latter part of his imprisonment he was allowed somebooks.

CHAPTER XIII

Socialism

The rest of 1883 passed in the usual way of hard work; the Affirmation Bill was rejected, and the agitation for Constitutional right grew steadily; the Liberal Press was won over, and Mr. Bradlaugh was beginning to earn golden opinions on all sides for his courage, his tenacity, and his self-control. A successful International Congress at Amsterdam took some of us over to the Northern Venice, where a most successful gathering was held. To me, personally, the year has a special interest, as being the one in which my attention was called, though only partially, to the Socialist movement. I had heard Louise Michelle lecture in the early spring; a brief controversy in the *National Reformer* had interested me, but I had not yet concerned myself with the economic basis of Socialism; I had realised that the land should be public property, but had not gone into the deeper economic causes of poverty, though the question was pressing with ever-increasing force on heart and brain. Of Socialist teaching I knew nothing, having studied only the older English Economists in my younger days. In 1884 a more definite call to consider 299 these teachings was to come, and I may perhaps open the record of 1884 with the words of greeting spoken by me to our readers in the first number of the *Reformer* for that year: "What tests 1884 may have for our courage, what strains on our endurance, what trials of our loyalty, none can tell. But this we know—that every test of courage successfully met, every strain of endurance steadily borne, every trial of loyalty nobly surmounted, leaves courage braver, endurance stronger, loyalty truer, than each was before. And therefore, for our own and for the world's sake, I will not wish you, friends, an 1884 in which there shall be no toil and no battling; but I will wish you, each and all, the hero's heart and the hero's patience, in the struggle for the world's raising that will endure through the coming year."

On February 3rd I came for the first time across a paper called *Justice*, in which Mr. Bradlaugh was attacked, and which gave an account of a meeting of the Democratic Federation—not yet the Social Democratic—in which a man had, apparently unrebuked, said that "all means were justifiable to attain" working-class ends. I protested strongly against the advocacy of criminal means, declaring that those who urged the use of such means were the worst foes of social progress. A few weeks later the

Echo repeated a speech of Mr. Hyndman's in which a "bloodier revolution" than that of France was prophesied, and the extinction of "book-learning" seemed coupled with the success of Socialism, and this again I commented on. But I had the pleasure, a week later, of reprinting from *Justice* a sensible paragraph, condemning the advocacy of violence so long as free agitation was allowed.

The spring was marked by two events on which I have not time or space to dwell—the resignation by Mr. Bradlaugh of his seat, on the reiteration of the resolution of exclusion, and his triumphant return for the fourth time by an increased majority, a vote of 4,032, a higher poll than that of the general election; and the release of Mr. Foote, on February 25th, from Holloway, whence he was escorted by a procession a quarter of a mile in length. On the 12th of March he and his fellow-prisoners received a magnificent reception and were presented with valuable testimonials at the Hall of Science.

Taking up again the thread of Socialism, the great debate in St. James's Hall, London, between Mr. Bradlaugh and Mr. Hyndman on April 17th, roused me to a serious study of the questions raised. Socialism has in England no more devoted, no more self-sacrificing advocate than Henry Hyndman. A man of wide and deep reading, wielding most ably a singularly fascinating pen, with talents that would have made him wealthy in any career he adopted, he has sacrificed himself without a murmur to the people's cause. He has borne obloquy from without, suspicion and unkindness from those he served, and surrounded by temptations to betray the people, he has never swerved from his integrity. He has said rash things, has been stirred to passionate outbursts and reckless phrases, but love to the people and sympathy with suffering lay at the root of his wildest words, and they count but little as against his faithful service. Personally, my debt to him is of a mixed character; he kept me from Socialism for some time by his bitter and very unjust antagonism to Mr. Bradlaugh; but it was the debate at St. James's Hall that, while I angrily resented his injustice, made me feel that there was something more in practical Socialism than I had imagined, especially when I read it over afterwards, away from the magic of Mr. Bradlaugh's commanding eloquence and personal magnetism. It was a sore pity that English Socialists, from the outset of their movement, treated Mr. Bradlaugh so unfairly, so that his friends were set against Socialists ere they began to examine their arguments. I must confess that my deep attachment to him led me into injustice to his Socialist foes in those early days, and often made me ascribe to them calculated malignity instead of hasty and prejudiced assertion. Added to this, their uncurbed violence in discussion, their constant interruptions during the speeches of opponents, their reckless inaccuracy in matters of fact, were all bars standing in the way of the thoughtful. When I came to know them better, I found that the bulk of their speakers were very young men, overworked and underpaid, who spent their scanty leisure in efforts to learn, to educate themselves, to train themselves, and I learned to pardon faults which grew out of the bitter sense of injustice, and which were due largely to the terrible pressure of our system on characters not yet strong enough—how few are strong enough!—to bear grinding injustice without loss of balance and of impartiality. None save those who have worked with them know how much of real nobility, of heroic self-sacrifice, of constant self-denial, of brotherly affection, there is among the Social Democrats.

At this time also I met George Bernard Shaw, one of the most brilliant of Socialist writers and most provoking of men; a man with a perfect genius for "aggravating" the enthusiastically earnest, and with a passion for representing himself as a scoundrel. On my first experience of him on the platform at South Place Institute he described himself as a "loafer," and I gave an angry snarl at him in the *Reformer*, for a loafer was my detestation, and behold! I found that he was very poor, because he was a writer with principles and preferred starving his body to starving his conscience; that he gave time and earnest work to the spreading of Socialism, spending night after night in workmen's clubs; and that "a loafer" was only an amiable way of describing himself because he did not carry a hod. Of course I had to apologise for my sharp criticism as doing him a serious injustice, but privately felt somewhat injured at having been entrapped into such a blunder. Meanwhile I was more and more turning aside from politics and devoting myself to the social condition of the people I find myself, in June, protesting against Sir John Lubbock's Bill which fixed a twelve-hour day as the limit of a "young person's" toil. "A 'day' of twelve hours is brutal," I wrote; "if the law fixes twelve hours as a 'fair day' that law will largely govern custom. I declare that a 'legal day' should be eight hours on five days in the week and not more than five hours on the sixth. If the labour is of an exhausting character these hours are too long." On every side now the Socialist controversy grew, and I listened, read, and thought much, but said little. The inclusion of John Robertson in the staff of the *Reformer* brought a highly intellectual Socialist into closer touch with us, and slowly I found that the case for Socialism was intellectually complete and ethically beautiful. The trend of my thought was shown by urging the feeding of Board School children, breaking down under the combination of education and starvation, and I asked, "Why should people be pauperised by a rate-supported meal, and not pauperised by, state-supported police, drainage, road-mending, street-lighting, &c? "Socialism in its splendid ideal appealed to my heart, while the economic soundness of its basis convinced my head. All my life was turned towards the progress of the people, the helping of man, and it leaped forward to meet the stronger hope, the lofty ideal of social brotherhood, the rendering possible to all of freer life; so long had I been striving thitherward, and here there opened up a path to the yearned-for goal! How strong were the feelings surging in my heart may be seen in a brief extract from an article published second week of January, 1885: "Christian charity? We know its work. It gives a hundred-weight of coal and five pounds of beef once a year to a family whose head could earn a hundred such doles if Christian justice allowed him fair wage for the work he performs. It plunders the workers of the wealth they make, and then flings back at them a thousandth part of their own product as 'charity.' It builds hospitals for the poor whom it has poisoned in filthy courts and alleys, and workhouses for the worn-out creatures from whom it has wrung every energy, every hope, every joy. Miss Cobbe summons us to admire Christian civilisation, and we see idlers flaunting in the robes woven by the toilers, a glittering tinselled super-structure founded on the tears, the strugglings, the grey, hopeless misery of the poor."

This first month of January, 1885, brought on me the first attack for my Socialistic tendencies, from the pen of Mr. W.P. Ball, who wrote to the *Reformer* complaining of my paragraph, quoted above, in which I had advocated rate-supported meals for Board School children. A brief controversy thus arose, in which I supported my opinion, waiving the question as to my being "at heart a Socialist." In truth, I dreaded to make the plunge of publicly allying myself with the advocates of Socialism, because of the attitude of bitter hostility they had adopted towards Mr. Bradlaugh. On his strong, tenacious nature, nurtured on self-reliant individualism, the arguments of the younger generation made no impression. He could not change his methods because a new tendency was rising to the surface, and he did not see how different was the Socialism of our day to the Socialist dreams of the past—noble ideals of a future not immediately realisable in truth, but to be worked towards and rendered possible in the days to come. Could I take public action which might bring me into collision with the dearest of my friends, which might strain the strong and tender tie so long existing between us? My affection, my gratitude, all warred against the idea of working with those who wronged him so bitterly. But the cry of starving children was ever in my ears; the sobs of women poisoned in lead works, exhausted in nail works, driven to prostitution by starvation, made old and haggard by ceaseless work. I saw their misery was the result of an evil system, was inseparable from private ownership of the instruments of wealth production; that while the worker was himself but an instrument, selling his labour under the law of supply and demand, he must remain helpless in the grip of the employing classes, and that trade combinations could only mean increased warfare—necessary, indeed, for the time as weapons of defence—but meaning war, not brotherly co-operation of all for the good of all. A conflict which was stripped of all covering, a conflict between a personal tie and a call of duty could not last long, and with a heavy heart I made up my mind to profess Socialism openly and work for it with all my energy. Happily, Mr. Bradlaugh was as tolerant as he was strong, and our private friendship remained unbroken; but he never again felt the same confidence in my judgment as he felt before, nor did he any more consult me on his own policy, as he had done ever since we first clasped hands.

A series of articles in *Our Corner* on the "Redistribution of Political Power," on the "Evolution of Society," on "Modern Socialism," made my position clear. "Over against those who laud the present state of Society, with its unjustly rich and its unjustly poor, with its palaces and its slums, its millionaires and its paupers, be it ours to proclaim that there is a higher ideal in life than that of being first in the race for wealth, most successful in the scramble for gold. Be it ours to declare steadfastly that health, comfort, leisure, culture, plenty for every individual are far more desirable than breathless struggle for existence, furious trampling down of the weak by the strong, huge fortunes accumulated out of the toil of others, to be handed down to those who had done nothing to earn them. Be it ours to maintain that the greatness of a nation depends not on the number of its great proprietors, on the wealth of its great capitalists, or the splendour of its great nobles, but on the absence of poverty among its people, on the education and refinement of its masses, on the universality of enjoyment in life. Enough for each of work, of leisure, of joy; too little for none, too much for none—such is the Social ideal. Better to strive after it worthily and fail, than to die without striving for it at all."

Then I differentiated the methods of the Socialist and the Radical Individualist, pleading for union among those who formed the wings of the army of Labour, and urging union of all workers against the idlers. For the weakness of the people has ever been in their divisions, in the readiness of each section to turn its weapons against other sections instead of against the common foe. All privileged classes, when they are attacked, sink their differences and present a serried front to their assailants; the people alone fight with each other, while the battle between themselves and the privileged is raging.

I strove, as so many others were striving, to sound in the ears of the thoughtless and the careless the cry of the sufferings of the poor, endeavouring to make articulate their misery. Thus in a description of Edinburgh slums came the following: "I saw in a 'house' which was made by boarding up part of a passage, which had no window, and in which it was necessary to burn an oil lamp all day, thus adding to the burden of the rent, a family of three— man, wife, and child—whose lot was hardly 'of their own making.' The man was tall and bronzed, but he was dying of heart disease; he could not do hard work, and he was too clumsy for light work; so he sat there, after two days' fruitless search, patiently nursing his miserable, scrofulous baby in his dim and narrow den. The cases of individual hopeless suffering are heartbreaking. In one room lay a dying child, dying of low fever brought on by want of food. 'It hae no faither,' sobbed the mother; and for a moment I did not catch the meaning that the father had left to the mother all the burden of a child unallowed by law. In another lay the corpse of a mother, with the children round her, and hard-featured, gentle-hearted women came in to take back to their overcrowded beds 'the mitherless bairns.' In yet another a woman, shrunken and yellow, crouched over a glimmer of fire; "I am dying of cancer of the womb," she said, with that pathetic resignation to the inevitable so common among the poor. I sat chatting for a few minutes. 'Come again, deary,' she said as I rose to go; 'it's gey dull sitting here the day through.'"

The article in which these, among other descriptions, occurred was closed with the following: "Passing out of the slums into the streets of the town, only a few steps separating the horror and the beauty, I felt, with a vividness more intense than ever, the fearful contrasts between the lots of men; and with more pressing urgency the question seemed to ring in my ears, 'Is there no remedy? Must there always be rich and poor?' Some say that it must be so; that the palace and the slum will for ever exist as the light and the shadow. Not so do I believe. I believe that the poverty is the result of ignorance and of bad social arrangements, and that therefore it may be eradicated by knowledge and by social change. I admit that for many of these adult dwellers in the slums there is no hope. Poor victims of a civilisation that hides its brutality beneath a veneer of culture and of grace, for them individually there is, alas! no salvation. But for their children, yes! Healthy surroundings, good food, mental and physical training, plenty of play, and carefully chosen work—these might save the young and prepare them for happy life. But they are being left to grow up as their parents were, and even when a few hours of school are given them the home half-neutralises what the education effects. The scanty aid given is generally begrudged, the education is to be but elementary, as little as possible is doled out. Yet these children have each one of them hopes and fears, possibilities of virtue and of crime, a life to be made or marred. We shower money on generals and on nobles, we keep high-born paupers living on the national charity, we squander wealth with both hands on army and navy, on churches and palaces; but we grudge every halfpenny that increases the education rate and howl down every proposal to build decent houses for the poor. We cover our heartlessness and indifference with fine phrases about sapping the independence of the poor and destroying their self-respect. With loathsome hypocrisy we repair a prince's palace for him, and let him live in it rent-free, without one word about the degradation involved in his thus living upon charity; while we refuse to 'pauperise' the toiler by erecting decent buildings in which he may live—not rent-free like the prince, but only paying a rent which shall cover the cost of erection and maintenance, instead of one which gives a yearly profit to a speculator. And so, year after year, the misery grows, and every great city has on its womb a cancer; sapping its vitality, poisoning its life-blood. Every great city is breeding in its slums a race which is reverting through the savage to the brute—a brute more dangerous in that degraded humanity has possibilities of evil in it beyond the reach of the mere wild beast. If not for Love's sake, then for fear; if not for justice or for human pity, then for sheer desire of self-preservation; I appeal to the wise and to the wealthy to set their hands to the cure of social evil, ere stolidity gives place to passion and dull patience vanishes before fury, and they

"'Learn at last, in some wild hour, how much the wretched dare.'"

Because it was less hotly antagonistic to the Radicals than the two other Socialist organisations, I joined the Fabian Society, and worked hard with it as a speaker and lecturer. Sidney Webb, G. Bernard Shaw, Hubert and Mrs. Bland, Graham Wallas—these were some of those who gave time, thought, incessant work to the popularising of Socialist thought, the spreading of sound economics, the effort to turn the workers' energy toward social rather than merely political reform. We lectured at workmen's clubs wherever we could gain a hearing, till we leavened London Radicalism with Socialist thought, and by treating the Radical as the unevolved Socialist rather than as the anti-Socialist, we gradually won him over to Socialist views. We circulated questions to be put to all candidates for parliamentary or other offices, stirred up interest in local elections, educated men and women into an understanding of the causes of their poverty, won recruits for the army of propagandists from the younger of the educated middle class. That the London working classes to-day are so largely Socialist is greatly due to the years of work done among them by members of the Fabian Society, as well to the splendid, if occasionally too militant, energy of the Social Democratic Federation, and to the devotion of that noble and generous genius, William Morris.

During this same year (1885) a movement was set on foot in England to draw attention to the terrible sufferings of the Russian political prisoners, and it was decided at a meeting held in my house to form a society of the friends of Russia, which should seek to spread accurate and careful information about the present condition of Russia. At that meeting were present Charles Bradlaugh, "Stepniak," and many others, E.R. Pease acting as honorary secretary. It is noteworthy that some of the most prominent Russian exiles—such as Kropotkin—take the view that the Tzar himself is not allowed to know what occurs, and is very largely the victim of the bureaucracy that surrounds him.

Another matter, that increased as the months went on, was the attempt of the police authorities to stop Socialist speaking in the open air. Christians, Freethinkers, Salvationists, agitators of all kinds were, for the most part, left alone, but there was a regular crusade against the Socialists. Liberal and Tory journals alike condemned the way in which in Dod Street, in September, the Socialists' meetings were attacked. Quiet persistence was shown by the promoters—members of the Social Democratic Federation—and they were well supported by other Socialists and by the Radical clubs. I volunteered to speak on October 4th (my first Sunday in London after the summoning and imprisoning of the speakers had commenced), but the attitude of the people was so determined on the preceding Sunday that all interference was withdrawn.

Herbert Burrows stood for the School Board for the Tower Hamlets in the November of this year, and I find a paragraph in the *Reformer* in which I heartily wished him success, especially as the first candidate who had put forward a demand for industrial education. In this, as in so many practical proposals, Socialists have led the way. He polled 4,232 votes, despite the furious opposition of the clergy to him as a Freethinker, of the publicans to him as a teetotaler, of the maintainers of the present social system to him as a Socialist. And his fight did much to make possible my own success in 1888.

With this autumn, too, began, in connection with the struggle for the right of meeting, the helping of the workmen to fair trial by providing of bail and legal defence. The first case that I bailed out was that of Lewis Lyons, sent to gaol for two months with hard labour by Mr. Saunders, of the Thames Police Court. Oh, the weary, sickening waiting in the court for "my prisoner," the sordid vice, the revolting details of human depravity to which my unwilling eyes and ears were witnesses. I carried Lyons off in triumph, and the Middlesex magistrates quashed the conviction, the evidence being pronounced by them to be "confusing, contradictory, and worthless." Yet but for the chance of one of us stepping forward to offer bail and to provide the means for an appeal (I acted on Mr. Bradlaugh's suggestion and advice, for he acted as counsellor to me all through the weary struggles that lasted till 1888, putting his great legal knowledge at my disposal, though he often disapproved my action, thinking me Quixotic)—but for this, Lewis Lyons would have had to suffer his heavy sentence.

The general election took place this autumn, and Northampton returned Mr. Bradlaugh for the fifth time, thus putting an end to the long struggle, for he took the oath and his seat in the following January, and at once gave notice of an Oaths Bill, to give to all who claimed it, under all circumstances, the right to affirm. He was returned with the largest vote ever polled for him—4,315—and he entered Parliament with all the prestige of his great struggle, and went to the front at once, one of the recognised forces in the House. The action of Mr. Speaker Peel promptly put an end to an attempted obstruction. Sir Michael Hicks Beach, Mr. Cecil Raikes, and Sir John Hennaway had written to the Speaker asking his interference, but the Speaker declared that he had no authority, no right to stand between a duly elected member and the duty of taking the oath prescribed by statute. Thus ended the constitutional struggle of six years, that left the victor well-nigh bankrupt in health and in purse, and sent him to a comparatively early grave. He lived long enough to justify his election, to prove his value to the House and to his country, but he did not live long enough to render to England all the services which his long training, his wide knowledge, his courage, and his honesty so eminently fitted him to yield.

NORWICH BRANCH OF THE SOCIALIST LEAGUE.

Our Corner now served as a valuable aid in Socialist propaganda, and its monthly "Socialist Notes" became a record of Socialist progress in all lands. We were busy during the spring in organising a conference for the discussion of "The Present Commercial System, and the Better Utilisation of National Wealth for the Benefit of the Community," and this was successfully held at South Place Institute on June 9th, 10th, 11th, the three days being given respectively, to the "Utilisation of Land," the "Utilisation of Capital," and the "Democratic Policy." On the 9th Mr. Bradlaugh spoke on the utilisation of waste lands, arguing that in a thickly populated country no one had the right to keep cultivable land uncultivated, and that where land was so kept there should be compulsory expropriation, the state taking the land and letting it out to cultivating tenants. Among the other speakers were Edward Carpenter, William Morris, Sidney Webb, John Robertson, William Saunders, W. Donnisthorpe, Edward Aveling, Charlotte Wilson, Mrs. Fenwick Miller, Hubert Bland, Dr. Pankhurst, and myself—men and women of many views, met to compare methods, and so help on the cause of social regeneration.

Bitter attacks were made on me for my Socialist advocacy by some of the Radicals in the Freethought party, and looking back I find myself condemned as a "Saint Athanasius in petticoats," and as possessing a "mind like a milk-jug." This same courteous critic remarked, "I have heard Mrs. Besant described as being, like most women, at the mercy of her last male acquaintance for her views on economics." I was foolish enough to break a lance in self-defence with this assailant, not having then learned that self-defence was a waste of time that might be better employed in doing work for others. I certainly should not now take the trouble to write such a paragraph as the following: "The moment a man uses a woman's sex to discredit her arguments, the thoughtful reader knows that he is unable to answer the arguments themselves. But really these silly sneers at woman's ability have lost their force, and are best met with a laugh at the stupendous 'male self-conceit' of the writer. I may add that such shafts are specially pointless against myself. A woman who thought her way out of Christianity and Whiggism into Freethought and Radicalism absolutely alone; who gave up every old friend, male and female, rather than resign the beliefs she had struggled to in solitude; who, again, in embracing active Socialism, has run counter to the views of her nearest 'male friends'; such a woman may very likely go wrong, but I think she may venture, without conceit, to at least claim independence of judgment. I did not make the acquaintance of one of my present

Socialist comrades, male or female, until I had embraced Socialism." A foolish paragraph, as are all self-defences, and a mischievous one, as all retort breeds fresh strife. But not yet had come the self-control that estimates the judgments of others at their true value, that recks not of praise and blame; not yet had I learned that evil should not be met with evil, wrath with wrath; not yet were the words of the Buddha the law to which I strove to render obedience: "Hatred ceases not by hatred at any time; hatred ceases by love." The year 1886 was a terrible one for labour, everywhere reductions of wages, everywhere increase of the numbers of the unemployed; turning over the pages of *Our Corner*, I see "Socialist Notes" filled, month after month, with a monotonous tale, "there is a reduction of wages at" such and such a place; so many "men have been discharged at ——-, owing to the slackness of trade." Our hearts sank lower and lower as summer passed into autumn, and the coming winter threatened to add to starvation the bitter pains of cold. The agitation for the eight hours' day increased in strength as the unemployed grew more numerous week by week "We can't stand it," a sturdy, quiet fellow had said to me during the preceding winter; "flesh and blood can't stand it, and two months of this bitter cold, too." "We may as well starve idle as starve working," had said another, with a fierce laugh. And a spirit of sullen discontent was spreading everywhere, discontent that was wholly justified by facts. But ah! how patient they were for the most part, how sadly, pathetically patient, this crucified Christ, Humanity; wrongs that would set my heart and my tongue afire would be accepted as a matter of course. O blind and mighty people, how my heart went out to you; trampled on, abused, derided, asking so little and needing so much; so pathetically grateful for the pettiest services; so loving and so loyal to those who offered you but their poor services and helpless love. Deeper and deeper into my innermost nature ate the growing desire to succour, to suffer for, to save. I had long given up my social reputation, I now gave up with ever-increasing surrender ease, comfort, time; the passion of pity grew stronger and stronger, fed by each new sacrifice, and each sacrifice led me nearer and nearer to the threshold of that gateway beyond which stretched a path of renunciation I had never dreamed of, which those might tread who were ready wholly to strip off self for Man's sake, who for Love's sake would surrender Love's return from those they served, and would go out into the darkness for themselves that they might, with their own souls as fuel, feed the Light of the World.

As the suffering deepened with the darkening months, the meetings of the unemployed grew in number, and the murmurs of discontent became louder. The Social Democratic Federation carried on an outdoor agitation, not without making blunders, being composed of human beings, but with abundant courage and self-sacrifice. The policy of breaking up Socialist meetings went on while other meetings were winked at, and John Williams, a fiery speaker, but a man with a record of pathetic struggle and patient heroism, was imprisoned for two months for speaking in the open air, and so nearly starved in gaol that he came out with his health broken for life.

1887 dawned, the year that was to close so stormily, and Socialists everywhere were busying themselves on behalf of the unemployed, urging vestries to provide remunerative work for those applying for relief, assailing the Local Government Board with practicable proposals for utilising the productive energies of the unemployed, circulating suggestions to municipalities and other local representative bodies, urging remedial measures. A four days' oral debate with Mr. Foote, and a written debate with Mr. Bradlaugh, occupied some of my energies, and helped in the process of education to which public opinion was being subjected. Both these debates were largely circulated as pamphlets. A series of afternoon debates between representative speakers was organised at South Place Institute, and Mr. Corrie Grant and myself had a lively discussion, I affirming "That the existence of classes who live upon unearned incomes is detrimental to the welfare of the community, and ought to be put an end to by legislation." Another debate—in this very quarrelsome spring of 1887—was a written one in the *National Reformer* between the Rev. G.F. Handel Rowe and myself on the proposition, "Is Atheism logically tenable, and is there a satisfactory Atheistic System for the guidance of Human Conduct." And so the months went on, and the menace of misery grew louder and louder, till in September I find myself writing: "This one thing is clear—Society must deal with the unemployed, or the unemployed will deal with Society. Stormier and stormier becomes the social outlook, and they at least are not the worst enemies of Society who seek to find some way through the breakers by which the ship of the Commonwealth may pass into quiet waters."

Some amusement turned up in the shape of a Charing Cross Parliament, in which we debated with much vigour the "burning questions" of the day. We organised a compact Socialist party, defeated a Liberal Government, took the reins of office, and—after a Queen's Speech in which her Majesty addressed her loyal Commons with a plainness of speech never before (or since) heard from the throne—we brought in several Bills of a decidedly heroic character. G. Bernard Shaw, as President of the Local Government Board, and I, as Home Secretary, came in for a good deal of criticism in connection with various drastic measures. An International Freethought Congress, held in London, entailed fairly heavy work, and the science classes were ever with us. Another written debate came with October, this time on the "Teachings of Christianity," making the fifth of these set discussions held by me during the year. This same month brought a change, painful but just: I resigned my much-prized position as co-editor of the *National Reformer,* and the number for October 23rd bore Charles Bradlaugh's name alone. The change did not affect my work on the paper, but I became merely a subordinate, though remaining, of course, joint proprietor. The reason cannot be more accurately given than in the paragraph penned at the time: "For a considerable time past, and lately in increasing number, complaints have reached me from various quarters of the inconvenience and uncertainty that result from the divided editorial policy of this paper on the question of Socialism. Some months ago I proposed to avoid this difficulty by resigning my share in the editorship; but my colleague, with characteristic liberality, asked me to let the proposal stand over and see if matters would not adjust themselves. But the difficulty, instead of disappearing, has only become more pressing; and we both feel that our readers have a right to demand that it be solved.

"When I became co-editor of this paper I was not a Socialist; and, although I regard Socialism as the necessary and logical outcome of the Radicalism which for so many years the *National Reformer* has taught, still, as in avowing myself a Socialist I have taken a distinct step, the partial separation of my policy in labour questions from that of my colleague has been of my own making, and not of his, and it is, therefore, for me to go away. Over by far the greater part of our sphere of action we are still substantially agreed, and are likely to remain so. But since, as Socialism becomes more and more a question of practical politics, differences of theory tend to produce differences in conduct; and since a political paper must have a single editorial programme in practical politics, it would obviously be most inconvenient for me to retain my position as co-editor. I therefore resume my former position as contributor only, thus clearing the *National Reformer* of all responsibility for the views I hold."

To this Mr. Bradlaugh added the following:—

"I need hardly add to this how very deeply I regret the necessity for Mrs. Besant's resignation of the joint editorship of this Journal, and the real grief I feel in accepting this break in a position in which she has rendered such enormous service to the Freethought and Radical cause. As a most valued contributor I trust the *National Reformer* may never lose the efficient aid of her brain and pen. For thirteen years this paper has been richer for good by the measure of her never-ceasing and most useful work. I agree with her that a journal must have a distinct editorial policy; and I think this distinctness the more necessary when, as in the present case, every contributor has the greatest freedom of expression. I recognise in the fullest degree the spirit of self-sacrifice in which the lines, to which I add these words, have been penned by Mrs. Besant. "CHARLES BRADLAUGH."

It was a wrench, this breaking of a tie for which a heavy price had been paid thirteen years before, but it was just. Any one who makes a change with which pain is connected is bound, in honour and duty, to take that pain as much as possible on himself; he must not put his sacrifice on others, nor pay his own ransom with their coin. There must be honour kept in the life that reaches towards the Ideal, for broken faith to that is the only real infidelity.

And there was another reason for the change that I dared not name to him, for his quick loyalty would then have made him stubbornly determined against change. I saw the swift turning of public opinion, the gradual approach to him among Liberals who had hitherto held aloof, and I knew that they looked upon me as a clog and a burden, and that were I less prominently with him his way would be the easier to tread. So I slipped more and more into the background, no longer went with him to his meetings; my use to him in public was over, for I had become hindrance instead of help. While he was outcast and hated I had the pride of standing at his side; when all the fair-weather friends came buzzing round him I served him best by self-effacement, and I never loved him better than when I stood aside. But I continued all the literary work unaltered, and no change of opinions touched his kindness to me, although when, a little later, I joined the Theosophical Society, he lost his trust in my reasoning powers and judgment.

In this same month of October the unemployed began walking in procession through the streets, and harshness on the part of the police led to some rioting. Sir Charles Warren thought it his duty to dragoon London meetings after the fashion of Continental prefects, with the inevitable result that an ill-feeling grew up between the people and the police.

At last we formed a Socialist Defence Association, in order to help poor workmen brought up and sentenced on police evidence only, without any chance being given them of proper legal defence, and I organised a band of well-to-do men and women, who promised to obey a telegraphic summons, night or day, and to bail out any prisoner arrested for exercising the ancient right of walking in procession and speaking. To take one instance: Mr. Burleigh, the well-known war correspondent, and Mr. Winks were arrested and "run in" with Mr. J. Knight, a workman, for seditious language. I went down to the police-station to offer bail for the latter: Chief-Constable Howard accepted bail for Messrs. Burleigh and Winks, but refused it for Mr. Knight. The next day, at the police-court, the preposterous bail of £400 was demanded for Mr. Knight and supplied by my faithful band, and on the next hearing Mr. Poland, solicitor to the Treasury, withdrew the charge against him for lack of evidence!

Then came the closing of Trafalgar Square, and the unexpected and high-handed order that cost some men their lives, many their liberty, and hundreds the most serious injuries. The Metropolitan Radical Federation had called a meeting for November 13th to protest against the imprisonment of Mr. O'Brien, and as Mr. Matthews, from his place in the House, had stated that there was no intention of interfering with *bonâ fide* political meetings, the Radical clubs did not expect police interference. On November 9th Sir Charles Warren had issued an order forbidding all meetings in the Square, but the clubs trusted the promise of the Home Secretary. On Saturday evening only, November 12th, when all arrangements were completed, did he issue a peremptory order, forbidding processions within a certain area. With this trap suddenly sprung upon them, the delegates from the clubs, the Fabian Society, the Social Democratic Federation, and the Socialist League, met on that same Saturday evening to see to any details that had been possibly left unsettled. It was finally decided to go to the Square as arranged, and, if challenged by the police, to protest formally against the illegal interference, then to break up the processions and leave the members to find their own way to the Square. It was also decided to go Sunday after Sunday to the Square, until the right of public meetings was vindicated.

The procession I was in started from Clerkenwell Green, and walked with its banner in front, and the chosen speakers, including myself, immediately behind the flag. As we were moving slowly and quietly along one of the narrow streets debouching on Trafalgar Square, wondering whether we should be challenged, there was a sudden charge, and without a word the police were upon us with uplifted truncheons; the banner was struck down, and men and women were falling under a hail of blows. There was no attempt at resistance, the people were too much astounded at the unprepared attack. They scattered, leaving some of their number on the ground too much injured to move, and then made their way in twos and threes to the Square. It was garrisoned by police, drawn up in serried rows, that could only have been broken by a deliberate charge. Our orders were to attempt no violence, and we attempted none. Mr. Cunninghame Graham and Mr. John Burns, arm-in-arm, tried to pass through the police, and were savagely cut about the head and arrested. Then ensued a scene to be remembered; the horse police charged in squadrons at a hand-gallop, rolling men and women over like ninepins, while the foot police struck recklessly with their truncheons, cutting a road through the crowd that closed immediately behind them. I got on a waggonette and tried to persuade the driver to pull his trap across one of the roads, and to get others in line, so as to break the charges of the mounted police; but he was afraid, and drove away to the Embankment, so I jumped out and went back to the Square. At last a rattle of cavalry, and up came the Life Guards, cleverly handled but hurting none, trotting their horses gently and shouldering the crowd apart; and then the Scots Guards with bayonets fixed marched through and occupied the north of the Square. Then the people retreated as we passed round the word, "Go home, go home." The soldiers were ready to fire, the people unarmed; it would have been but a massacre. Slowly the Square emptied and all was still. All other processions were treated as ours had been, and the injuries inflicted were terrible. Peaceable, law-abiding workmen, who had never dreamed of rioting, were left with broken legs, broken arms, wounds of every description. One man,

Linnell, died almost immediately, others from the effect of their injuries. The next day a regular court-martial in Bow Street Police Court, witnesses kept out by the police, men dazed with their wounds, decent workmen of unblemished character who had never been charged in a police-court before, sentenced to imprisonment without chance of defence. But a gallant band rallied to their rescue. William T. Stead, most chivalrous of journalists, opened a Defence Fund, and money rained in; my pledged bail came up by the dozen, and we got the men out on appeal. By sheer audacity I got into the police-court, addressed the magistrate, too astounded by my profound courtesy and calm assurance to remember that I had no right there, and then produced bail after bail of the most undeniable character and respectability, which no magistrate could refuse. Breathing-time gained, a barrister, Mr. W.M. Thompson, worked day after day with hearty devotion, and took up the legal defence. Fines we paid, and here Mrs. Marx Aveling did eager service. A pretty regiment I led out of Millbank Prison, after paying their fines; bruised, clothes torn, hatless, we must have looked a disreputable lot. We stopped and bought hats, to throw an air of respectability over our *cortège*, and we kept together until I saw the men into train and omnibus, lest, with the bitter feelings now roused, conflict should again arise. We formed the Law and Liberty League to defend all unjustly assailed by the police, and thus rescued many a man from prison; and we gave poor Linnell, killed in Trafalgar Square, a public funeral. Sir Charles Warren forbade the passing of the hearse through any of the main thoroughfares west of Waterloo Bridge, so the processions waited there for it. W.T. Stead, R. Cunninghame Graham, Herbert Burrows, and myself walked on one side the coffin, William Morris, F. Smith, R. Dowling, and J. Seddon on the other; the Rev. Stewart D. Headlam, the officiating clergyman, walked in front; fifty stewards carrying long wands guarded the coffin. From Wellington Street to Bow Cemetery the road was one mass of human beings, who uncovered reverently as the slain man went by; at Aldgate the procession took three-quarters of an hour to pass one spot, and thus we bore Linnell to his grave, symbol of a cruel wrong, the vast orderly, silent crowd, bareheaded, making mute protest against the outrage wrought.

It is pleasant to put on record here Mr. Bradlaugh's grave approval of the heavy work done in the police-courts, and the following paragraph shows how generously he could praise one not acting on his own lines: "As I have on most serious matters of principle recently differed very widely from my brave and loyal co-worker, and as the difference has been regrettably emphasised by her resignation of her editorial functions on this Journal, it is the more necessary that I should say how thoroughly I approve, and how grateful I am to her for, her conduct in not only obtaining bail and providing legal assistance for the helpless unfortunates in the hands of the police, but also for her daily personal attendance and wise conduct at the police-stations and police-courts, where she has done so much to abate harsh treatment on the one hand and rash folly on the other. While I should not have marked out this as fitting woman's work, especially in the recent very inclement weather, I desire to record my view that it has been bravely done, well done, and most usefully done, and I wish to mark this the more emphatically as my views and those of Mrs. Besant seem wider apart than I could have deemed possible on many of the points of principle underlying what is every day growing into a most serious struggle." Ever did I find Charles Bradlaugh thus tolerant of difference of opinion, generously eager to approve what to him seemed right even in a policy he disapproved.

The indignation grew and grew; the police were silently boycotted, but the people were so persistent and so tactful that no excuse for violence was given, until the strain on the police force began to tell, and the Tory Government felt that London was being hopelessly alienated; so at last Sir Charles Warren fell, and a wiser hand was put at the helm.

CHAPTER XIV

Through Storm To Peace

Out of all this turmoil and stress rose a Brotherhood that had in it the promise of a fairer day. Mr. Stead and I had become close friends—he Christian, I Atheist, burning with one common love for man, one common hatred against oppression. And so in *Our Corner* for February, 1888, I wrote:—"Lately there has been dawning on the minds of men far apart in questions of theology, the idea of founding a new Brotherhood, in which service of Man should take the place erstwhile given to service of God—a brotherhood in which work should be worship and love should be baptism, in which none should be regarded as alien who was willing to work for human good. One day as I was walking towards Millbank Gaol with the Rev. S.D. Headlam, on the way to liberate a prisoner, I said to him: 'Mr. Headlam, we ought to have a new Church, which should include all who have the common ground of faith in and love for man.' And a little later I found that my friend Mr. W.T. Stead, editor of the *Pall Mall Gazette,* had long been brooding over a similar thought, and wondering whether men 'might not be persuaded to be as earnest about making this world happy as they are over saving their souls.' The teaching of social duty, the upholding of social righteousness, the building up of a true commonwealth—such would be among the aims of the Church of the future. Is the hope too fair for realisation? Is the winning of such beatific vision yet once more the dream of the enthusiast? But surely the one fact that persons so deeply differing in theological creeds as those who have been toiling for the last three months to aid and relieve the oppressed, can work in absolute harmony side by side for the one end—surely this proves that there is a bond which is stronger than our antagonisms, a unity which is deeper than the speculative theories which divide."

How unconsciously I was marching towards the Theosophy which was to become the glory of my life, groping blindly in the darkness for that very brotherhood, definitely formulated on these very lines by those Elder Brothers of our race, at whose feet I was so soon to throw myself. How deeply this longing for something loftier than I had yet found had wrought itself into my life, how strong the conviction was growing that there was something to be sought to which the service of man was the road, may be seen in the following passage from the same article:—

"It has been thought that in these days of factories and of tramways, of shoddy, and of adulteration, that all life must tread with even rhythm of measured footsteps, and that the glory of the ideal could no longer glow over the greyness of a modern horizon. But signs are not awanting that the breath of the older heroism is beginning to stir men's breasts, and that the passion for justice and for liberty, which thrilled through the veins of the world's greatest in the past, and woke our pulses to responsive throb, has not yet died wholly out of the hearts of men. Still the quest of the Holy Grail exercises its deathless fascination, but the seekers no longer raise eyes to heaven, nor search over land and sea, for they know that it waits them in the suffering at their doors, that the consecration of the holiest is on the agonising masses of the poor and the despairing, the cup is crimson with the blood of the

"'People, the grey-grown speechless Christ.'

If there be a faith that can remove the mountains of ignorance and evil, it is surely that faith in the ultimate triumph of Right in the final enthronement of Justice, which alone makes life worth the living, and which gems the blackest cloud of depression with the rainbow-coloured arch of an immortal hope."

As a step towards bringing about some such union of those ready to work for man, Mr. Stead and I projected the *Link*, a halfpenny weekly, the spirit of which was described in its motto, taken from Victor Hugo: "The people are silence. I will be the advocate of this silence. I will speak for the dumb. I will speak of the small to the great and of the feeble to the strong. I will speak for all the despairing silent ones. I will interpret this stammering; I will interpret the grumblings, the murmurs, the tumults of crowds, the complaints ill-pronounced, and all these cries of beasts that, through ignorance and through suffering, man is forced to utter I will be the Word of the People. I will be the bleeding mouth whence the gag is snatched out. I will say everything." It announced its object to be the "building up" of a "New Church, dedicated to the service of man," and "what we want to do is to establish in every village and in every street some man or woman who will sacrifice time and labour as systematically and as cheerfully in the temporal service of man as others do in what they believe to be the service of God." Week after week we issued our little paper, and it became a real light in the darkness. There the petty injustices inflicted on the poor found voice; there the starvation wages paid to women found exposure; there sweating was brought to public notice. A finisher of boots paid 2s. 6d. per dozen pairs and "find your own polish and thread"; women working for 10-1/2 hours per day, making shirts—"fancy best"—at from 10d. to 3s. per dozen, finding their own cotton and needles, paying for gas, towel, and tea (compulsory), earning from 4s. to 10s. per week for the most part; a mantle finisher 2s. 2d. a week, out of which 6d. for materials; "respectable hard-working woman" tried for attempted suicide, "driven to rid herself of life from want." Another part of our work was defending people from unjust landlords, exposing workhouse scandals, enforcing the Employers' Liability Act, Charles Bradlaugh's Truck Act, forming "Vigilance Circles" whose members kept watch in their own district over cases of cruelty to children, extortion, insanitary workshops, sweating, &c., reporting each case to me. Into this work came Herbert Burrows, who had joined hands with me over the Trafalgar Square defence, and who wrote some noble articles in the *Link*. A man loving the people with passionate devotion, hating oppression and injustice with equal passion, working himself with remorseless energy, breaking his heart over wrongs he could not remedy. His whole character once came out in a sentence when he was lying delirious and thought himself dying: "Tell the people how I have loved them always."

In our crusade for the poor we worked for the dockers." To-morrow morning, in London alone 20,000 to 25,000 adult men," wrote Sidney Webb, "will fight like savages for permission to labour in the docks for 4d. an hour, and one-third of them will fight in vain, and be turned workless away." We worked for children's dinners. "If we insist on these children being educated, is it not necessary that they shall be fed? If not, we waste on them knowledge they cannot assimilate, and torture many of them to death. Poor waifs of humanity, we drive them into the school and bid them learn; and the pitiful, wistful eyes question us why we inflict this strange new suffering, and bring into their dim lives this new pang. 'Why not leave us alone? 'ask the pathetically patient little faces. Why not, indeed, since for these child martyrs of the slums, Society has only formulas, not food." We cried out against "cheap goods," that meant "sweated and therefore stolen goods." "The ethics of buying should surely be simply enough. We want a particular thing, and we do not desire to obtain it either by begging or by robbery; but if in becoming possessed of it, we neither beg it nor steal, we must give for it something equivalent in exchange; so much of our neighbour's labour has been put into the thing we desire; if we will not yield him fair equivalent for that labour, yet take his article, we defraud him, and if we are not willing to give that fair equivalent we have no right to become the owners of his product."

This branch of our work led to a big fight—a fight most happy in its results. At a meeting of the Fabian Society, Miss Clementina Black gave a capital lecture on Female Labour, and urged the formation of a Consumers' League, pledged only to buy from shops certificated "clean" from unfair wage. H.H. Champion, in the discussion that followed, drew attention to the wages paid by Bryant & May (Limited), while paying an enormous dividend to their shareholders, so that the value of the original £5 shares was quoted at £18 7s. 6d. Herbert Burrows and I interviewed some of the girls, got lists of wages, of fines, &c. "A typical case is that of a girl of sixteen, a piece-worker; she earns 4s. a week, and lives with a sister, employed by the same firm, who 'earns good money, as much as 8s. or 9s. a week.' Out of the earnings 2s. a week is paid for the rent of one room. The child lives only on bread and butter and tea, alike for breakfast and dinner, but related with dancing eyes that once a month she went to a meal where 'you get coffee and bread and butter, and jam and marmalade, and lots of it.'" We published the facts under the title of "White Slavery in London," and called for a boycott of Bryant & May's matches. "It is time some one came and helped us," said two pale-faced girls to me; and I asked: "Who will help? Plenty of people wish well to any good cause; but very few care to exert themselves to help it, and still fewer will risk anything in its support. 'Some one ought to do it, but why should I?' is the ever re-echoed phrase of weak-kneed amiability. 'Some one ought to do it, so why *not* I?' is the cry of some earnest servant of man, eagerly forward springing to face some perilous duty. Between those two sentences lie whole centuries of moral evolution."

I was promptly threatened with an action for libel, but nothing came of it; it was easier to strike at the girls, and a few days later Fleet Street was enlivened by the irruption of a crowd of match-girls, demanding Annie Besant. I couldn't speechify to match-girls in Fleet Street, so asked that a deputation should come and explain what they wanted. Up came three women and told their story: they had been asked to sign a paper certifying that they were well treated and contented, and that my statements were untrue; they refused. "You had spoke up for us," explained one, "and we weren't going back on you." A girl, pitched on as their leader, was threatened with dismissal; she stood firm; next day she was discharged for some trifle, and they all threw down their work, some 1,400 of them, and then a crowd of them started off to me to ask what to do next. If we ever worked in our lives, Herbert Burrows and I worked for the next fortnight. And a pretty hubbub we created; we asked for money, and it came pouring in; we registered the girls to receive strike pay, wrote articles, roused the clubs, held public meetings, got Mr. Bradlaugh to ask questions in Parliament, stirred up constituencies in which shareholders were members, till the whole country rang with the struggle. Mr. Frederick Charrington lent us a hall for registration, Mr. Sidney Webb and others moved the National Liberal Club to action; we led a procession of the girls to the House of Commons, and interviewed, with a deputation of them, Members of Parliament who cross-questioned them. The girls behaved splendidly, stuck together, kept brave and bright all through. Mr. Hobart of the Social Democratic Federation, Messrs. Shaw, Bland, and Oliver, and Headlam of the Fabian Society, Miss Clementina Black, and many another helped in the heavy work. The London Trades Council finally consented to act as arbitrators and a satisfactory settlement was arrived at; the girls went in to work, fines and deductions were abolished, better wages paid; the Match-makers' Union was established, still the strongest woman's Trades Union in England, and for years I acted as secretary, till, under press of other duties, I resigned, and my work was given by the girls to Mrs. Thornton Smith; Herbert Burrows became, and still is, the treasurer. For a time there was friction between the Company and the Union, but it gradually disappeared under the influence of common sense on both sides, and we have found the manager ready to consider any just grievance and to endeavour to remove it, while the Company have been liberal supporters of the Working Women's Club at Bow, founded by H.P. Blavatsky.

STRIKE COMMITTEE OF THE MATCHMAKERS' UNION.

The worst suffering of all was among the box-makers, thrown out of work by the strike, and they were hard to reach. Twopence-farthing per gross of boxes, and buy your own string and paste, is not wealth, but when the work went more rapid starvation came. Oh, those trudges through the lanes and alleys round Bethnal Green Junction late at night, when our day's work was over; children lying about on shavings, rags, anything; famine looking out of baby faces, out of women's eyes, out of the tremulous hands of men. Heart grew sick and eyes dim, and ever louder sounded the question, "Where is the cure for sorrow, what the way of rescue for the world?"

In August I asked for a "match-girls' drawing-room." "It will want a piano, tables for papers, for games, for light literature; so that it may offer a bright, homelike refuge to these girls, who now have no real homes, no playground save the streets. It is not proposed to build an 'institution' with stern and rigid discipline and enforcement of prim behaviour, but to open a home, filled with the genial atmosphere of cordial comradeship, and self-respecting freedom—the atmosphere so familiar to all who have grown up in the blessed shelter of a happy home, so strange, alas! to too many of our East London girls." In the same month of August, two years later, H.P. Blavatsky opened such a home.

Then came a cry for help from South London, from tin-box makers, illegally fined, and in many cases grievously mutilated by the non-fencing of machinery; then aid to shop assistants, also illegally fined; legal defences by the score still continued; a vigorous agitation for a free meal for children, and for fair wages to be paid by all public bodies; work for the dockers and exposure of their wrongs; a visit to the Cradley Heath chain-makers, speeches to them, writing for them; a contest for the School Board for the Tower Hamlets division, and triumphant return at the head of the poll. Such were some of the ways in which the autumn days were spent, to say nothing of scores of lectures—Secularist, Labour, Socialist—and scores of articles written for the winning of daily bread. When the School Board work was added I felt that I had as much work as one woman's strength could do.

Thus was ushered in 1889, the to me never-to-be-forgotten year in which I found my way "Home," and had the priceless good fortune of meeting, and of becoming the pupil of, H.P. Blavatsky. Ever more and more had been growing on me the feeling that something more than I had was needed for the cure of social ills. The Socialist position sufficed on the economic side, but where to gain the inspiration, the motive, which should lead to the realisation of the Brotherhood of Man? Our efforts to really organise bands of unselfish workers had failed. Much indeed had been done, but there was not a real movement of self-sacrificing devotion, in which men worked for Love's sake only, and asked but to give, not to take. Where was the material for the nobler Social Order, where the hewn stones for the building of the Temple of Man? A great despair would oppress me as I sought for such a movement and found it not.

MEMBERS OF THE MATCHMAKERS' UNION.

Not only so; but since 1886 there had been slowly growing up a conviction that my philosophy was not sufficient; that life and mind were other than, more than, I had dreamed. Psychology was advancing with rapid strides; hypnotic experiments were revealing unlooked-for complexities in human consciousness, strange riddles of multiplex personalities, and, most startling of all, vivid intensities of mental action when the brain, that should be the generator of thought, was reduced to a comatose state. Fact after fact came hurtling in upon me, demanding explanation I was incompetent to give. I studied the obscurer sides of consciousness, dreams, hallucinations, illusions, insanity. Into the darkness shot a ray of light—A.P. Sinnett's "Occult World," with its wonderfully suggestive letters, expounding not the supernatural but a nature under law, wider than I had dared to conceive. I added Spiritualism to my studies, experimenting privately, finding the phenomena indubitable, but the spiritualistic explanation of them incredible. The phenomena of clairvoyance, clairaudience, thought-reading, were found to be real. Under all the rush of the outer life, already sketched, these questions were working in my mind, their answers were being diligently sought. I read a variety of books, but could find little in them that satisfied me. I experimented in various ways suggested in them, and got some (to me) curious results. I finally convinced myself that there was some hidden thing, some hidden power, and resolved to seek until I found, and by the early spring of 1889 I had grown desperately determined to find at all hazards what I sought. At last, sitting alone in deep thought as I had become accustomed to do after the sun had set, filled with an intense but nearly hopeless longing to solve the riddle of life and mind, I heard a Voice that was later to become to me the holiest sound on earth, bidding me take courage for the light was near. A fortnight passed, and then Mr. Stead gave into my hands two large volumes. "Can you review these? My young men all fight shy of them, but you are quite mad enough on these subjects to make something of them." I took the books; they were the two volumes of "The Secret Doctrine," written by H.P. Blavatsky.

Home I carried my burden, and sat me down to read. As I turned over page after page the interest became absorbing; but how familiar it seemed; how my mind leapt forward to presage the conclusions, how natural it was, how coherent, how subtle, and yet how intelligible. I was dazzled, blinded by the light in which disjointed facts were seen as parts of a mighty whole, and all my puzzles, riddles, problems, seemed to disappear. The effect was partially illusory in one sense, in that they all had to be slowly unravelled later, the brain gradually assimilating that which the swift intuition had grasped as truth. But the light had been seen, and in that flash of illumination I knew that the weary search was over and the very Truth was found.

I wrote the review, and asked Mr. Stead for an introduction to the writer, and then sent a note asking to be allowed to call. I received the most cordial of notes, bidding me come, and in the soft spring evening Herbert Burrows and I—for his aspirations were as mine on this matter—walked from Netting Hill Station, wondering what we should meet, to the door of 17, Lansdowne Road. A pause, a swift passing through hall and outer room, through folding-doors thrown back, a figure in a large chair before a table, a voice, vibrant, compelling, "My dear Mrs. Besant, I have so long wished to see you," and I was standing with my hand in her firm grip, and looking for the first time in this life straight into the eyes of "H.P.B." I was conscious of a sudden leaping forth of my heart—was it recognition?—and then, I am ashamed to say, a fierce rebellion, a fierce withdrawal, as of some wild animal when it feels a mastering hand. I sat down, after some introductions that conveyed no ideas to me, and listened. She talked of travels, of various countries, easy brilliant talk, her eyes veiled, her exquisitely moulded fingers rolling cigarettes incessantly. Nothing special to record, no word of

Occultism, nothing mysterious, a woman of the world chatting with her evening visitors. We rose to go, and for a moment the veil lifted, and two brilliant, piercing eyes met mine, and with a yearning throb in the voice: "Oh, my dear Mrs. Besant, if you would only come among us!" I felt a well-nigh uncontrollable desire to bend down and kiss her, under the compulsion of that yearning voice, those compelling eyes, but with a flash of the old unbending pride and an inward jeer at my own folly, I said a commonplace polite good-bye, and turned away with some inanely courteous and evasive remark. "Child," she said to me long afterwards, "your pride is terrible; you are as proud as Lucifer himself." But truly I think I never showed it to her again after that first evening, though it sprang up wrathfully in her defence many and many a time, until I learned the pettiness and the worthlessness of all criticism, and knew that the blind were objects of compassion not of scorn.

Once again I went, and asked about the Theosophical Society, wishful to join, but fighting against it. For I saw, distinct and clear—with painful distinctness, indeed—what that joining would mean. I had largely conquered public prejudice against me by my work on the London School Board, and a smoother road stretched before me, whereon effort to help should be praised not blamed. Was I to plunge into a new vortex of strife, and make myself a mark for ridicule—worse than hatred—and fight again the weary fight for an unpopular truth? Must I turn against Materialism, and face the shame of publicly confessing that I had been wrong, misled by intellect to ignore the Soul? Must I leave the army that had battled for me so bravely, the friends who through all brutality of social ostracism had held me dear and true? And he, the strongest and truest friend of all, whose confidence I had shaken by my Socialism—must he suffer the pang of seeing his co-worker, his co-fighter, of whom he had been so proud, to whom he had been so generous, go over to the opposing hosts, and leave the ranks of Materialism? What would be the look in Charles Bradlaugh's eyes when I told him that I had become a Theosophist? The struggle was sharp and keen, but with none of the anguish of old days in it, for the soldier had now fought many fights and was hardened by many wounds. And so it came to pass that I went again to Lansdowne Road to ask about the Theosophical Society. H.P. Blavatsky looked at me piercingly for a moment. "Have you read the report about me of the Society for Psychical Research?" "No; I never heard of it, so far as I know." "Go and read it, and if, after reading it, you come back—well."

And nothing more would she say on the subject, but branched off to her experiences in many lands.

I borrowed a copy of the Report, read and re-read it. Quickly I saw how slender was the foundation on which the imposing structure was built. The continual assumptions on which conclusions were based; the incredible character of the allegations; and—most damning fact of all—the foul source from which the evidence was derived. Everything turned on the veracity of the Coulombs, and they were self-stamped as partners in the alleged frauds. Could I put such against the frank, fearless nature that I had caught a glimpse of, against the proud fiery truthfulness that shone at me from the clear, blue eyes, honest and fearless as those of a noble child? Was the writer of "The Secret Doctrine" this miserable impostor, this accomplice of tricksters, this foul and loathsome deceiver, this conjuror with trap-doors and sliding panels? I laughed aloud at the absurdity and flung the Report aside with the righteous scorn of an honest nature that knew its own kin when it met them, and shrank from the foulness and baseness of a lie. The next day saw me at the Theosophical Publishing Company's office at 7, Duke Street, Adelphi, where Countess Wachtmeister—one of the lealest of H.P.B.'s friends—was at work, and I signed an application to be admitted as fellow of the Theosophical Society.

On receiving my diploma I betook myself to Lansdowne Road, where I found H.P.B. alone. I went over to her, bent down and kissed her, but said no word. "You have joined the Society?" "Yes." "You have read the report?" "Yes." "Well?" I knelt down before her and clasped her hands in mine, looking straight into her eyes. "My answer is, will you accept me as your pupil, and give me the honour of proclaiming you my teacher in the face of the world?" Her stern, set face softened, the unwonted gleam of tears sprang to her eyes; then, with a dignity more than regal, she placed her hand upon my head. "You are a noble woman. May Master bless you."

From that day, the 10th of May, 1889, until now—two years three and half months after she left her body on May 8, 1891—my faith in her has never wavered, my trust in her has never been shaken. I gave her my faith on an imperious intuition, I proved her true day after day in closest intimacy living by her side; and I speak of her with the reverence due from a pupil to a teacher who never failed her, with the passionate gratitude which, in our School, is the natural meed of the one who opens the gateway and points out the path. "Folly! fanaticism!" scoffs the Englishman of the nineteenth century. Be it so. I have seen, and I can wait. I have been told that I plunged headlong into Theosophy and let my enthusiasm carry me away. I think the charge is true, in so far as the decision was swiftly taken; but it had been long led up to, and realised the dreams of childhood on the higher planes of intellectual womanhood. And let me here say that more than all I hoped for in that first plunge has been realised, and a certainty of knowledge has been gained on doctrines seen as true as that swift flash of illumination. I *know*, by personal experiment, that the Soul exists, and that my Soul, not my body, is myself; that it can leave the body at will; that it can, disembodied, reach and learn from living human teachers, and bring back and impress on the physical brain that which it has learned; that this process of transferring consciousness from one range of being, as it were, to another, is a very slow process, during which the body and brain are gradually correlated with the subtler form which is essentially that of the Soul, and that my own experience of it, still so imperfect, so fragmentary, when compared with the experience of the highly trained, is like the first struggles of a child learning to speak compared with the perfect oratory of the practised speaker; that consciousness, so far from being dependent on the brain, is more active when freed from the gross forms of matter than when encased within them; that the great Sages spoken of by H.P. Blavatsky exist; that they wield powers and possess knowledge before which our control of Nature and knowledge of her ways is but as child's play. All this, and much more, have I learned, and I am but a pupil of low grade, as it were in the infant class of the Occult School; so the first plunge has been successful, and the intuition has been justified. This same path of knowledge that I am treading is open to all others who will pay the toll demanded at the gateway—and that toll is willingness to renounce everything for the sake of spiritual truth, and willingness to give all the truth that is won to the service of man, keeping back no shred for self.

On June 23rd, in a review of "The Secret Doctrine" in the *National Reformer,* the following passages occur, and show how swiftly some of the main points of the teaching had been grasped. (There is a blunder in the statement that of the seven modifications of Matter Science knows only four, and till lately knew only three; these four are sub-states only, sub-divisions of the lowest plane.)

After saying that the nineteenth-century Englishman would be but too likely to be repelled if he only skimmed the book, I went on: "With telescope and with microscope, with scalpel and with battery, Western Science interrogates nature, adding fact to fact, storing experience after experience, but coming ever to gulfs unfathomable by its plummets, to heights unscalable by its ladders. Wide and masterful in its answers to the 'How?' the 'Why?' ever eludes it, and causes remain enwrapped in gloom. Eastern Science uses as its scientific instrument the penetrating faculties of the mind alone, and regarding the material plane as *Maya*—illusion—seeks in the mental and spiritual planes of being the causes of the material effects. There, too, is the only reality; there the true existence of which the visible universe is but the shadow.

"It is clear that from such investigations some further mental equipment is necessary than that normally afforded by the human body. And here comes the parting of the ways between East and West. For the study of the material universe, our five senses, aided by the instruments invented by Science, may suffice. For all we can hear and see, taste and handle, these accustomed servitors, though often blundering, are the best available guides to knowledge. But it lies in the nature of the case that they are useless when the investigation is to be into modes of existence which cannot impress themselves on our nerve-ends. For instance, what we know as colour is the vibration frequency of etheric waves striking on the retina of the eye, between certain definite limits—759 trillions of blows from the maximum, 436 trillions from the minimum—these waves give rise in us to the sensation which the brain translates into colour. (Why the 436 trillion blows at one end of a nerve become 'Red' at the other end we do not know; we chronicle the fact but cannot explain it.) But our capacity to respond to the vibration cannot limit the vibrational capacity of the ether; to *us* the higher and lower rates of vibration do not exist, but if our sense of vision were more sensitive we should see where now we are blind. Following this line of thought we realise that matter may exist in forms unknown to us, in modifications to which our senses are unable to respond. Now steps in the Eastern Sage and says: 'That which you say *may* be, *is*; we have developed and cultivated senses as much superior to yours as your eye is superior to that of the jelly-fish; we have evolved mental and spiritual faculties which enable us to investigate on the higher planes of being with as much certainty as you are investigating on the physical plane; there is nothing *supernatural* in the business, any more than your knowledge is supernatural, though much above that accessible to the fish; we do not speculate on these higher forms of existence; we *know* them by personal study, just as you know the fauna and flora of your world. The powers we possess are not supernatural, they are latent in every human being, and will be evolved as the race progresses. All that we have done is to evolve them more rapidly than our neighbours, by a procedure as open to you as it was to us. Matter is everywhere, but it exists in seven modifications of which you only know four, and until lately only knew three; in those higher forms reside the causes of which you see the effects in the lower, and to know these causes you must develop the capacity to take cognisance of the higher planes.'"

Then followed a brief outline of the cycle of evolution, and I went on: "What part does man play in this vast drama of a universe? Needless to say, he is not the only living form in a Cosmos, which for the most part is uninhabitable by him. As Science has shown living forms everywhere on the material plane, races in each drop of water, life throbbing in every leaf and blade, so the 'Secret Doctrine' points to living forms on higher planes of existence, each suited to its environment, till all space thrills with life, and nowhere is there death, but only change. Amid these myriads are some evolving towards humanity, some evolving away from humanity as we know it, divesting themselves of its grosser parts. For man is regarded as a sevenfold being, four of these parts belonging to the animal body, and perishing at, or soon after, death; while three form his higher self, his true individuality, and these persist and are immortal. These form the Ego, and it is this which passes through many incarnations, learning life's lesson as it goes, working out its own redemption within the limits of an inexorable law, sowing seeds of which it ever reaps the harvest, building its own fate with tireless fingers, and finding nowhere in the measureless time and space around it any that can lift for it one weight it has created, one burden it has gathered, unravel for it one tangle it has twisted, close for it one gulf it has digged."

Then after noting the approaches of Western Science to Eastern, came the final words: "it is of curious interest to note how some of the latest theories seem to catch glimpses of the occult Doctrines, as though Science were standing on the very threshold of knowledge which shall make all her past seem small. Already her hand is trembling towards the grasp of forces beside which all those now at her command are insignificant. How soon will her grip fasten on them? Let us hope not until social order has been transformed, lest they should only give more to those who have, and leave the wretched still wretcheder by force of contrast. Knowledge used by selfishness widens the gulf that divides man from man and race from race, and we may well shrink from the idea of new powers in Nature being yoked to the car of Greed. Hence the wisdom of those 'Masters,' in whose name Madame Blavatsky speaks, has ever denied the knowledge which is power until Love's lesson has been learned, and has given only into the hands of the selfless the control of those natural forces which, misused, would wreck society."

This review, and the public announcement, demanded by honesty, that I had joined the Theosophical Society, naturally raised somewhat of a storm of criticism, and the *National Reformer* of June 30th contained the following: "The review of Madame Blavatsky's book in the last *National Reformer*, and an announcement in the *Star*, have brought me several letters on the subject of Theosophy. I am asked for an explanation as to what Theosophy is, and as to my own opinion on Theosophy—the word 'theosoph' is old, and was used among the Neo-platonists. From the dictionary its new meaning appears to be, 'one who claims to have a knowledge of God, or of the laws of nature by means of internal illumination.' An Atheist certainly cannot be a Theosophist. A Deist might be a Theosophist. A Monist cannot be a Theosophist. Theosophy must at least involve Dualism. Modern Theosophy, according to Madame Blavatsky, as set out in last week's issue, asserts much that I do not believe, and alleges some things that, to me, are certainly not true. I have not had the opportunity of reading Madame Blavatsky's two volumes, but I have read during the past ten years many publications from the pen of herself, Colonel Olcott, and of other Theosophists. They appear to me to have sought to rehabilitate a kind of Spiritualism in Eastern phraseology. I think many of their allegations utterly erroneous, and their reasonings wholly unsound. I very deeply regret indeed that my colleague and co-worker has, with somewhat of suddenness, and without any interchange of ideas with myself, adopted as facts matters which seem to me to be as unreal as it is possible for any fiction to be. My regret is greater as I know Mrs. Besant's devotion to any course she believes to be true. I know that she will always be earnest in the advocacy of any views she undertakes to defend, and I look to possible developments of her Theosophic views with the very gravest misgiving. The editorial policy of this paper is unchanged, and is directly antagonistic to all forms of Theosophy. I would have preferred on this subject to have held my peace, for the public disagreeing with Mrs. Besant on her adoption of Socialism has caused pain to both; but on reading her article and taking the public announcement made of her having joined the Theosophical organisation, I owe it to those who look to me for guidance to say this with clearness. "CHARLES BRADLAUGH."

"It is not possible for me here to state fully my reasons for joining the Theosophical Society, the three objects of which are: To found a Universal Brotherhood without distinction of race or creed; to forward the study of Aryan literature and philosophy; to investigate unexplained laws of nature and the physical powers latent in man. On matters of religious opinion the members are absolutely free. The founders of the society deny a personal God, and a somewhat subtle form of Pantheism is taught as the Theosophic view of the universe, though even this is not forced on members of the society. I have no desire to hide the fact that this form of Pantheism appears to me to promise solution of some problems, especially problems in psychology, which Atheism leaves untouched.

"ANNIE BESANT."

Theosophy, as its students well know, so far from involving Dualism, is based on the One, which becomes Two on manifestation, just as Atheism posits one existence, only cognisable in the duality force and matter, and as philosophic— though not popular—Theism teaches one Deity whereof are spirit and matter. Mr. Bradlaugh's temperate disapproval was not copied in its temperance by some other Freethought leaders, and Mr. Foote especially distinguished himself by the bitterness of his attacks. In the midst of the whirl I was called away to Paris to attend, with Herbert Burrows, the great Labour Congress held there from July 15th to July 20th, and spent a day or two at Fontainebleau with H.P. Blavatsky, who had gone abroad for a few weeks' rest. There I found her translating the wonderful fragments from "The Book of the Golden Precepts," now so widely known under the name of "The Voice of the Silence." She wrote it swiftly, without any material copy before her, and in the evening made me read it aloud to see if the "English was decent." Herbert Burrows was there, and Mrs. Candler, a staunch American Theosophist, and we sat round H.P.B. while I read. The translation was in perfect and beautiful English, flowing and musical; only a word or two could we find to alter, and she looked at us like a startled child, wondering at our praises— praises that any one with the literary sense would endorse if they read that exquisite prose poem.

A little earlier in the same day I had asked her as to the agencies at work in producing the taps so constantly heard at Spiritualistic *Séances*. "You don't use spirits to produce taps," she said; "see here." She put her hand over my head, not touching it, and I heard and felt slight taps on the bone of my skull, each sending a little electric thrill down the spine. She then carefully explained how such taps were producible at any point desired by the operator, and how interplay of the currents to which they were due might be caused otherwise than by conscious human volition. It was in this fashion that she would illustrate her verbal teachings, proving by experiment the statements made as to the existence of subtle forces controllable by the trained mind. The phenomena all belonged to the scientific side of her teaching, and she never committed the folly of claiming authority for her philosophic doctrines on the ground that she was a wonder-worker. And constantly she would remind us that there was no such thing as "miracle"; that all the phenomena she had produced were worked by virtue of a knowledge of nature deeper than that of average people, and by the force of a well-trained mind and will; some of them were what she would describe as "psychological tricks," the creation of images by force of imagination, and in pressing them on others as a "collective hallucination"; others, such as the moving of solid articles, either by an astral hand projected to draw them towards her, or by using an Elemental; others by reading in the Astral Light, and so on. But the proof of the reality of her mission from those whom she spoke of as Masters lay not in these comparatively trivial physical and mental phenomena, but in the splendour of her heroic endurance, the depth of her knowledge, the selflessness of her character, the lofty spirituality of her teaching, the untiring passion of her devotion, the incessant ardour of her work for the enlightening of men. It was these, and not her phenomena, that won for her our faith and confidence— we who lived beside her, knowing her daily life—and we gratefully accepted her teaching not because she claimed any authority, but because it woke in us powers, the possibility of which in ourselves we had not dreamed of, energies of the Soul that demonstrated their own existence.

Returning to London from Paris, it became necessary to make a very clear and definite presentment of my change of views, and in the *Reformer* of August 4th I find the following: "Many statements are being made just now about me and my beliefs, some of which are absurdly, and some of which are maliciously, untrue. I must ask my friends not to give credence to them. It would not be fair to my friend Mr. Bradlaugh to ask him to open the columns of this Journal to an exposition of Theosophy from my pen, and so bring about a long controversy on a subject which would not interest the majority of the readers of the *National Reformer*. This being so I cannot here answer the attacks made on me. I feel, however, that the party with which I have worked for so long has a right to demand of me some explanation of the step I have taken, and I am therefore preparing a pamphlet dealing fully with the question. Further, I have arranged with Mr. R.O. Smith to take as subject of the lectures to be delivered by me at the Hall of Science on August 4th and 11th 'Why I became a Theosophist.' Meanwhile I think that my years of service in the ranks of the Freethought party give me the right to ask that I should not be condemned unheard, and I even venture to suggest, in view of the praises bestowed on me by Freethinkers in the past, that it is possible that there may be something to be said, from the intellectual standpoint, in favour of Theosophy. The caricatures of it which have appeared from some Freethinkers' pens represent it about as accurately as the Christian Evidence caricatures of Atheism represent that dignified philosophy of life; and, remembering how much they are themselves misrepresented, I ask them to wait before they judge."

The lectures were delivered, and were condensed into a pamphlet bearing the same title, which has had a very great circulation. It closed as follows:—

"There remains a great stumblingblock in the minds of many Freethinkers which is certain to prejudice them against Theosophy, and which offers to opponents a cheap subject for sarcasm—the assertion that there exist other living beings than the men and animals found on our own globe. It may be well for people who at once turn away when such an assertion is made to stop and ask themselves whether they really and seriously believe that throughout this mighty universe, in which our little planet is but as a tiny speck of sand in the Sahara, this one planet only is inhabited by living things? Is all the universe dumb save for *our* voices? eyeless save for *our* vision? dead save for *our* life? Such a preposterous belief was well enough in the days when Christianity regarded our world as the centre of the universe, the human race as the one for which the Creator had deigned to die. But now that we are placed in our proper position, one among countless myriads of worlds, what ground is there for the preposterous conceit which arrogates as ours all sentient existence? Earth, air, water, all are teeming with living things suited to their environment; our globe is overflowing with life. But the moment we pass in thought beyond our atmosphere everything is to be changed. Neither reason nor analogy support such a supposition. It was one of Bruno's crimes that he dared to teach that other worlds than ours were inhabited; but he was wiser than the monks who burned him. All the Theosophists aver is that each phase of matter has living things suited to it, and that all the universe is pulsing with life. 'Superstition!' shriek the bigoted. It is no more superstition than the belief in Bacteria, or in any other living thing invisible to the ordinary human eye. 'Spirit' is a misleading word, for, historically, it connotes immateriality and a supernatural kind of existence, and the Theosophist believes neither in the one nor the other. With him all living things act in and through a material basis, and 'matter' and 'spirit' are not found dissociated. But he alleges that matter exists in states other than those at present known to science. To deny this is to be about as sensible as was the Hindû prince who denied the existence of ice because water, in his experience, never became solid. Refusal to believe until proof is given is a rational position; denial of all outside of our own limited experience is absurd.

"One last word to my Secularist friends. If you say to me, 'Leave our ranks,' I will leave them; I force myself on no party, and the moment I feel myself unwelcome I will go.[29] It has cost me pain enough and to spare to admit that the Materialism from which I hoped all has failed me, and by such admission to bring on myself the disapproval of some of my nearest friends. But here, as at other times in my life, I dare not purchase peace with a lie. An imperious necessity forces me to speak the truth, as I see it,

---

[29] I leave these words as they were written in 1889. I resigned my office in the N.S.S. in 1890, feeling that the N.S.S. was so identified with Materialism that it had no longer place for me.

whether the speech please or displease, whether it bring praise or blame. That one loyalty to Truth I must keep stainless, whatever friendships fail me or human ties be broken. She may lead me into the wilderness, yet I must follow her; she may strip me of all love, yet I must pursue her; though she slay me, yet will I trust in her; and I ask no other epitaph on my tomb but

"'SHE TRIED TO FOLLOW TRUTH.'"

Meanwhile, with this new controversy on my hands, the School Board work went on, rendered possible, I ought to say, by the generous assistance of friends unknown to me, who sent me, £150 a year during the last year and a half. So also went on the vigorous Socialist work, and the continual championship of struggling labour movements, prominent here being the organisation of the South London fur-pullers into a union, and the aiding of the movement for shortening the hours of tram and 'bus men, the meetings for which had to be held after midnight. The feeding and clothing of children also occupied much time and attention, for the little ones in my district were, thousands of them, desperately poor. My studies I pursued as best I could, reading in railway carriages, tramcars, omnibuses, and stealing hours for listening to H.P.B. by shortening the nights.

In October, Mr. Bradlaugh's shaken strength received its death-blow, though he was to live yet another fifteen months. He collapsed suddenly under a most severe attack of congestion and lay in imminent peril, devotedly nursed by his only remaining child, Mrs. Bonner, his elder daughter having died the preceding autumn. Slowly he struggled back to life, after four weeks in bed, and, ordered by his physician to take rest and if possible a sea voyage, he sailed for India on November 28th, to attend the National Congress, where he was enthusiastically acclaimed as "Member for India."

In November I argued a libel suit, brought by me against the Rev. Mr. Hoskyns, vicar of Stepney, who had selected some vile passages from a book which was not mine and had circulated them as representing my views, during the School Board election of 1888. I had against me the Solicitor-General, Sir Edward Clarke, at the bar, and Baron Huddleston on the bench; both counsel and judge did their best to browbeat me and to use the coarsest language, endeavouring to prove that by advocating the limitation of the family I had condemned chastity as a crime. Five hours of brutal cross-examination left my denial of such teachings unshaken, and even the pleadings of the judge for the clergyman, defending his parishioners against an unbeliever and his laying down as law that the statement was privileged, did not avail to win a verdict. The jury disagreed, not, as one of them told me afterwards, on the question of the libel, but on some feeling that a clergyman ought not to be mulcted in damages for his over-zeal in defence of his faith against the ravening wolf of unbelief, while others, regarding the libel as a very cruel one, would not agree to a verdict that did not carry substantial damages. I did not carry the case to a new trial, feeling that it was not worth while to waste time over it further, my innocence of the charge itself having been fully proved.

Busily the months rolled on, and early in the year 1890 H.P.Blavatsky had given to her £1,000, to use in her discretion for human service, and if she thought well, in the service of women. After a good deal of discussion she fixed on the establishment of a club in East London for working girls, and with her approval Miss Laura Cooper and I hunted for a suitable place. Finally we fixed on a very large and old house, 193, Bow Road, and some months went in its complete renovation and the building of a hall attached to it. On August 15th it was opened by Madame Blavatsky, and dedicated by her to the brightening of the lot of hardworking and underpaid girls. It has nobly fulfilled its mission for the last three years. Very tender was H.P.B.'s heart to human suffering, especially to that of women and children. She was very poor towards the end of her earthly life, having spent all on her mission, and refusing to take time from her Theosophical work to write for the Russian papers which were ready to pay highly for her pen. But her slender purse was swiftly emptied when any human pain that money could relieve came in her way. One day I wrote a letter to a comrade that was shown to her, about some little children to whom I had carried a quantity of country flowers, and I had spoken of their faces pinched with want. The following characteristic note came to me:—

"MY DEAREST FRIEND,—I have just read your letter to —— and my heart is sick for the poor little ones! Look here; I have but 30s. of *my own money* of which I can dispose (for as you know I am a pauper, and proud of it), but I want you to take them and *not say a word*. This may buy thirty dinners for thirty poor little starving wretches, and I may feel happier for thirty minutes at the thought. Now don't say a word, and do it; take them to those unfortunate babies who loved your flowers and felt happy. Forgive your old uncouth friend, *useless* in this world!

"Ever yours,

"H.P.B."

It was this tenderness of hers that led us, after she had gone, to found the "H.P.B. Home for little children," and one day we hope to fulfil her expressed desire that a large but homelike Refuge for outcast children should be opened under the auspices of the Theosophical Society.

The lease of 17, Lansdowne Road expiring in the early summer of 1890, it was decided that 19, Avenue Road should be turned into the headquarters of the Theosophical Society in Europe. A hall was built for the meetings of the Blavatsky Lodge—the lodge founded by her—and various alterations made. In July her staff of workers was united under one roof; thither came Archibald and Bertram Keightley, who had devoted themselves to her service years before, and the Countess Wachtmeister, who had thrown aside all the luxuries of wealth and of high social rank to give all to the cause she served and the friend she loved with deep and faithful loyajty; and George Mead, her secretary and earnest disciple, a man of strong brain and strong character, a fine scholar and untiring worker; thither, too, Claude Wright, most lovable of Irishmen, with keen insight underlying a bright and sunny nature, careless on the surface, and Walter Old, dreamy and sensitive, a born psychic, and, like many such, easily swayed by those around him; Emily Kislingbury also, a studious and earnest woman; Isabel Cooper Oakley, intuitional and studious, a rare combination, and a most devoted pupil in Occult studies; James Pryse, an American, than whom none is more devoted, bringing practical knowledge to the help of the work, and making possible the large development of our printing department. These, with myself, were at first the resident staff, Miss Cooper and Herbert Burrows, who were also identified with the work, being prevented by other obligations from living always as part of the household.

The rules of the house were—and are—very simple, but H.P.B. insisted on great regularity of life; we breakfasted at 8 a.m., worked till lunch at 1, then again till dinner at 7. After dinner the outer work for the Society was put aside, and we gathered in H.P.B.'s room where we would sit talking over plans, receiving instructions, listening to her explanation of knotty points. By 12 midnight all the lights had to be extinguished. My public work took me away for many hours, unfortunately for myself, but such was the regular run of our busy lives. She herself wrote incessantly; always suffering, but of indomitable will, she drove her body through its tasks, merciless to its weaknesses and its pains. Her pupils she treated very variously, adapting herself with nicest accuracy to their differing natures; as a teacher she was marvellously patient, explaining a thing over and over again in different fashions, until sometimes after prolonged failure she would throw herself back in her chair: "My God!" (the easy "Mon Dieu" of the foreigner) "am I a fool that you can't understand? Here, So-and-so"—to some one on whose countenance a faint gleam of comprehension was discernible—"tell these flapdoodles of the ages what I mean." With vanity, conceit, pretence of knowledge, she was merciless, if the pupil were a promising one; keen shafts of irony would pierce the sham. With some she would get very angry, lashing them out of their lethargy with fiery scorn; and in truth she made herself a mere instrument for the training of her pupils, careless what they, or any one else thought of her, providing that the resulting benefit to them was secured. And we, who lived around her, who in closest intimacy watched her day after day, we bear witness to the unselfish beauty of her life, the nobility of her character, and we lay at her feet our most reverent gratitude for knowledge gained, lives purified, strength developed. O noble and heroic Soul, whom the outside purblind world misjudges, but whom your pupils partly saw, never through lives and deaths shall we repay the debt of gratitude we owe to you.

And thus I came through storm to peace, not to the peace of an untroubled sea of outer life, which no strong soul can crave, but to an inner peace that outer troubles may not avail to ruffle—a peace which belongs to the eternal not to the transitory, to the depths not to the shallows of life. It carried me scatheless through the terrible spring of 1891, when death struck down Charles Bradlaugh in the plenitude of his usefulness, and unlocked the gateway into rest for H. P. Blavatsky. Through anxieties and responsibilities heavy and numerous it has borne me; every strain makes it stronger; every trial makes it serener; every assault leaves it more radiant. Quiet confidence has taken the place of doubt; a strong security the place of anxious dread. In life, through death, to life, I am but the servant of the great Brotherhood, and those on whose heads but for a moment the touch of the Master has rested in blessing can never again look upon the world save through eyes made luminous with the radiance of the Eternal Peace.

PEACE TO ALL BEINGS.

THE END.

Lightning Source UK Ltd.
Milton Keynes UK
05 October 2010

160782UK00004B/28/A